# Families and Social Workers

# Families and Social Workers
## The Work of Family Service Units
## 1940–1985

**Pat Starkey**

LIVERPOOL UNIVERSITY PRESS

First published 2000 by
Liverpool University Press
4 Cambridge Street
Liverpool
L69 7ZU

**British Library Cataloguing-in-Publication Data**
A British Library CIP Record is available

ISBN 0–85323–656–9  hardback
      0–85323–666-6  paperback

Typeset in Plantin by Koinonia, Bury
Printed and bound in Great Britain by Bell and Bain Limited, Glasgow

# Contents

# Acronyms and abbreviations

| | |
|---|---|
| CCETSW | Central Council for the Education and Training of Social Workers |
| CCU | Combined Casework Unit |
| CPF | City Parochial Foundation |
| FSU | Family Service Units |
| FWA | Family Welfare Association |
| ICAA | Invalid Children's Aid Association |
| ILEA | Inner London Education Authority |
| LCC | London County Council |
| LPSS | Liverpool Personal Service Society |
| MOH | Medical Officer of Health |
| PNCMH | Provisional National Council for Mental Health |
| PSU | Pacifist Service Units |
| STU | student training unit |
| ULSCA | University of Liverpool Special Collections and Archives |

# Introduction

It has never been one of the giants of voluntary social work. Management consultants called in to comment on its structure in 1988 noted its relatively small size and 'hand to mouth' financial existence.[1] What was true at the end of the 1980s was equally true 40 years earlier, but in spite of its small size and its recent arrival in the social work field, Family Service Units (FSU) had been more confident of its role in the immediate post-war period than in 1988. In the intervening years it had exercised an influence on the development of social work practice and training which was out of all proportion to its size and financial resources.

Its important place in the history of a developing profession could not easily have been predicted. Originating in the activities of a small group of conscientious objectors who attempted to respond to the demands of wartime suffering by involving themselves in relief work, it came to the attention of politicians and the public alike with the publication of an account of the activities of the Liverpool, Manchester and Stepney Pacifist Service Units (PSU) during the war.[2] The book attracted both national and international publicity. The active interest of Lord Balfour of Burleigh led the PSUs in Liverpool and Manchester to abandon the creed which had motivated their wartime work and to set up a more conventional voluntary social work agency, renamed Family Service Units, in 1948. The agency consisted of no more than a handful of young, untrained workers. Although confident of the value of their work, and convinced of the existence of the social phenomenon of the problem family, they were surprised to find themselves in receipt of invitations to establish units in towns and cities throughout Britain. They rose to the challenge, however, and throughout the next decade, units were set up and workers trained. FSU slowly and steadily positioned itself within post-war welfare arrangements.

Its lack of history proved to be one of FSU's major advantages. Facing what were feared to be major attacks on their autonomy by Labour government legislation in the years after the end of the war, other agencies working with families – especially those working with children – believed that their futures were in jeopardy. The Church of England Waifs and Strays Society (later the Children's Society) feared for its future.[3] So did Dr Barnardo's.[4] The passing of the Children Act in 1948 and the appointment of local authority children's officers reinforced that fear, but FSU did not share it. Its members were convinced that the work they had pioneered was such that no local authority in the late 1940s would have the resources to undertake it. Their wartime resistance to fighting because they believed it to be wrong, and their readiness to accept the consequences of that resistance up to and including a prison sentence, gave them the confidence and courage to oppose what they perceived to be the inappropriate approaches of established social work agencies. Their relative lack of experience, their determination and, perhaps, their naivety led them to forge ahead, without any clear idea of the way in which the work might develop.

In the short term, their assessment of local authority capacity was correct. The reconstruction of cities and communities severely damaged by bombing prompted local authorities to recognise their inability to meet the needs of a small number of poor and disadvantaged families. FSU was invited to work alongside other agencies, both voluntary (for example the National Society for the Prevention of Cruelty to Children (NSPCC)) and statutory (for example the newly established children's departments). However, the area of public well-being in which officials most clearly perceived the value of an organisation like PSU/FSU was public health. In many local authorities, rural as well as urban, it was the medical officers of health who assumed responsibility for what was seen to be a serious threat to the work of reconstruction – the problem family. Staff in these departments, most frequently the health visitors, undertook the care of problem families. The relationships between PSU/FSU and medical officers of health throw light on the extent to which PSU/FSU's own practices were influenced by the social theory of the pre-war years which was characterised by an emphasis on biological determinism. As these ideas became diluted by the environmentalism which increasingly influenced social theory after the war, workers became understandably anxious to distance themselves from eugenics; but in spite of the demonisation of eugenicism, there can be little doubt that a group of untrained social workers during the 1940s could not avoid being influenced by elements of it. Moreover, some of PSU/FSU's most enthusiastic supporters were themselves adherents of eugenicist philosophy.

The post-war years saw significant advances in the professionalisation of social work. This long and sometimes difficult process, begun in the early years of the twentieth century, was documented by Eileen Younghusband in the mid-1940s and early 1950s[5] and updated in the late 1970s.[6] It was expressed in the introduction of new college- and university-based courses and a new emphasis on the value of training. FSU, by offering to take students on placement and building relationships with key social work educators, found itself contributing to both the theory and practice of social work. The significance of FSU's contribution to social work education can be seen in the numbers of its workers who left the organisation for academic social work, its importance as a provider of experience to student social workers, and its contribution to discussions surrounding developments in social work education.

Relationships between voluntary organisations and what was perceived to be an increasingly interventionist state have led commentators to try to plot the negotiating positions adopted by each side, and to interrogate the ways in which social need, political motivation and the self-preservation impulses of voluntary organisations have determined the extent of voluntary activity. For example, Maria Brenton,[7] Geoffrey Finlayson,[8] Rodney Lowe[9] and Nicholas Deakin[10] have all considered the role of the voluntary sector within the British welfare system, as has June Rose in her study of Dr Barnardo's.[11] Jane Lewis has discussed the changing part played by the Charity Organisation Society/Family Welfare Association, on the surface an agency which has more in common with FSU than child rescue agencies.[12] FSU, no less and no more sure-footed than other agencies, found itself forced to move from a position in which it could confidently expect financial help from local authorities to one in which it had regularly to justify its claims for support and to demonstrate that it gave value for money. The ability to experiment and innovate, and to challenge local authority policy, became seriously circumscribed in the face of an increasing emphasis on accountability, to some extent brought about by the serious financial difficulties in which local authorities found themselves from the 1970s onwards.

By the second half of the period covered by this book, FSU was having to learn the painful lesson that failure to recognise the reality of its dependent position would result in the withdrawal of essential statutory funding and the closure of local units.

Each unit's necessary and close relationship with its locality, part of the original conception of FSU's supporters in the 1940s, had an adverse effect on its relationship with the national body; a management consultant in the 1960s proclaimed FSU to be a fascinating organisation, because it was so nearly not an organisation at all.[13] Its inability to delineate clear lines of management and to distinguish between matters of national and local importance led to confused and confusing relationships between local units and the national office. The emphasis on the local also ensured that individual units developed in a wide variety of different ways, and that there is no such thing as a typical Family Service Unit. For that reason, it has proved impossible to give a full account of every unit and to detail the various ways in which it has attempted to serve its community. The material presented here reflects the accident of survival as well as those developments in post-war social work which appear to be have been most significant to FSU and to have shaped its history. Some units have kept little in the way of documentary material, others have carefully saved everything; some material has been destroyed or lost; some units preferred not to deposit their records but to shred them in the interests of confidentiality. However, most units have deposited some material at the University of Liverpool so that a picture of an important and influential, though sometimes quirky, organisation can be built up. The story peters out in 1985, which also reflects the state of the archive; when this research was started, little post-1985 material had been deposited. More recent deposits have included such material, although much of it has yet to be listed.

The spur to this attempt to record the history of FSU came in the late 1980s with the discovery of boxes of documents taking up valuable space in a cupboard in the Liverpool FSU offices. They turned out to be the complete records, including the grocery bills, of the Liverpool and District Pacifist Service Unit, which had operated in the city from 1940 until the end of the Second World War. Fearful that any one of their number might suddenly fall victim to enemy action, the keeping of detailed and accurate records was enjoined on every member. The result is a complete set of minutes of every meeting held by the committee and the caseworkers, notes on every person visited, and even a blow-by-blow account of their work during the Blitz. Carefully logged by a group of always independent, sometimes bloody-minded, conscientious objectors, a picture emerges of amateur social workers gradually becoming aware of the problems faced since before the war by a small group of poor families, and of the process of developing mechanisms to help them.

The University of Liverpool already housed the archives of Dr Barnardo's, the Fairbridge Trust and the NCH Action for Children (formerly National Children's Homes). Michael Cook, the university archivist, was enthusiastic at the prospect of adding FSU to this valuable collection, and the university formally took responsibility for the FSU archive in 1992. Collecting the records entailed many visits to individual units to rescue case notes and administrative records. Social workers have more important things to do than ensure careful records management, and there were occasions when we had to make decisions about which black bags held archival material and which the goods for the next jumble sale. We were not always successful, and on occasion returned to Liverpool with the jumble as well as the case notes.

The award of a research grant from the Economic and Social Research Council in 1993 enabled some remission of teaching responsibilities and provided time to explore FSU's past. Many friends and colleagues have contributed in one way or another to this work; some may not realise how much they have helped. A list of names holds dangers; I want to record my thanks to individuals, but there are so many of them – supposing I forget to mention someone? A long list also makes for tedious reading, even for those whose names are included. I have decided, therefore, to group together those whose advice, encouragement and criticism have been invaluable and trust that they will appreciate the extent of my gratitude. Members of Pacifist Service Units based in Liverpool, Manchester and Stepney during the war have provided information of all sorts, most usefully about their own time in the organisation. A reunion in York in 1989, to which I was invited, enabled a very useful discussion to take place. FSU administrators, fieldwork organisers, unit organisers and social workers have shared their experiences and opinions. Rex Halliwell died before the research was started, but it has been possible to talk with all the other national secretaries and directors who were in post in the period I have studied. Social workers who did student placements in units have also discussed their experiences. I did not formally interview any service users, although visits to units have facilitated casual conversations and enabled impressions to be gained. Members of both national and local committees have given generously of their time, and social workers who have viewed FSU from the perspective of local authority children's and social services departments have also helped to me to understand the organisation. At the University of Liverpool, the staff of the Special Collections and Archives Department have been unfailingly helpful, and my colleagues in the School of History, especially those on the top corridor, must be included. What would I have done without their friendship and cups of tea? Alan Cohen, Peter Hennock, Adah Kay, John Lansley, Anne Pope and Rose Pyle have all shown interest in the work and have read sections while the book was in preparation. I'm grateful to each of them for their thoughtful comments. Not all those who have helped me will like what I have written. I may have misunderstood the points that they were trying to make. On occasion I have chosen to interpret things differently. The responsibility for mistakes and errors of interpretation is, of course, wholly mine.

## NOTES

**1.** Coopers and Lybrand, *Organising for a Purpose: Roles and relationships* (London, 1988).

**2.** T. Stephens, *Problem Families: An experiment in social rehabilitation* (London, 1945).

**3.** Church of England Waifs and Strays Society, *Annual Report for 1948.*

**4.** Council Minutes of Dr Barnardo's Homes, April 1946. University of Liverpool Special Collections and Archives (hereafter ULSCA) D239/B1/2. I am grateful to Julie Grier for this reference.

**5.** E. Younghusband, *Report on the Employment and Training of Social Workers* (Edinburgh, 1947) and *Social Work in Britain: A Supplementary Report on the Employment and Training of Social Workers* (Edinburgh, 1951).

**6.** E. Younghusband, *Social Work in Britain: 1950–1975*, 2 vols (London, 1978).

**7.** M. Brenton, *The Voluntary Sector in British Social Services* (London, 1985).

**8.** G. Finlayson, *Citizen, State and Social Welfare in Britain, 1830–1990* (Oxford, 1994).

**9.** R. Lowe, *The Welfare State in Britain Since 1945* (London, 1993).

**10.** N. Deakin, 'The perils of partnership: The voluntary sector and the state, 1945–1992', in J. Davis Smith, C. Rochester and R. Hedley (eds), *An Introduction to the Voluntary Sector* (London, 1995).

**11.** J. Rose, *For the Sake of the Children: Inside Dr Barnardo's: 120 years of caring for children* (London, 1987).

**12.** J. Lewis, *The Voluntary Sector, the State and Social Work in Britain* (London, 1995).

**13.** Derek Newman, *Report on Two Years' Work with FSU* (London, 1969).

# 1

# Pacifist Service

The Liverpool and District Pacifist Service Unit was part of a loosely knit national network of pacifist groups based at Dick Sheppard House at 6 Endsleigh Street in London (in 1940 the recently purchased headquarters of the Peace Pledge Union), which at its first meeting in May 1940 had committed its members to '... train for relief and other social work and thereafter give their services for the benefit of the community at large'.[1] It was a vague and open-ended commitment, but although the type and extent of their work had not been decided – and possibly could not have been decided during the first, uncertain months of the Second World War – the statement of intent carried the implicit ambition that service initiated during the war should continue when it was over, and was an important element in the whole notion of pacifist service exemplified by the establishment of Pacifist Service Units (PSU). As might be expected, in the early years of the war the emphasis was on emergency and first aid work, but some members nursed the vision of a network of voluntary, pacifist groups which would strive to improve society through activities motivated by human sympathy and the desire to serve others, and which would become a permanent feature of British life.[2] In 1940, members of the Liverpool unit shared such dreams with their colleagues elsewhere, but could not have foreseen the impact that their work would have. They neither set out to work with those who came to be called problem families, nor to found a voluntary social work agency, but by the end of the war they had established themselves as social workers with skills that other agencies wished to emulate.

Many PSUs, including Liverpool, were composed of men and women already committed to other pacifist groups. Their existence reflected the rise in the number of new organisations, and the growth of previously established ones, that had been a feature of the inter-war period. As Martin Caedel has shown, the shock of the First World War and the horror which the destructive potential of the bomber plane had aroused in the minds of ordinary people contributed in no small measure to the birth of organisations dedicated to the pursuit of peace. In the mid-1930s, as the international situation appeared to become more dangerous, these organisations experienced a rapid growth in membership.[3] Once war had been declared, most of those who chose to join PSUs engaged in some form of emergency work, much of it directed towards helping those who were using air-raid shelters. They gave first aid treatment where necessary and provided simple refreshments – mainly cups of tea, and soup and bread – as well as helping with activities in the clubs and play centres that had been set up in some areas. By 1942, there were 14 such units. Nine were in London; the remainder were in Bristol, Cardiff, Liverpool, Manchester and Sheffield. In addition to providing emergency aid, each unit developed other activities in response to local needs. The unit based at the Dick Sheppard Centre formed a first aid patrol which travelled by bicycle.[4] In Hampstead, the local group undertook buildings maintenance and engaged in welfare work with infants in the nursery school run by Anna Freud and Dorothy Burlingham. On the Honor Oak estate, PSU workers were involved in community work and became very familiar with the layout of the estate. They were to provide vital assistance during the flying bomb raids, becoming responsible for helping with evacuation arrangements. Members of the Sheffield unit became guinea pigs for medical research; they allowed themselves to be infected with a number of diseases, including scabies, and to be subjected to a variety of experimental treatments. In Bristol and Cardiff the units helped in hospitals and youth clubs.[5]

Each local unit enjoyed a degree of autonomy, but was accountable to the national committee in London, which exercised control over some aspects of organisation in the provincial branches. All appointments had to be approved by the national committee, which insisted that all volunteers should be prepared to undertake some form of training. It was also expected that they would agree to be moved to new areas should the need arise.[6] There is no suggestion that the units entertained any anxiety about the possible curbs on their freedom, at least at the outset, and there were times when units were glad of the support of the central committee, although from time to time disagreements did arise. Often these were prompted by the national committee's attempts to exercise control over work outside London, in spite of local units' conviction that they were better placed to understand and respond to local needs. Resentment against the London committee's tendency to issue instructions was exacerbated by the fact that local units were responsible for finding the money for their own activities, and received no financial help from the central committee. Understandably, those who raised the money felt that they had the right to say how it was spent. Throughout the war, strenuous efforts were made to repair relationships between the centre and the periphery by ensuring proper representation of all units on the national committee, but that did not stop occasional bouts of grumbling.[7]

The half-formed hope that ideals of service developed during the Second World War would inform some sort of community work in time of peace came to be realised when the Liverpool unit, almost by accident, began to engage in an activity which was to continue long after the war was over – even though it was to entail the abandonment of the goal of an exclusively pacifist enterprise. The unit's origins lay in decisions taken at a meeting in the city in October 1940 attended by representatives of local branches of pacifist groups already active in the area, including the Peace Pledge Union, the Fellowship of Reconciliation, the Anglican Pacifist Fellowship, and the Society of Friends.[8] An agreement to combine in order to engage in useful service was made, and recruitment was very satisfactory. Within a few weeks, over 60 applications for membership – both full- and part-time – had been received, even though there was as yet no clear idea about the sort of work that needed to be done. Deciding what that work should be proved to be more difficult. Although the right to conscientious objection was enshrined in law, and attitudes towards conscientious objectors ('conchies') were more relaxed than they had been during the First World War,[9] pacifists could expect to attract little popular favour. Liverpudlians, living in daily fear of enemy attack, might be forgiven for viewing them with some suspicion. Liverpool was Britain's second port and a target for attack, not only because of its vital role in the handling of food imports and arms but, more particularly, because of its strategic position as a base for naval operations in the Atlantic. Pacifists, reluctant to take part in any activity which would support the war effort – even such vital and potentially lifesaving tasks as fire-watching, in some cases – laid themselves open to accusations that they put the safety and welfare of the city and its inhabitants at risk. Those who did not share the principles informing pacifist belief understandably failed to comprehend the sometimes tortuous process by which some conscientious objectors came to decide the issues on which they intended to make a stand. Moreover, the PSU workers' implied criticism of the city council could not have helped their cause in official circles. Suspecting that, like other local authorities, Liverpool was not fully prepared for the likely effects of mass bombing, one of their first acts was to offer to help as volunteers in official air-raid shelters, believing that even by assisting in menial tasks like the provision of refreshments they could go some way to compensate for the city's organisational deficiencies.[10]

The deficiencies were real enough. As in many other British cities, insufficient thought had been given either to the provision of temporary shelter or to the organisation of permanent or semi-permanent accommodation for those whose houses had been made uninhabitable by the bombing. As Richard Titmuss noted there was a general assumption that, for instance, all slightly injured persons would return immediately to their homes once they had been given treatment. Little consideration had been given to ways of ameliorating the plight of those whose homes were no longer standing or were so badly damaged as to be unsafe,[11] nor were adequate plans in place for the emergency supply of food and clothing. In Liverpool the situation was exacerbated by a long tradition of sectarian politics and a degree of antipathy to voluntary organisations, especially to those which requested help in carrying out their functions. Even so forceful a person as Lady Reading, requesting office space from which to organise the services of her newly founded Women's Voluntary Services for Air Raid Precautions, was given short shrift by the local Air Raid Precautions (ARP) (Special) Committee. A similar response greeted the offers of help from an organisation known as ARP Voluntary Services, which had a membership of about 400, nearly all of whom were trained air-raid wardens and possessed skills which might have been put to good use.[12] In such a climate, it was not surprising that PSU's offer to service air-raid shelters met with outright rejection. The Liverpool Civil Defence Emergency Committee was not prepared to grant permission for PSU to organise canteens in any of its shelters. In reply to a request from PSU that he consider overturning the committee's decision, the Lord Mayor, Alderman Sydney Jones, claimed that provision in the city was adequate.

Moreover, he argued that it was inappropriate for conscientious objectors to involve themselves in civil defence work.[13] Faced with so unequivocal a rejection, unit members were left casting round for useful things to do.

Even though there was little to report, the unit established a system of careful record keeping. Minute books for the last weeks of 1940 and the early part of the following year tell of the frustration of young men and women who were certain that they had something to offer, but had no one to whom to offer it. The opportunity to assist in an ill-equipped and unofficial shelter situated beneath Holy Trinity Church in the city centre was their first break. Officially, the shelter provided refuge for 350 people, although twice as many were frequently to be found there. The vicar, who spent most nights in the shelter so as to offer support to anxious local people, shared none of the city council's suspicions of pacifists and their intentions, and was only too pleased to accept the help they offered. At his invitation the PSU workers began to provide hot drinks and food for sale at a moderate cost. They also tried to improve the sanitary conditions by making themselves responsible for emptying the chemical lavatories and for sweeping and cleaning the shelter.[14] Some unit members joined the fire-watching teams that had been set up by local businesses and community groups which were anxious to limit any damage to their property. These teams were unofficial in the sense that they did not operate under the auspices of the Civil Defence Committee, and so membership neither invited the antagonism of the Lord Mayor nor excited the consciences of those scrupulous objectors for whom belonging to an 'official' team would have been tantamount to supporting the war effort.[15] Unit workers found occupation during the day, too; because most city centre schools had been closed by government order, there were large numbers of children on the local streets with nothing to do. Many of them were evacuees who had returned from their rural billets, preferring the familiarity of the city streets to the strangeness of the countryside, in spite of the danger of bombing. They, too, became the objects of unit concern; walks and other activities were organised for them,[16] and in some cases bathing arrangements were offered on Saturday afternoons to those whose homes lacked hot running water.[17]

Those activities were short-lived, though, and the Holy Trinity shelter in St Anne's Street was soon abandoned for more urgent and dramatic work. Liverpool was subjected to more than a week of enemy raids in May 1941. After eight nights of bombing, nearly 90,000 houses had been damaged, more than 1,400 people killed and at least 1,000 seriously wounded.[18] The experiences of those who were the immediate victims of this onslaught confirmed PSU's conviction that the city was poorly prepared for the consequences of mass bombing. A two-stage relief scheme had been planned by the city authorities: initially, those who had been bombed out of their homes but had escaped injury were to be taken to emergency rest centres, usually large halls situated in areas of the city distant from the docks and other enemy targets. The function of these centres was simply to provide short-term shelter – in many cases for little more than a few hours – until temporary accommodation could be arranged, possibly with friends or relatives. The second stage was the allocation of places in dispersal rest centres, similarly situated in suburban areas but intended to provide basic, but longer-term, accommodation for those who continued to find themselves homeless. It quickly became clear, however, that although the necessary buildings had been requisitioned, the city was not able to call upon the services of the numbers of people who were required to staff them adequately. Faced with the responsibility for making on-the-spot decisions, and working under considerable pressure, Public Assistance Committee officers gratefully accepted PSU's suggestion that it send some of its members to help to staff one of the emergency rest centres. Civic objections to the use of pacifists evaporated. PSU members rapidly became the valued colleagues of the emergency services, and their assistance began to be enlisted on a regular basis.[19] Some of their colleagues from the unit in Manchester travelled to Liverpool to help them; the local laundry, which was owned by a Quaker family, provided a van that was used to transport goods, food and people around the city. As the weeks went by the unit extended its activities in an attempt to plug gaps in the second phase of the city's relief organisation by assisting local authority officials in the longer-term task of providing services in dispersal rest centres for families whose homes were so badly damaged that they had to be rehoused.[20]

By working in shelters and refuges the Liverpool PSU was adopting the pattern followed by its sister units in other cities. As a result of their experience in the dispersal rest centres, however, members of the Liverpool unit began to develop a distinctive type of work that was soon to spread to the units in Manchester and Stepney and laid the foundations for an approach to work with needy families that was to continue after 1945. The degree of chronic need was not immediately apparent though, and was secondary to the urgent necessity of removing people to areas deemed to be safe from enemy bombardment. However, once the initial emergency had ended, conditions in the dispersal rest centres quickly demonstrated the extent to which insufficient consideration had been given either to the sort of people who were likely to have to use them or to their requirements. Little support was provided. Families were allocated a small amount of space (usually one room to each family), provided with some basic household equipment, and then expected to fend for themselves in stressful circumstances and in an unfamiliar part of the city, away from what remained of family and neighbourhood support networks.[21] Many had lived in very poor conditions long before the bombing exposed their plight. By herding together families who had become accustomed to sub-standard housing and poor sanitation, the authorities ensured that the efficient and clean administration of the dispersal rest centres would be difficult to achieve. Furthermore, although efforts to billet some families with the owners of large houses in the suburbs had some success, as did attempts to move other families into temporary dwellings, it was impossible to find alternative accommodation for everybody. Family size played an important part; many families had four or five children, some had eight or ten. In a city whose housing stock had been severely depleted by the bombing, there was little readily available accommodation that was large enough for them. To make matters more difficult, the lifestyle of some families was such that they were unlikely to be welcomed, even as temporary lodgers, into other people's homes. Consequently, large or antisocial families tended to be concentrated in the dispersal rest centres.[22]

PSU members' first attempts at what might be called social work ended in failure. Invited to staff some dispersal rest centres, they appointed a few of their number as resident wardens with responsibility for managing the hostels and maintaining cleanliness and good order. They were not able to do so. Conditions in all the hostels deteriorated and the PSU members appeared incapable of doing anything to influence the behaviour of the residents, or to uphold even basic standards of cleanliness. As a result, the system was abandoned in favour of a different approach. Instead of acting as resident wardens, PSU workers became peripatetic and visited the hostels several times a day, offering support and help to one another as well as to the families. By substituting a support role for a policing one, unit members found themselves better able to establish good relationships with the families, to help them to cope with the problems caused by the loss of their homes, and to assist in the care of the children.[23] Very soon, unit members became aware that they were engaged in work that the statutory services were either unable or unwilling to undertake.

The last bomb was dropped on Merseyside in November 1941. During the months of bombardment, 3,370 people had been killed and 2,955 seriously injured, and more than 200,000 houses had been either destroyed or damaged.[24] Further attacks were expected but none materialised and the cessation of the bombing, together with the gradual emptying of the dispersal rest centres, prompted a change of focus for the unit's work. From providing short- and medium-term relief, it began to engage in longer-term support. By then, the character of the unit membership had also begun to change. In October 1940, the Liverpool unit had consisted mainly of part-time volunteers who had used the city centre Friends Meeting House as their base. Conditions there had been cramped, though luxurious compared with those in Stepney, where some PSU members slept in a lavatory.[25] By 1942, the Liverpool unit had a core of full-time workers. Some of these had joined in 1940 as part-timers but, having lost their jobs because of their status as conscientious objectors, had begun to work with the unit on a full-time basis. Edgar McCoy, whose involvement with the work in both Manchester and Liverpool lasted throughout the war, was dismissed from his employment as a clerk in the department of education in Bootle because he was a conscientious objector.[26] Others had given up their employment voluntarily because it involved contributing to the war effort. Michael Lee, his parents, Chris and Honor Lee, and his brother, Roger, all gave up their employment at the family's tapestry works in Birkenhead for the duration of the war because the firm accepted orders to make military uniforms. Chris, Honor and Michael assisted the Liverpool and Manchester PSUs, Chris and Honor acting as housekeepers from 1943.[27] Roger joined the Friends Relief Service.[28] Yet others had been sent to work in Liverpool by the PSU headquarters in London. An example is David Jones (who was to become an important influence on the post-war organisation) who had worked with both the Bristol and Cardiff units before being sent to Liverpool.[29] Fred Philp, another key figure whose contribution was to stretch over 20 years, had been invited to consider joining PSU after he placed an advertisement in the *New Statesman* suggesting that a young man suffering from 'agricultural atrophy' (he had been directed to work on a farm in Leicestershire) was looking for work suitable for a conscientious objector.[30]

They were a mixed group of people from a variety of backgrounds; most were under 25. Although PSU and its successor organisation, Family Service Units, have been closely linked with the Society of Friends in FSU mythology, this is not borne out by the evidence. Local Quakers supported the work of the unit, but with the exception of Chris and Honor Lee, few of the Liverpool and Manchester workers had ever attended Quaker meetings, and none was a member of the Society.[31] Nor were Quakers represented on the local committee. Although his parents were members of the Society of Friends, Michael Lee did not become a member until towards the end of the war. Like many other young people linked to the Society through family affiliation, he preferred to plead the case for conscientious objection on grounds other than membership of a religious organisation. This behaviour was motivated by the belief that they would appear before tribunals in exactly the same way as other 'conchies' and could not be seen to have an unfair advantage.[32] The religious affiliations of unit members, and the strength of those affiliations, were varied; some professed no faith at all. If there was a unifying philosophy it was broadly humanist, seeing the resolution of social problems in political rather than religious terms. Many members held left-wing views.

Working through the PSU committee, and acting on instructions from London, local pacifists supported the full-time workers by allowing them 2s 6d per week for pocket money[33] and providing for their keep. From May 1942 a house for the full-time workers was rented from the Liverpool Corporation. This became the workers' hostel, enabling them to move out of the Friends Meeting House which they had used since 1940 and providing them with a more secure and comfortable base for the next phase of their work.[34] The move came as a great relief to the members of the local Society of Friends, whose patience with the untidiness and chaos had been thinning. Similar arrangements were made for the Manchester unit.[35] The Liverpool PSU committee, which had been chaired from its earliest days by Eric McKie, an administrator at the University of Liverpool, began to take on a greater day-to-day management role. McKie regularly visited the unit house, which was near the university. He supported, cajoled and encouraged the workers, and helped to direct the focus of their work. He also exerted considerable control over the appointment of workers to the unit and insisted on helping to interview every applicant. McKie's certainty about the value of the work in which the unit was engaged, and his conviction that he knew the best way to carry it forward, sometimes alienated other committee members, and some found it difficult to cope with his inability to delegate responsibility. He may not always have been an easy colleague, but without him it is unlikely that the Liverpool unit would have survived to develop family casework and to make an important contribution to post-war social work practice. McKie shared with other founders of PSU the vision of a national organisation that would continue its work after the war. There can be little doubt that it was because of this vision that members of the Liverpool unit were moved elsewhere in the country. When key Liverpool workers were moved to London and Manchester in 1942, it was because McKie was aware of the work that they could do to spread the PSU philosophy as it was developing in Liverpool.[36] He retained his position as chair of the local committee until 1967, but by that time the organisational centre of gravity had moved to London and the Liverpool unit was fighting to continue to exert influence.

Developments in management and organisation which occurred in the aftermath of the Blitz came into operation as the unit's task for the rest of the war gradually became clear. A PSU tradition holds that when most families had been rehoused and the dispersal rest centres were all but empty, a breakfast-time conversation in the unit hostel resulted in a plan to follow up some of the families in their new homes and to offer them support.[37] The young pacifists' contribution to emergency relief had served to allay, or at least to render of little consequence, many of the anxieties previously voiced by the Liverpool Corporation, and few objections were raised to their continued involvement in relief work. Once engaged in this new task of visiting, the unit members concentrated on improving what they perceived to be unacceptably low standards of personal and domestic hygiene among some of the families. The impulse to involve themselves with those who were to become known as problem families appears to have arisen from the suspicion that there had been, and still were, those in need who were untouched by other agencies, whether statutory or voluntary.[38] This flew in the face of a long-standing belief that such families were likely to be attended by a number of agencies with differing functions, all visiting independently, sometimes offering conflicting advice and always failing to coordinate what they were doing.[39] This does not seem to have been the case in Liverpool in the 1940s. In a pamphlet produced in 1944, the Liverpool and District PSU claimed that of the 80 families with whom they were working, fewer than half were known to any other organisation. Of the remainder, only eight families had received help from other voluntary agencies in the previous six months.[40] A document sent from the Liverpool unit to PSU's London headquarters in the same year in response to complaints from the long-established and highly respected Liverpool Personal Service Society asserted that it worked exclusively with people in whom no other agency had any interest.[41] That is partly contradicted by the unit's own case records, which make it clear that many families did have some contact with other welfare organisations; by the end of 1943 most of the families with whom the unit was working had been referred by a statutory body, most commonly by relieving officers employed by the National Assistance Board, the education department, the housing department or the probation service.[42] However, the fact of referral was not necessarily an indication of anything more than minimal contact with the family. Some of those referred to PSU appear to have been families for whom statutory agencies believed that they could do nothing. Voluntary organisations, like the Discharged Prisoners' Aid Society, were only too pleased to be able to pass some of their more difficult cases to the unit, with whom they built up close links.[43] Close working relationships also grew up with the Liverpool Child Welfare Association, the Liverpool Diocesan Board of Moral Welfare and the Liverpool Society for the Prevention of Cruelty to Children. Nor did PSU's pacifism put any obstacles in the way of cooperation with the Soldiers', Sailors' and Airmen's Families Association, which was often glad of the support that the unit could give to men and women discharged from the forces, and to the families of men absent on active service. There was little competition for the privilege of working with problem families among the more conventional voluntary social work organisations.[44] Some may have criticised PSU methods, but none suggested that clients were being poached or that there was any great overlap in provision. Casenotes confirm that, whatever the national pattern, Liverpool problem families could not be described as 'over-visited'; most were not, and never had been, in receipt of concerned attention from anyone.

This was a cause for pride on the part of PSU members who derived satisfaction from their association with those presumed to be difficult, if not hopeless, cases, and who were pleased to be seen servicing people who others might designate the 'undeserving poor'. It exemplified the humanitarian impulse which informed their pacifism and gave expression to their belief in the worth of every human being. In addition, it provided some workers with the means of identifying with those clients who felt themselves to be social outcasts. Conscientious objectors often experienced a similar sense of rejection by and isolation from 'respectable' society.[45]

This sense of shared experience was sometimes heightened by poor relationships with the law. Among those with whom PSU worked were men and women who had been convicted of a variety of offences, from burglary to the failure to ensure their children's regular attendance at school. Occasionally a family sheltered a deserter from the armed forces. Their criminality may have been of a different order, but many pacifists, too, had criminal records resulting from their refusal to keep to the rules which governed the registration of conscientious objectors. PSU minute books record a number of occasions on which members found themselves in the local magistrates' courts to answer such charges as infringing the terms of their exemption from military service, or refusing to fire-watch with official teams.[46] Conscientious objectors were required to register with the authorities before they could gain exemption from military service. Applicants had to appear before a tribunal to defend their stance and to plead for the right to be allowed to engage in activity which did not support the war effort. The chairmen of some local tribunals were reputed to give 'conchies' a bad time. Judge Burgis, chairman of the north-western tribunal in Manchester, enjoyed a degree of notoriety for his overt hostility towards pacifists, as did his colleague, Judge Frankland.[47] This was not purely a northern phenomenon. The disdain which conscientious objectors and their organisations aroused in official circles was also voiced by a magistrate of the Thames Police Court, who made a disparaging reference to Pacifist Service Units during one member's trial for refusing to abide by the terms of his exemption from the armed forces. He was given a six-month prison sentence.[48] If officials could be harsh, conscientious objectors could be uncooperative. Some refused to accept the tribunal's decision that they should take up alternative occupations, especially if this would deny them opportunities to work with urban pacifist units or to involve themselves in activities which they believed to be more socially useful than forestry or landwork. For some, their understanding of conscientious objection entailed the adoption of a non-participatory stance towards all official civil defence activity, including fire-watching.

Like some of their clients, several PSU members had served time in local prisons.[49] One was discharged from the Pioneer Corps, to which he had been unwillingly recruited, having served a prison sentence for refusing to name the parts of a rifle.[50] Some refused to pay fines for offences resulting from their stance, because to do so would be to acknowledge the authority of the court which imposed them; these people were often given custodial sentences. Units found their manpower suddenly reduced as their members paid the penalty for refusing to comply with court orders. Not all served their time in full; supporters could often be relied upon to pay the fine money into the court, or an impromptu bring-and-buy sale might produce the necessary funds, but all sorts of moral gymnastics had then to be performed in order to persuade the prisoner to accept his freedom.[51]

Experience of prison provided a point of contact with families that was not available to workers in the more respectable agencies. Other differences between the more traditional approach and that of PSU stemmed from the novel methods employed by the latter. One of the earliest tasks the unit undertook in Liverpool received the active encouragement of the education department. Unit members devised a system of calling early in the morning at the homes of reluctant school attenders in order to help parents to get their children washed and dressed and ready for the worker to escort them to school.[52] Sometimes they were successful, but PSU workers were no match for those resourceful Liverpool children who had no intention of spending the day in the classroom and who were adept at giving their escorts the slip. But by combining escort duties with other methods of helping the family, unit workers hoped to encourage parents to reorganise their lives so as to take seriously the educational and other needs of their children.

It was all part of the 'friendship with a purpose' approach, which entailed setting socially accepted standards of domestic organisation and child-care, and providing what PSU members believed to be appropriate support in helping families to meet them. This friendship, 'without condescension or professional aloofness; not forced or superficial but a relationship of mutual trust as between equals'[53] was based on a false premise. It could not fail to be condescending, and it was certainly not between equals. That the families were described as exhibiting 'obtuseness of mind and degenerate habits'[54] in an account of PSU activity calls into question any real mutuality. In spite of his disclaimers, Tom Stephens's 1945 account of PSU work describes relationships between needy clients and authoritarian professionals; an essential element was the right assumed by the worker to 'make it his duty to see that the treatment he prescribes is carried out... whatever happens, the responsibility for the family's welfare is his'.[55] Even the encouragement to their clients to use the workers' first names, while the workers always addressed formally the adults whom they were trying to help, reinforced the distance between them. Its distortion of the normal convention, however well-intentioned, resulted in a confused and artificial relationship between client and worker. The quasi-professional relationship between 'the case' (the term used throughout the war to describe any family with whom PSU was involved, and in itself a denial of the mutuality and friendship that the workers professed) and the worker was between someone who could cope with the demands of his everyday life[56] and a family who could not. That the day-to-day income of the PSU workers and the families appeared to be roughly equivalent, and their relationship with officialdom equally strained, might have been a matter of pride for the workers; it also reinforced the personal and social differences between them and the families. PSU members had access to personal and other resources not available to most of their 'cases' and they enjoyed the practical and emotional backing of a highly motivated network of supporters. They may have been working in return for a small amount of pocket money, but their hostel was adequately, if frugally, furnished and their rent and household bills paid. Essential clothing was also supplied.[57] Money was put aside for any medical treatment that might be needed by a unit worker.[58] The clients, on the other hand, were usually socially isolated and often displayed characteristics that made them unpopular neighbours. In addition, they were frequently at the mercy of unscrupulous landlords, who paid scant attention to the maintenance of their property. Nevertheless, although PSU workers may have been confused about their own underlying motives, and have failed to consider more than one side of the 'friendship' they offered, they provided a range of services hitherto unavailable to families whose difficulties had been noted but rarely addressed.

While the Liverpool and Manchester units pursued their work with families, other units became involved in activities which had their genesis in the evacuation of children from cities to rural and suburban places of safety. These units attempted to fill the gaps in local authority schemes by giving more personal attention than the hard-pressed officials were able to offer. By the time that state evacuation programmes were suspended in September 1941, a department of PSU based in London had developed a wide network of contacts among billeting officers and others throughout the country, making it possible to offer assistance to families and to give children the benefit of a holiday in the country. One version of this was what PSU came to call 'applied evacuation', a process which involved the removal of children from poor home conditions for what might be termed therapeutic reasons. Their somewhat telegraphic notes describe the sort of arrangement that was made:

> Young woman of 27, husband serving overseas, four children aged 8, 6, 4 and 3 living in very bad conditions and depressed, demoralised and exasperated by the disobedience of the children, who were largely out of control and suffering in health. We arranged for the two older boys to be evacuated to billets with a party from their school and they settled down and stayed away 12 months. In the meantime their mother made a great improvement in the home conditions and affairs generally and gained control of the younger boys. The husband has now returned from foreign service and the home and all four boys are now well-managed.[59]

The happy ending masks what might be seen as insensitivity to the woman's condition and criticism of her ability to exercise the maternal functions of providing a clean and healthy home and exerting adequate control over her children. Another case study of a family whose child members were evacuated for a year suggests that an underlying reason for the evacuation was to impress upon the mother the reason for their absence. 'She was not allowed to forget them and was fully conscious of the purpose of their temporary absence.' On their return, the boys found a 'mother more able to keep their respect and affection'.[60] The success claimed by PSU was attributed to the evacuation organised for the children and measured in terms of what the workers perceived to be improved parental control. It failed to consider the children's ability to adapt to different situations or to take into account the difficulties for them attendant on the process of removal from one home to another. Moreover, the significance of the father's return for the achievement of improved conditions, maternal morale and parental control is not discussed. Little consideration appears to have been given to the need to alleviate the underlying conditions of poverty in which some families lived, although bedding or clothing met some of the more urgent needs. There was, however, no agreement among the workers about the wisdom of such treatment. Justification for what was recognised to be an extreme procedure is given at the end of PSU's 1944 newsletter, with an acknowledgement that even among themselves PSU members entertained a number of different opinions as to the circumstances which might justify the separation of children from their parents. Some were totally opposed to any separation while others believed that temporary removal from an unhealthy environment was the only opportunity some children might have to experience a standard of life, defined in purely physical terms, which was better than that in their own homes. However, on the whole – and not surprisingly – PSU was eager to claim success for its methods and to record such achievements in the newsletters sent to its supporters. While workers recognised the importance of environmental factors in the mental and physical development of the children, they appear to have believed that improved environmental conditions could only be achieved by removing children from their parents.

> The value to children of periods in the country is strikingly illustrated... by a boy of eleven whose parents are separated and who was living with his mother and younger sisters in extreme poverty. He was out of control and rarely attended school, running wild in the streets, uncouth, uncivil, showing respect for no one. The unit arranged for his evacuation to a camp school... where the children enjoy an open-air life in huts. He has been away only four months but the regular and balanced meals, proper sleep and fresh air have brought about a great improvement. He is fitter and mentally brighter, and his manners and general attitude to other people have been transformed... Other children have been sent for varying periods to hostels catering for difficult children and several have gone to a remarkable farm-training colony for young people, which is run mainly by pacifists, and where astonishing improvements have taken place in the children, mentally and physically.[61]

In such reports, the contrast between pacifist and non-pacifist communities and between inadequate parents and competent carers is reinforced by the distinctions made between the presumed environmental purity of the countryside and the dirt, squalor and potential for contamination of the town. The comments unconsciously reveal anti-urban sentiments that had influenced theories of child-care since the nineteenth century. As Nikolas Rose has demonstrated, fears that moral contagion could spread like an epidemic through urban communities had influenced the development of reformatory and industrial schools in order to provide supervision for children thought to be in 'need of care and protection' from 1854 onwards. The underlying justification for the removal of children to such institutions lay in the belief that they would act as substitutes for the families who had failed properly to encourage moral values, and introduce the children to habits of cleanliness, work and obedience.[62] Such ambitions for schemes for separating children from parents found an echo in the justifications put forward by advocates of applied evacuation. Contemporary studies, however, did not necessarily support the contention that time spent in the country resulted in improved physical and emotional health. Although the School Medical Officer for Oxfordshire claimed that evacuees had put on weight, while his colleague in the City of Oxford asserted confidently that country life was more attractive to children than a more restricted existence in towns, John Welshman has shown that such impressionistic claims were not borne out by rigorous studies of evacuated children. A London County Council investigation which suggested that a period of evacuation did not cause any significant difference in the rate of children's growth was confirmed by research carried out for the Ministry of Health.[63] Lucy Faithfull, who was involved with evacuee children during the war, noted that those who stayed with their parents through the Blitz were 'taller, despite missing school meals, were heavier and were emotionally better balanced' than those who had been separated from them.[64] For John Bowlby, evacuation confirmed what was already known about small children; that there was a demonstrable link between early separation of child and parent (generally assumed to be the mother) and later antisocial behaviour.[65]

In Stepney, some PSU members put time and energy into working with pre-school children who, although living with their families, spent their days playing unsupervised in the streets and on bomb sites.[66] Supplied with toys and equipment by friends in the local Peace Pledge Union and the Save the Children Fund, the unit opened a nursery in its house and used methods of child management learned by those of their number who had worked in Anna Freud's nursery in Hampstead.[67] Freud's ideals found an echo in the non-violent ethos espoused by the unit and, although some of her practices were modified slightly to meet the needs of inner-city children, they formed the basis of the unit's approach to the children's activities. The terms in which children's behaviour is described and explained, as well as the workers' justification for methods of discipline which eschewed the violence to which some children had been accustomed at home, clearly owes a great deal to Freud's methods.[68] Unit members also used their contacts with the children to build relationships with their parents and to open up conversations about the difficulties faced as a result of air raids, evacuation and paternal absence. Their child-centred approach differed significantly from that being employed in the other key units of Manchester and Liverpool, which, although equally committed to non-violence, saw the solution of family problems primarily in terms of improvement of standards of housewifery and parental control.

In the north-western units the work of raising standards of domestic hygiene and child-care involved regular visits to families, often as frequently as two or three times a day. No other agency was able to offer such intensive supervisory care, nor was any other agency prepared to engage in the sort of work that PSU workers were happy to undertake. They helped parents, often lone mothers, to scrub and decorate their homes. They used what appears to have been a highly toxic spray to rid rooms of the bugs and fleas which had bred in them, and occasionally removed and burned furniture which had been so badly infested that incineration was the only solution. Protective clothing, secured with elastic bands at the wrists and ankles, was worn in an attempt to limit the numbers of bugs, lice and fleas which settled on workers' own skin.[69] Workers also deloused children, acquired second-hand furniture to supply to families, and helped parents to budget so that they were better able to feed and clothe their children. When necessary they helped families to move house, using a handcart to transport their furniture; until they could afford to buy one of their own, members of the Liverpool unit hired a cart at the cost of 6d a day.[70] The active cooperation of the families was believed to be essential: workers would only help to decorate a room if members of the family also wielded whitewash brushes, and when they fine-combed the heads of lousy children, it was with the assistance of the mother. The aim was not just to get the family out of a particular set of difficulties but to help family members to learn skills which would enable them to meet acceptable standards.[71] In addition, unit workers performed more conventional social work tasks, such as ensuring that families in need received any financial help to which they were entitled in the form of pensions, army allotments or war damage claims; helping families to apply for free school dinners and free milk for their children; and assisting them in their dealings with official bodies like the local housing department or the Public Assistance Committee.[72]

PSU members and the families worked in difficult conditions. In some Liverpool houses, as in the poorer quarters of other British cities, there was no easy access to water, making the preparation of food, especially vegetables, difficult. In order to wash cooking utensils and crockery, let alone children or clothing, the women had to carry water from a communal tap. If they were lucky, the tap was on the landing; if they were not, they might find that the nearest source of water was across a yard. Most women had to heat water on an open fire. One PSU newsletter in 1944 carried a report from an unspecified unit describing the state of the property occupied by some of its clients:

> ... the coal has to be dumped at the side of the cooker which is contained in a very small space at the bottom of the stairs. From here there is a way out into an open passage in which there is a door to the communal lavatory shared with two other houses. An old man from one of these houses is unable to use the lavatory properly with the result that the seat is covered with excreta. The only usable bedroom has a hole in the ceiling through to the slates and leaks badly...There is no lock on either the front or the back door. The tap in the basement, the house's only water supply, has no drain beneath it. The tenants complain of rats...[73]

Similarly bad conditions are described regularly in the casenotes of Liverpool and Manchester PSUs. One family included a tubercular father who had recently discharged himself from hospital, and three children aged between six months and nine years, who

> were sleeping in one bed, which had no overlay mattress, and the spring had a hole in it, thro (sic) which the boys used to fall at night; very little bedding; their only furniture being one kitchen table, 1 chair and 1 bed... since we have known them the baby has died of pulmonary tuberculosis.[74]

Detailed notes on the work with this family describe the efforts made to try to persuade the father to resume treatment for his tuberculosis, and the visits made on behalf of the family to a range of agencies including the public health, sanitary, housing and billeting departments. Unit members also requested help from officials at the Employment Exchange, various clinics, the Food Office and a local doctor. Evacuation for the nine-year-old boy was arranged. In addition:

On the material level, we have supplied and have helped them to obtain from other sources clothing, furniture (including chairs, chest of drawers) beds and bedding and overlay mattress. Some of the clothing has been pawned from time to time; we have tried to stop this habit, by advice, by helping her to save to redeem articles, and by providing other articles when she redeems others. Some of the furniture – chairs and the bottom of the couch – were used for firewood. We have seen that the children received the free meals and milk to which they were entitled, by helping them complete application forms, even obtaining these on occasion and seeing they were handed in. Contacts have been made with several official organisations on such matters as employment, income, lost clothing coupons, housing, sanitary defects, health of various members of family, school attendance...[75]

While the problems faced by that family were probably unusually severe, a similar lack of basic household equipment was noted frequently in casenotes and was an indication not of incompetence – although that might have made an unsatisfactory state of affairs worse – but of extreme poverty. In many cases the suffering of the family was exacerbated by the failure of landlords to maintain their property to a reasonable standard. The culpability of landlords is rarely considered, though, and caseworkers' notes frequently remark on the poor physical condition of the properties they have visited, without commenting on the landlords' responsibility for improving them. However, the tendency of tenants to fall behind with their rent payments is frequently noted.

Their home is a large old house which is shared with two old people who occupy a room each. It is in very bad structural condition, there is no lighting, no cooking facilities and only one tap with no sink for the whole house. Rent is 12s 6d a week and over a period of 15 months no arrears have accumulated. Equipment is meagre and consisted of two double beds, with one mattress, one blanket and a few rags in the bedroom; and in the living room one table, a chair, a broken sideboard, a chest of drawers with one drawer, a couch in bad condition and a kind of garden seat with one leg missing. They had only a few pieces of cutlery, two cups, a large meat dish, a kettle, a very large pot and a smaller one. The only clothing they had was what they stood in.

In that case, although the family income was about £2 12s 6d a week, they had managed to keep out of debt and to avoid the pawnshop and the money lenders.[76] Not all were so skilled, and keeping out of debt had been at great cost to their health and comfort.

The interventions employed by PSUs and their post-war successors, FSUs, came to be known as intensive family casework – although, as one commentator was to argue, the workers made negligible use of conventional professional casework skills.[77] Such a comment assumes the existence of a recognised armoury of specific techniques. It also misses the point. While it is unlikely that a group of untrained workers would have a range of professional skills at its command, one reason for the success of the PSU approach might be seen to lie in its rejection of professionalism. Workers did not set out to be professional; they believed themselves to be effective because they were non-professional – even anti-professional – and practised a type of intensive work with families which they believed to be innovatory. Their emphasis was on befriending poor families, an approach characterised by an informality unregulated by professional codes of conduct. To some extent the units consciously challenged the pattern of official relationships ordinarily experienced by such families. For example, PSU members tried to establish a relationship with their clients which combined friendly interest with respect; they did not keep to regular working hours; they refused to confine meetings to formal sessions in a client's home or in an office, as was the case with more traditional agencies. Callers to the unit house were made welcome at any time of day or night, and their problems were discussed over a cup of tea at the kitchen table.[78] Families were regularly invited to meals at the unit house. This was not just for purposes of education – although the opportunity to offer advice about cooking or hygiene was rarely missed – but, as Tom Stephens has explained, was also intended to make the family as welcome in the worker's home as he was in theirs.[79] While (as has been suggested) this notion of mutuality does not bear close examination, it has to be noted that this approach differed very significantly from that of other agencies, whether voluntary or statutory. It was, perhaps, this self-conscious sense of difference which made PSU decide, in 1944, that no useful purpose would be served by affiliating to the British Federation of Social Workers.[80]

The Liverpool unit also operated as an unofficial foster home until the local education department put a stop to it. The motivation behind this was to give hard-pressed mothers a break, provide an opportunity for strained family relationships to calm down, or to give children from disorganised homes the experience of regular meals and bedtimes. Sometimes the unit believed itself to be the only agency able to help in a family emergency.[81] The care offered was necessarily fairly basic; the workers were too busy to provide much in the way of supervision. The reason that the local education department insisted that the practice should stop was not inadequate supervision, however, but because there were no women living in the unit house and it was thought unsuitable that young children should be allowed to stay in a house full of men.[82]

The gender balance in the unit came to be used to demonstrate male superiority in caseworking because, it was later claimed, PSU believed that in some cases male workers were better able to influence a 'shiftless housewife' than women were.[83] The reality was more complicated. Working and living in the less attractive parts of the city, which were also more vulnerable to enemy attack, may have appealed more to men than to women and may have been more acceptable to men's families, but the PSU committee's decision to discourage women from becoming residential workers was informed both by the small number of female volunteers and by the limited accommodation available. Conscious that its pacifist stance already attracted hostility in some quarters, it was feared that a group of young unmarried women and men sharing a house might attract further criticism, and that accusations of sexual immorality might sully the unit's reputation. There were few full-time female members and it was agreed that none could be resident in the unit house unless a chaperone were provided. Any unchaperoned woman working in the unit was required to sleep in the home of a committee member,[84] which resulted in considerable inconvenience for the women, and, occasionally, dangerous night-time journeys across the blacked-out city in the interests of propriety.

It was not only the statutory authorities, such as the education department, which occasionally questioned PSU's unconventional style of work. Some established voluntary agencies thought them uncooperative;[85] others believed their approach to be harmful. Frances Peck, secretary of the Liverpool Personal Service Society (LPSS), used what she believed to be the weaknesses in their methods to try to persuade the PSU headquarters in London to curtail the activities of the Liverpool group. Miss Peck particularly disapproved of the way that PSU workers encouraged the use of given names by clients and thought that the practice of allowing young men to visit women in their homes was an undesirable one.[86] She may have been right, but a community which in its early days was almost entirely male, and which, even at the end of the war, had only two or three women attached to it at any one time, clearly had to confront the problems which resulted from the unequal gender balance of the team. Its dealings were very frequently with lone mothers and their children, while the male partners were in the forces, in prison, or just absent.[87] The unit's response to Miss Peck's criticism was to argue that if they did not try to help these families then no one else was likely to. In spite of Miss Peck's misgivings, nothing untoward seems to have happened, although she alleged that at least one woman had complained that she found the attentions of the young male workers embarrassing,[88] and one unit member later confessed to an infatuation with a young female client and to his sense of despair when he discovered her soliciting as a prostitute in the city.[89]

Miss Peck also believed the unit's methods to be misdirected. In her representations to the London committee, she cited an instance of PSU workers giving second-hand clothes to a needy family; the LPSS thought that the mother ought to have been encouraged to save a shilling a week for clothing for her children.[90] This revealing incident exposed a basic difference in approach between the two agencies: PSU, perhaps naively, responded to immediate need with immediate practical help, in this case the gift of some second-hand clothes; whereas the LPSS had a longer-term educational aim, and placed a greater emphasis on the encouragement of self-reliance than on the relief of present distress. Yet PSU and LPSS had more in common than they may have realised. Both groups were infused with a sense of moral purpose and the determination to improve standards of hygiene and child-care, and both were convinced that their methods held the clue to such improvement.

PSU workers' lack of professional education left them little defence against criticisms that they used inappropriate methods. Few PSU workers had done any sort of social work training;[91] a woman who became a Liverpool PSU resident in 1944 had completed part of a diploma course at the University of Manchester and hoped eventually to work as a hospital almoner, but she was unusual. However, although their approach may have been untutored and even overtly anti-professional, they sought to equip themselves intellectually for the task they had taken on. They read as widely as they could.[92] The Liverpool workers enrolled for a course of seminars with a sociologist who was living at the university settlement,[93] though it was not notably successful; the unit workers were nearly always too tired or too busy to spend much time writing essays, and their tutor was rarely sober enough to teach them properly.[94] Casework conferences provided a further opportunity for learning. These began to be held regularly towards the end of the war, when Manchester and

Liverpool caseworkers met to compare notes on the families with whom they were dealing, and to discuss the methods they employed. These meetings allowed the exchange of ideas and experiences and helped in the development of common patterns of intervention.[95]

Valuable though such meetings were, they did not constitute training. An opportunity to undertake more formal study presented itself towards the end of the war. The Provisional National Council for Mental Health devised a short course of instruction especially for PSU workers, several of whom were sent from the northern units to London to take advantage of it, alongside their colleagues from Stepney. The programme involved both theoretical instruction and supervised practical work with clients. The opportunity to work with a recognised agency employing trained staff reinforced the pacifists' confidence in what they had been doing,[96] and helped to shape their assessment of the ways in which some other agencies – especially statutory agencies – worked. On several occasions towards the end of the war, the actions of officials were criticised during PSU casework meetings, and it is clear that the units were confidently beginning to claim a distinctiveness of approach.[97]

Their claim, based on the conviction that their method had been shown to be effective, was also infused by a sense of moral superiority informed by their pacifism. The essence of the pacifist position involved a rejection of current social mores, extending from the refusal to engage in any violence to an informed criticism of welfare provision. One PSU document argues in almost evangelical tone that pacifists had cornered the market in morality and suggests a long-term aim of social improvement in the quest for moral progress, in line with the ambitions harboured for PSU by some of the founding members:

> ... the pacifist conception of the brotherhood of man is one the general acceptance of which needs a higher general level of human morality than mankind yet seems to have attained... its acceptance on a world-wide scale must therefore await the march of moral progress... pacifists have a direct interest in promoting those social conditions which further moral progress and in removing those which hinder it.[98]

Such sentiments were sometimes included in the notes they made on the families. Members of one Liverpool family, living in appalling conditions, were recognised as being victims of the British social system and, therefore, deserving of whatever help and encouragement PSU could give.[99] The environmentalism of such sentiments contrasts sharply with the eugenically inspired ideas of heredity which also appear to have informed much of their early casework, and to be indicative of a contradiction of which, at first, the workers seemed hardly aware.[100]

The methods employed by the original groups in Liverpool and Manchester were also less straightforward than they allowed themselves to believe. Judgmental attitudes lay behind worker–client friendships; the family was required to cooperate, and to allow a group of young men to criticise (however kindly) its standards of housekeeping, supervise the care of children, and decide how conditions which had been deemed unsatisfactory by the workers could best be remedied. Workers' perceptions of problem families indicate a middle-class and upper-working-class problematising of aspects of working-class life, based around the figure of the feckless mother. They were, although they did not appreciate it, well within a tradition informed by nearly a century of legislative and regulatory thought which underpinned a system of social work founded upon a classed construction of inadequate mothering.[101] As Philp and Timms were to observe in 1956, social work consisted of the application of standards of health and child-care espoused by middle-class social workers, and which had in previous generations been associated with the middle and upper classes.[102] Although PSU's successor organisation, FSU, was to build its reputation on the importance it attached to the integrity of the family, few PSU workers during the war believed that keeping the family together was their primary aim. The ease with which happy but dirty families were separated in order that children should experience the delights of soap and water and nourishing, if unfamiliar, food in a foster home was symptomatic of a controlling style of social work which largely ignored the psychological needs of children and, in the wake of the work of John Bowlby, Anna Freud and others, was later to go out of fashion. The workers were convinced, though, that the methods they used were right in the circumstances and that future events would vindicate them.

At the end of the war members of the PSU groups went their separate ways. Some became involved in post-war reconstruction in Europe, mainly through the work of the Friends' Relief Service, and others made plans to resume their peacetime careers.[103] However, a significant number elected to stay in their newly chosen employment and some made plans to enrol on courses which would furnish them with professional qualifications.[104] The organisation itself, in so far as it can be separated from its personnel, was very soon to begin a new life. A confident pamphlet published by *Peace News* in 1944 publicised the approach to helping families in difficulties which had been pioneered by the Liverpool, Manchester and Stepney units and suggested ways in which the lessons learned in wartime could be applied once the hostilities were over.[105] The confidence demonstrated by its author, a Liverpool PSU worker, was born of the conviction that the work PSU had done represented a new and effective approach to the solution of severe social problems.

Success, if measured in terms of families who developed parenting skills, managed to keep their children out of care, and kept their homes to the standards of cleanliness demanded by the PSU, does not seem to have been particularly high. Casenotes record an upturn in the fortunes of those families whose only need had been for friendly support and practical help in a time of crisis, but they also tell of families who did not respond, whose children remained dirty and ill-nourished and whose behaviour remained antisocial. It was reported, even by supporters of the PSU approach, that fewer than one in ten of the families they helped were able to maintain the improvements they had made for any length of time.[106] In spite of disappointments, however, by the end of the war the caseworking units of Stepney, Manchester and Liverpool had become convinced of the continued need for the sort of service they had begun to provide. At a joint meeting of the PSU executive and finance committees in London in March 1944, the post-war shape of the organisation was the main topic of discussion, and a measure of agreement on its role in society was reached. It appeared that a continuing core of workers could be assured; a questionnaire which elicited 47 replies from unit members revealed that 32 hoped to stay in some form of social service once the war was over, and 19 of those wanted to remain with PSU.[107] This commitment to social work was later to receive official approval with a statement on PSU policy which continued to express the moral contribution which members believed that pacifists could make to the development of an improved society, even if that necessitated a change in the philosophical basis of its own organisation. PSU believed its essential role to be:

> ... to offer pacifists the opportunity of applying their principles in trying to find solutions to the social problems they have seen and to achieve this end [it] is prepared to adapt its organisation in such ways as may seem appropriate...

to further necessary social reforms by all appropriate means, including those of creating social consciousness in those who will benefit by those reforms... to cooperate with other bodies as opportunity offers and circumstances permit... [to be] prepared to see those engaged on particular jobs or work break away from PSU, taking the jobs with them, if this will further the service being given... to continue in the post-war period on the basis of paying full-time members a living wage.[108]

The policy statement, generous though its outline appears to be, is less than clear about whether the adaptation of PSU as an organisation would have been so acceptable had it entailed the complete abandonment of pacifism, or the too-ready acceptance of 'co-operation with and absorption into the work of non-pacifists'.[109] Members probably approved this, believing it to mean a number of different things, but the painful decision to abandon the creed that had united a disparate group of workers lay not far into the future. In a report to the Manchester PSU committee contained in the minutes of the national executive committee in August 1944, possible ways forward were listed. Suggestions included: strengthening remaining units and attempting to open new ones in order to establish PSU as a permanent casework agency in its own right; keeping things as they were and making efforts to infiltrate other organisations by releasing trained men (sic); or abandoning all thought of permanency and concentrating on placing personnel in other agencies.[110] All were based on the ambition to retain, or even to increase, PSU influence over the development of social work with poor families.

Future plans were, however, out of step with present realities. Caseworking in Stepney had been temporarily abandoned because of a shortage of workers.[111] One proposal for remedying this was to put extra resources into developing the Manchester and Liverpool units so that they could eventually provide trained workers for London,[112] but resources were increasingly hard to come by. Solutions to local staff shortages, such as amalgamating the Liverpool PSU with the local Friends Service Centre, were proposed[113] only to be rejected. The shape of the future was eventually determined, however, not so much by committee decisions as by the unexpected consequences of publicity featuring PSU's wartime work. In 1945, Tom Stephens (then leader of the PSU in Manchester) edited an account of the work of the Liverpool, Manchester and Stepney units, based on disguised case studies and illustrated with undisguised photographs of families and the conditions in which they had to live. Entitled *Problem Families: An experiment in social rehabilitation*,[114] it described the methods which had been used. It was the latest in a number of publications exposing levels of deprivation in British cities, including David Caradog Jones's *Social Survey of Merseyside*;[115] Margery Spring Rice's *Working Class Wives*[116] (which uses some Merseyside examples); and most especially the report of the Women's Group on Public Welfare, *Our Towns: A close up*, published in 1943.[117] That last described the conditions brought to public notice when evacuees from British cities arrived in rural and suburban reception areas between 1939 and 1942. Although contemporaries suspected that some of the reports may have been exaggerated, and – as John Macnicol and others have demonstrated – they do need to be read with caution,[118] descriptions of the physical condition of evacuees had shocked many in the reception areas[119] and had occasioned a debate in the House of Commons.[120] The publication of *Our Towns* had confirmed the Liverpool PSU's conviction that it was working with a section of society widely represented in British cities and for whom the welfare services made little or no provision. The report identified the need for more sympathetic treatment for such families than that meted out by the NSPCC, whose practice of prosecuting neglectful parents often failed to take account of the physical and mental health of the parents concerned. Prosecution and imprisonment were condemned as appalling and criminally futile.[121]

The reception that *Problem Families* received was unexpected. At the time of its writing PSU had assumed that it would have to be published privately, suspecting that the material it contained was so unpalatable as to be unpublishable commercially and of interest only to those professionally concerned.[122] In the event, whatever its readership, the first edition of 1,890 copies was sold out within a few weeks and the agency was soon to be found negotiating with the publisher Gollancz for a second, and much larger, print run. A third printing appeared in 1947. Reviews – most of them favourable – appeared in more than 50 journals, and orders for copies were received from Belgium, the Netherlands and Sweden, in addition to Britain.[123]

It was as the result of a review of *Problem Families* in the *Manchester Guardian* that Lord Balfour of Burleigh – chairman of Lloyds Bank, the founder in 1926 of the Kensington Housing Trust, and a Kensington borough councillor – came to take an interest in the work. His experience of London housing had led him to believe that the 'subnormal, hopeless family' had hitherto presented an insoluble difficulty for welfare and housing workers. In correspondence with the Clerk to the Trustees of the City Parochial Foundation in 1947 he made reference to the 1938 *Report of the Central Housing Advisory Committee of the Ministry of Health* in which, in his view, the question had been glossed over because the authors could see no obvious solution. His reading of *Problem Families*, however, led him to hope that a solution had been found. In offering to support the foundation of a new, peacetime organisation, by making himself responsible for raising the necessary financial support provided that PSU produced an acceptable plan,[124] he had several objects in mind: to establish the extent of the problem; to study the causes of the disintegration of family life and the consequent burden on the social services (services for these families were a waste of money, time and effort, he opined); and to study the results obtained in terms of regenerated families or families in which disintegration had been averted by timely help.[125] PSU's emphasis on standards of housekeeping and general cleanliness accorded with his own. He argued that his experience with the Kensington Housing Trust had demonstrated that families were able to alter their way of life when their living conditions improved, and that constant hot water was a 'civilising influence'.[126] Lord Balfour's support was not entirely disinterested. It was conditional on the undertaking that the first 'new' unit to be established should be in the part of London in which he was a councillor and where he believed a large number of needy families were to be found.[127] A social work organisation focusing on a particular group of poor families might enhance the work of his own agency. Although the Kensington Housing Trust had achieved a great deal in terms of improved housing conditions, its supporters recognised that there was a hard core of families for whom better accommodation had proved inappropriate, either because their behaviour tended to make life unbearable for their neighbours or because they were in debt and under threat of eviction. Some of these families had been told that they must improve their behaviour in order to qualify for rehousing, but the trust also recognised that many families would not be able to achieve the targets they had been set without encouragement and supervision.[128] PSUs, with their experience of inner city deprivation and their commitment to domestic skills education, must have seemed a godsend.

The City Parochial Foundation responded to Lord Balfour's request by offering a grant of £500 towards the proposed centre in London on the understanding that an enquiry into problem families be conducted over a two-year period.[129] The possibility of putting their work on a permanent peacetime footing was discussed with leading PSU committee members and workers from Liverpool. In May 1946, a draft scheme was approved and plans were laid for a national committee whose membership would include representatives from the Liverpool, Manchester and Stepney units. A special general meeting in July 1946 agreed that Pacifist Service Units should cease to be organised on a national basis from September 30 1946 and that local committee members should assume responsibility for the workers in their units and for any work still in progress.[130] The first meeting to discuss the formation of Family Service Units, which would continue the intensive family casework pioneered by PSU, was scheduled to take place on July 25.[131]

The change in name signalled both the abandonment of pacifism as an essential qualification for workers and a recognition that pacifism was inappropriate for a peacetime organisation. Although the replacement of 'pacifist' in the organisation's name by a more generally acceptable word ('family') had been one of Lord Balfour's conditions, the decision was not taken lightly; it caused a division among the units and fuelled discussions which highlighted the distinctiveness which some members believed to be characteristic of pacifist endeavour. For some, cooperation with non-pacifists and the absorption of non-pacifists into work which, during the war, had been the expression of a quasi-religious, passionately held ideal threatened to dilute their witness. Workers in Stepney believed the proposal to be a betrayal and opted to remain pacifist, to continue their work under the sponsorship of the Peace Pledge Union and to stay outside the new organisation;[132] the Manchester unit, having originally expressed a preference for retaining the pacifist name in 1946,[133] eventually fell in with Lord Balfour's plans; only the Liverpool unit appears to have entertained few doubts about the way to proceed and to have acceded immediately. The names of PSU workers who wished to be considered as members of the new organisation were sent to the new national committee for consideration at the beginning of 1947.[134] Money for accommodation and wages (to replace pocket money) took longer to raise than expected and, although the PSU officially ceased to exist in the summer of 1946,[135] it was not until July 1948 that the Memorandum and Articles of Association of Family Service Units were signed and the first Family Service Units were functioning as parts of the new organisation.[136]

# NOTES

**1.** Minutes of an inaugural meeting, May 20 1940. ULSCA D495(HQ)PSU/1. See also H. Marsh, 'The agency: Its history and its clients', in J. Miller and T. Cook (eds), *Direct Work with Families* (London, 1981), p7. Pacifist Service Units were registered under the Charities Act 1940.

**2.** This was being actively discussed by 1943. See Minutes of the Liverpool PSU committee, February 10 1943. ULSCA D495(LI)M1/3.

**3.** M. Caedel, 'The peace movement between the wars: problems of definition', in R. Taylor and N. Young (eds), *Campaigns for Peace* (Manchester, 1987), pp75–6; P. Starkey, *'I Will Not Fight': Conscientious objectors and pacifists in the North West during the Second World War* (Liverpool, 1992), pp3–7.

**4.** Minutes of the PSU national committee, September 15 1940. ULSCA D495 (HQ)PSU/1.

**5.** A. Cohen, *The Revolution in Post-war Family Casework: The Story of Pacifist Service Units and Family Service Units 1940–1959* (Lancaster, 1998), p7.

**6.** Minutes of the PSU national committee, December 16 1940. ULSCA D495(HQ)PSU/1. Minutes of the Liverpool PSU management committee, November 27 1943; minutes of the Liverpool PSU finance sub-committee, January 8 1944. ULSCA D495(MA)M1/1.

**7.** Cohen, *Revolution in Post-war Family Casework*, p17.

**8.** Minutes of the Liverpool PSU committee, October 12 1940. ULSCA D495 (LI)M1/1.

**9.** R. Barker, *Conscience, Government and War* (London, 1982), p14.

**10.** Minutes of the Liverpool PSU committee, November 22 1940. ULSCA D495(LI)M1/1.

**11.** R. M. Titmuss, *Problems of Social Policy* (London, 1950), p50. See also J. N. Sissons, 'Planning Air Raid Precautions in the City of Liverpool, 1935–1940: A study of politics and administration' (unpublished MPhil thesis, University of Liverpool, 1985), p108; and J. Macnicol, 'The effect of the evacuation of British schoolchildren on official attitudes to state intervention', in H. L. Smith (ed.), *War and Social Change: British Society in the Second World War* (Manchester, 1986), p11.

**12.** Sissons, *Planning Air Raid Precautions*, p29.

**13.** Minutes of the Liverpool PSU committee, November 22 1940, November 29 1940, December 13 1940, January 3 1941, February 19 1941, March 12 1941. ULSCA D495(LI)M1/1. See also Cohen, *Revolution in Post-war Family Casework*, p17.

**14.** Cohen, *Revolution in Post-war Family Casework*, p17.

**15.** Personal communication from David Jones, April 1989.

**16.** Minutes of the Liverpool PSU meeting, March 20 1941. ULSCA D495(LI)M1/1. Cohen, *Revolution in Post-war Family Casework*, p17.

**17.** Minutes of the Liverpool PSU meeting, February 19 1941, March 20 1941, March 28 1941. ULSCA D495(LI)M1/1.

**18.** R. Whitworth, *Merseyside at War: A day-by-day diary of the 1940–1941 bombing* (Liverpool, 1988), p78.

**19.** The Liverpool unit kept a detailed log of these events, albeit written a few days after the emergency. ULSCA D495(HQ)PSU/2. A unit based at Westbourne Park,

London, kept a similar, but less detailed log. ULSCA D495(HQ)PSU/4. See also Cohen, *Revolution in Post-war Family Casework*, pp18–20.

**20.** Report of the Manchester PSU mobile section, May 4–12 1941. ULSCA D495(LI)M8/3. Minutes of the Liverpool PSU meeting, May 16 1941. ULSCA D495(LI)M1/2.

**21.** See notes in PSU log. ULSCA D495(HQ)PSU/2.

**22.** Cohen, *Revolution in Post-war Family Casework*, p21.

**23.** Cohen, *Revolution in Post-war Family Casework*, p21.

**24.** Whitworth, *Merseyside at War*, p81.

**25.** Personal communication from Dr Tony Gibson, a Stepney PSU worker, June 1995.

**26.** Personal communication from Edgar McCoy, June 1989.

**27.** Minutes of the Liverpool PSU committee, September 1 1943. ULSCA D495(LI)M1/3. Minutes of the Liverpool PSU committee, February 2 1944. ULSCA D495(LI)M1/5.

**28.** Personal communication from Michael Lee, June 1989. Cohen, *Revolution in Post-war Family Casework*, p17.

**29.** Personal communication from David Jones, April 1989. Cohen, *Revolution in Post-war Family Casework*, p15.

**30.** Personal communication from Fred Philp, April 1988. Cohen, *Revolution in Post-war Family Casework*, p15.

**31.** Personal communication from Michael Lee, May 1989. Cohen, *Revolution in Post-war Family Casework*, p29.

**32.** Personal communication from Michael Lee, May 1989. Starkey, *'I Will Not Fight'*, p12. See also minutes of the PSU national committee, October 21 1944. ULSCA D495(HQ)PSU/1.

**33.** This was increased to 5s during the course of the war. Although it was decided that it should be raised to £1 in 1944, funds were insufficient and workers had to be content with 10s. Minutes of the PSU national committee, June 24 1944, July 23 1944, September 23 1945. ULSCA D495(HQ)PSU/1.

**34.** Minutes of a general meeting, Liverpool PSU, June 4 1941. ULSCA D495(LI)M1/2.

**35.** The Manchester records are not as detailed as those from Liverpool, but from evidence in the Liverpool archive it is clear that similar arrangements were made for the accommodation of workers in both cities.

**36.** Cohen, *Revolution in Post-war Family Casework*, pp20–30.

**37.** Cohen, *Revolution in Post-war Family Casework*, pp8, 21ff.

**38.** Cohen, *Revolution in Post-war Family Casework*, p8.

**39.** See, for example, *Report of the Royal Commission on the Poor Laws and Relief of Distress, 1905–09*, Cd 4499 (HMSO, 1909), p1028. See also Women's Group on Public Welfare, *The Neglected Child and His Family: A study made in 1946–47 of the problem of the child neglected in his own home with certain recommendations* (Oxford, 1948), p88.

**40.** M. Lee, *Pacifism on the Doorstep* (London, 1944), pp5–6. Personal communication from Michael Lee, June 1989. Cohen, *Revolution in Post-war Family Casework*, p50.

**41.** Casework in Liverpool. ULSCA(HQ)PSU/7. See also minutes of the Liverpool PSU committee, December 6 1944. ULSCA D495(LI)M1/5.

**42.** PSU Newsletter, November 1943. ULSCA D495(LI)M13. T. Stephens, *Problem Families: An experiment in social rehabilitation* (London, 1945), p47.

**43.** See, for example, minutes of the Liverpool PSU committee, February 10 1943, February 24 1943, March 10 1943, March 31 1943, September 13 1944, October 4 1944; and minutes of the Liverpool PSU unit meeting, October 29 1942, December 3 1942, February 11 1943, February 25 1943, March 18 1943, April 15 1943, April 22 1943, May 6 1943. ULSCA D495(HQ)PSU/2.

**44.** Stephens, *Problem Families*, pp61–3.

**45.** P. Goldring, *Friend of the Family: The Work of Family Service Units* (Newton Abbott, 1973), p174.

**46.** The examples are numerous. See, for example, minutes of the Liverpool PSU committee, ULSCA(LI)M1/3, passim; and minutes of PSU national committee meetings for the duration of the war. ULSCA D495(HQ)PSU/1–8. Personal communication from Edgar McCoy, June 1988. See Cohen, *Revolution in Post-war Family Casework*, p9 and p14, n32. See also F. Rodger and M. Lawson, *Dear Heart: Letters to and from two conscientious objectors* (Sheffield, 1997), passim.

**47.** Barker, *Conscience, Government and War*, pp32ff; Starkey, *'I Will Not Fight'*, p24; Rodger and Lawson, *Dear Heart*, p3.

**48.** Minutes of the PSU management committee, November 23 1943. ULSCA D495(HQ)PSU/1.

**49.** Stephens, *Problem Families*, pp45 and 70.

**50.** Cohen, *Revolution in Post-war Family Casework*, p38.

**51.** See, for example, minutes of the Liverpool PSU committee, October 14 1942. ULSCA D495(LI)M1/2.

**52.** Stephens, *Problem Families*, pp18–19.

**53.** Stephens, *Problem Families*, p46.

**54.** Stephens, *Problem Families*, p46.

**55.** Stephens, *Problem Families*, p48. Minutes of the PSU committee February 10 1943. ULSCA D495(LI)M1/3.

**56.** During the war, nearly all PSU caseworkers were male.

**57.** See, for example, minutes of the Liverpool PSU committee, 21 October 1942, November 11 1942, February 10 1943. ULSCA D495(LI)M1/3. September 8 1943. ULSCA D495(LI)M1/4. December 8 1943. ULSCA(LI)M1/5.

**58.** See, for example, minutes of the Liverpool PSU committee, February 10 1943. ULSCA D495(LI)M1/3.

**59.** PSU Newsletter, May 1944. ULSCA D495(HQ)PSU/7.

**60.** Stephens, *Problem Families*, p10.

**61.** PSU Newsletter, May 1944. ULSCA D495(HQ)PSU/7.

**62.** N. Rose, *Governing the Soul: The shaping of the private self* (London, 1989), pp152–53.

**63.** J. Welshman, 'Evacuation and social policy: Myth and reality', *Twentieth-Century British History*, 9 (1998), pp44ff.

**64.** Quoted in B. Holman, *The Corporate Parent: Manchester Children's Department 1948–71* (London, 1996), p118. Lucy Faithfull was later to become children's officer for the City of Oxford.

**65.** J. Bowlby, 'Forty-four juvenile thieves: Their character and home life', *International Journal of Psycho-Analysis*, 25 (1944), pp19–53 and 107–28.

**66.** Stepney PSU Nursery Report; from internal evidence it is clear that this was produced some time after 1942. ULSCA D495(HQ)PSU/7.

**67.** One PSU had been based there. It finally withdrew its services in October 1944. Minutes of the PSU national committee, October 21 1944. ULSCA D495(HQ)PSU/1.

**68.** A. Freud and D. Burlingham, *Young Children in War-time: A year's work in a residential nursery* (London, 1942). A. Freud, *Infants Without Families and Reports on the Hampstead War Nurseries 1939–1945* (London, 1973), pxxiv. See also Rose, *Governing the Soul*, pp159–60.

**69.** Cohen, *Revolution in Post-war Family Casework*, p21.

**70.** Stephens, *Problem Families*, p50.

**71.** Stephens, *Problem Families*, p50.

**72.** Liverpool Pacifist Service Unit and case work; no date. ULSCA D495 (LI)M1/6.

**73.** PSU Newsletter, April 1944. ULSCA D495(HQ)PSU/7.

**74.** Casenotes Liverpool PSU, no date but after October 1943. ULSCA D495 (LI)M1.

**75.** Casenotes Liverpool PSU, no date but after October 1943. ULSCA D495 (LI)M1.

**76.** Casenotes Liverpool PSU, no date but after October 1943. ULSCA D495 (LI)M1.

**77.** E. Howarth, 'The present dilemma of social casework', *Social Work*, 8 (1951), p529.

**78.** Women's Group on Public Welfare, *The Neglected Child*, p90.

**79.** Women's Group on Public Welfare, *The Neglected Child*, p90. Stephens, *Problem Families*, p46.

**80.** Minutes of the PSU national committee, January 22 1944. ULSCA D495 (HQ)PSU/1.

**81.** Stephens, *Problem Families*, pp26–27.

**82.** Minutes of the Liverpool PSU committee, October 18 1944. ULSCA D495(LI)M1/5.

**83.** Women's Group on Public Welfare, *The Neglected Child*, p92. Cohen, *Revolution in Post-war Family Casework*, pp27–8.

**84.** Personal communication from Gwen Hall. Minutes of the Liverpool PSU committee meeting, September 7 1942. ULSCA (LI)M1/2. Minutes of the Liverpool PSU committee, July 7 1943. ULSCA D495(LI)M11/4. Cohen, *Revolution in Post-war Family Casework*, p28.

**85.** Minutes of the Liverpool PSU committee, June 23 1943. ULSCA D495(LI)M1/4. Liverpool Council of Social Service, *The Outlook for Voluntary Social Service on Merseyside* (Liverpool, 1950), p17.

**86.** Minutes of the PSU national committee, September 3 1942, and minutes of the PSU executive committee extraordinary meeting, September 6 1942. ULSCA D495(HQ)PSU/1.

**87.** Stephens, *Problem Families*, p11.

**88.** Minutes of the PSU executive committee, September 3 1942, and minutes of the PSU extraordinary meeting, September 6 1942. ULSCA D495(HQ)PSU/1.

**89.** Personal communication from a former Liverpool PSU worker, July 1988.

**90.** Minutes of the PSU executive committee, September 3 1942, and minutes of the PSU executive committee extraordinary meeting, September 6 1942. ULSCA D495(HQ)PSU/1. Cohen, *Revolution in Post-war Family Casework*, pp24–5.

**91.** Stephens, *Problem Families*, p69. Cohen, *Revolution in Post-war Family Casework*, p31.

**92.** Stephens, *Problem Families*, p72.

**93.** Minutes of the Liverpool PSU committee, September 14 1942. ULSCA D495(LI)M1/2. Cohen, *Revolution in Post-war Family Casework*, p32. Settlements were established in a number of urban centres and gave middle-class people, often university graduates, the opportunity to serve poor neighbourhoods by living there and giving time to local activities.

**94.** Personal communication from David Jones, April 1989. Cohen, *Revolution in Post-war Family Casework*, p32.

**95.** Minutes of the Liverpool PSU committee, 12 May 1943. ULSCA D495(LI)M1/4. Stephens, *Problem Families*, p71.

**96.** Cohen, *Revolution in Post-war Family Casework*, pp32–3.

**97.** Notes of combined casework meeting, 1944. Comments from Jack Marsden. ULSCA D495(HQ)PSU/7.

**98.** An unsigned, undated paper in the Liverpool PSU file. Because it refers specifically to the Pacifist Service Unit and to events of the war, it must date from before 1945. ULSCA D495(HQ)PSU/7.

**99.** Casenotes Liverpool PSU, no date but after October 1943. ULSCA D495 (HQ)PSU/7.

**100.** See below, ch. 2.

**101.** C. Smart, 'Disruptive bodies and unruly sex: The regulation of reproduction and sexuality in the nineteenth century', in C. Smart (ed.), *Regulating Womanhood: Historical essays on marriage, motherhood and sexuality* (London, 1992), pp23–4. A. Davin, 'Imperialism and motherhood', *History Workshop*, 5 (1978), passim.

**102.** A. F. Philp and N. Timms, *The Problem of 'The Problem Family': A critical review of the literature concerning the 'problem family' and its treatment* (London, 1957), pp3 and 9.

**103.** Minutes of the Liverpool PSU committee, June 24 1944. ULSCA D495(MA)M1/1.

**104.** For example, Ken Richardson engaged in correspondence with the London School of Economics to enquire whether PSU workers would be considered as students on the psychiatric social work course. See below, pp145, 146.

**105.** Lee, *Pacifism on the Doorstep*; ULSCA D495(HQ)PSU/7.

**106.** Stephens, *Problem Families*, pp9 and 15; Women's Group on Public Welfare, *The Neglected Child*, p100; R . C. Wofinden, 'Homeless Children: A survey of children in the scattered homes, Rotherham', *The Medical Officer* (May, 1947), p186.

**107.** Minutes of the PSU national committee, June 24 1944. ULSCA D495 (HQ)PSU/1.

**108.** Minutes of the joint meeting of PSU executive and finance committees, March 4 1944. Revised draft statement on PSU policy, no date but probably April 1944. ULSCA D495(MA)M1/1.

**109.** Minutes of the Manchester PSU executive committee, 20 December 1945. ULSCA D495(MA)M1/1.

**110.** Report to Manchester PSU committee on minutes of national executive committee and report of PSU general secretary, August 1944. ULSCA D495(MA) M1/1.

**111.** Minutes of the PSU national committee, August 26 1944, October 21 1944. ULSCA D495(HQ)PSU/1. See also secretary's report to the PSU national committee, no date but probably late 1944. ULSCA D495(MA)M1/1.

**112.** Minutes of the PSU national committee, October 21 1944. ULSCA D495 (HQ)PSU/1.

**113.** Liverpool's proposal regarding amalgamation. Manchester PSU unit meeting, May 10 1945. ULSCA D495(MA)M1/1. See also the discussions about the future of the Manchester unit. Minutes of the Manchester PSU unit meeting, June 6 1945. ULSCA D495(MA)M1/1.

**114.** Stephens, *Problem Families*.

**115.** D. Caradog Jones, *A Social Survey of Merseyside*, 3 vols (Liverpool, 1934).

**116.** M. Spring-Rice, *Working-class Wives: Their health and conditions* (London, 1939).

**117.** Women's Group on Public Welfare, *Our Towns, A Close Up: A study made during 1939–42 with certain recommendations* (Oxford, 1943).

**118.** J. Macnicol, 'The evacuation of schoolchildren', in Smith (ed.) *War and Social Change* pp3ff; Hendrick, *Child Welfare*, p194; Welshman, 'Evacuation and social policy', pp28ff. See also Richard Titmuss's foreword to Philp and Timms, *The Problem of 'The Problem Family'*, ppv–vi.

**119.** Women's Group on Public Welfare, *Our Towns*, pp1ff.

**120.** House of Commons Debates, *Hansard*, September 14 1939, cols802ff.

**121.** Women's Group on Public Welfare, *Our Towns*, pp52 and 123.

**122.** Minutes of the Manchester PSU executive committee, July 14 1945. ULSCA D495(MA)M1/1.

**123.** Manchester and Salford PSU, annual report for 1945–46. ULSCA D495(MA)M1/1.

**124.** Minutes of the Manchester PSU executive committee, March 30 1946. ULSCA D495(MA)M1/1.

**125.** Minutes of the Manchester PSU executive committee, March 30 1946. ULSCA D495(MA)M1/1.

**126.** City Parochial Foundation file, ULSCA unlisted. See also O. M. Blyth, 'Housing in Kensington: An account of the Kensington Housing Trust Ltd', *Social Work*, 2 (1942), pp214–24.

**127.** Notes of meeting with Lord Balfour of Burleigh, July 18 1946. ULSCA D495(HQ)M2/1.

**128.** Blyth, 'Housing in Kensington', pp214ff.

**129.** Copy of letter to Lord Balfour of Burleigh, April 27 1947. ULSCA D495 (HQ)PSU/9. V. Belcher, *The City Parochial Foundation 1891–1991: A trust for the poor of London* (Aldershot, 1991), p284.

**130.** Minutes of meeting with Lord Balfour of Burleigh, July 18 1946. ULSCA D495(HQ)PSU/9. Cohen, *Revolution in Post-war Family Casework*, p49.

**131.** Minutes of the Manchester PSU executive committee, July 22 1946. ULSCA D495(MA)M1/1.

**132.** The Stepney unit eventually joined FSU in 1953; see below, p78. The Brockley unit, too, intended to continue its pacifist service and reconstituted itself as Fellowship House, with the wartime fieldwork leader as warden. PSU report for 1945–46. ULSCA D495(MA)M1/1.

**133.** Minutes of the Manchester PSU committee, February 2 1946. PSU annual report for 1945–46. ULSCA D495(MA)M1/1. See also minutes of the Manchester PSU unit meeting, January 23 1946. ULSCA D495(MA)M1/3.

**134.** Minutes of the Manchester PSU committee, February 2 1946. ULSCA D495(MA)M1/1.

**135.** Minutes of the Manchester PSU executive committee. ULSCA D495 (MA)M1/1.

**136.** Notes of meeting of signatories of Memorandum and Articles of Association of Family Service Units, July 23 1948. ULSCA D495(HQ)M2/2.

# 2
# Problem Families, Eugenics and FSU

The publication of *Problem Families* in 1945 marked the end of a process of redefinition. The PSUs of Liverpool, Manchester and Stepney, having originated in the activities of a disparate group of conscientious objectors who were united in their aim to engage in humanitarian action which did not further the war effort, had developed into an organisation which had started to lay claim to considerable expertise in social work. Their sense of their own status was both confused and ambitious. Although they referred to themselves as 'willing volunteers', their apparent modesty was belied by their assertion that they were also 'pioneers of social work'.[1] Moreover, the field they had chosen was one that had assumed an urgency in both official and popular circles. This urgency was informed by the sense that the post-war reconstruction of British cities would be adversely affected by the lifestyles of a minority of poor families. PSU's work with such families had attracted the admiration and active support of Lord Balfour as well as medical and welfare workers, and reinforced the sense that the group had embarked on new and effective methods of intervention. FSU faced the post-war world with considerable confidence. Furthermore, as Michael Rustin has shown, the development of the professional status of social work – which accelerated in the decades after the Second World War – was intimately linked to the process of making the family an object of positive social policy.[2] PSU/FSU had, perhaps without realising it, positioned itself within the ambitions of a developing profession and within concerns about the health of the family.

However innovative their methods of working with problem families, PSU workers, and their successors in FSU, had also positioned themselves within a long-standing discussion about poorly functioning families, and were heirs to deeply rooted ideas.

Anxiety about the family, which exercised the minds of social commentators and national and local government workers in the 1940s, was part of a recurring pattern. As Jacques Donzelot has noted, the ritual scrutiny of the family as part of an attempt to discover the destiny of the society in which it is set has a long history. On one hand, the possible death of traditional family patterns and organisation has often fuelled fears of an impending return to barbarism; while on the other, the family's capacity for survival has provided reassurance for the future.[3] Scrutiny of the family in the 1940s appeared to reveal, if not an impending return to barbarism, at least a suggestion that the standards of some families threatened the stability and health of urban societies, and gave rise to the fear that they would have a deleterious effect on the quality of life enjoyed by the population as a whole. Such views did not seem to offer much in the way of encouragement for the future.

The designation problem family may have been a new one, but its 1940s manifestation had well-recognised antecedents. Tom Stephens's choice of title for his book about the work of Liverpool, Manchester and Stepney PSUs utilised the most recent term to come into vogue, although Stephens and his PSU colleagues also suggested that the families with whom they worked were part of the 'social problem group'. This was the appellation favoured by commentators in the 1930s, and implied that the families constituted part of a wider category of people, with whom they shared certain characteristics. As a quasi-technical term, problem families appears to have been used consciously for the first time during the course of the Second World War. Some date it precisely to 1943, when it was employed by the hygiene committee of the Women's Group on Public Welfare in its report on conditions brought to light during the evacuation of city children to places of safety in 1939.[4] In succeeding years, it came to be used to categorise those living in squalid conditions who were unable or unwilling to make appropriate use of the social services,[5] but whatever the subtleties of terminological distinction, it was the persistence of the phenomenon which impressed the Women's Group for Public Welfare and informed its plea for serious consideration to be given to the plight of the problem family and that of its neighbours:

> The 'submerged tenth' described by Charles Booth still exists in our towns like a hidden sore, poor, dirty and crude in its habits, an intolerable and degrading burden to decent people forced by poverty to neighbour with it.

Within this group are the 'problem families', always on the brink of pauperism and crime, riddled with mental and physical defects, in and out of the Courts for child neglect, a menace to the community of which the gravity is out of all proportion to their numbers. It is a serious matter that no study of this class of the population exists.[6]

The Women's Group on Public Welfare was not entirely correct; some studies did exist. As its own comments reveal, at the turn of the century Charles Booth had described a section of the population which the Women's Group believed to have been a forerunner of the group which was causing them such concern; presumably they equated this group with Booth's classes A and B.[7] If Booth's description did not answer their cry for a serious study – it was, after all, a generation and more out of date – then there had been more recent work. For example, E. J. Lidbetter, a Poor Law official, had identified a 'race of subnormals' in a study of an area in East London which was published in 1933. His analysis of the family histories of people on poor relief on a particular day in 1923 had led him confidently to assert that most, if not all, of those claiming long-term relief suffered from a genetic predisposition to incapacity for self-support, making them a persistent strain on the public purse. He made three overarching comments: that there was some evidence that such families had so many characteristics in common that they constituted a class by themselves; that members of affected families often closely intermarried; and that they exhibited a surprising degree of latent 'mental defectiveness' which appeared frequently to be transmitted from one generation to another, through the apparently normal members.[8]

Lidbetter was not alone in his suspicions that the families deemed inadequate by Poor Law officials and welfare workers were afflicted with inherited mental deficiency, and that this rendered them incapable of escaping their difficulties. The Report of the Wood Committee on Mental Deficiency in 1929 had posited innate inferiority in the lowest social stratum whose members, it suggested, lived in the inner areas of cities. This group – designated the 'social problem group' by the committee – consisted of about 10 per cent of any population and was characterised by 'a high proportion of insane persons, epileptics, paupers, unemployables, habitual slum-dwellers, prostitutes and inebriates'.[9] C. P. Blacker, general secretary of the Eugenics Society in the 1930s and 1940s, had also detected an hereditary element in the aetiology and pathology of the 'social problem group';[10] and its characteristics, similarly described, featured in the writings of David Caradog Jones who, like Lidbetter, presented the choice of sexual partner as a pathological act which perpetuated the existence of a section of society

> ... from which the majority of criminals and paupers, unemployables and defectives of all kinds are recruited. It is reasonable to suppose that the individuals who comprise this group would not be attractive to normally intelligent persons and hence they would tend to marry among themselves, as indeed they do. This goes far to explain why clusters of them should be found... in certain districts; and, seeing that so many of the group are clearly below the average in physique and mentality, it is no matter for surprise that these districts should in course of time deteriorate into slums... While external conditions ... largely determine the attitude of mind of the parents... it is the inherent quality of the parental stock that determines the kind of children they have... Those who have a serious concern for the future must direct their attention also to the quality of the people from whom that society is increasingly recruited.[11]

Such commentators, whose works were all to be found in the Liverpool PSU's house, branded families which exhibited symptoms of weakness and social failure as an undesirable but almost unavoidable feature of some neighbourhoods, and used the language of medical science and the law to describe their characteristics. Such families were held to be genetically deficient and to display criminal tendencies; poorly developed both mentally and physically, they were unattractive to normal members of the population; and their weaknesses were inherited by their children. 'Inheritance' could, of course, have a variety of meanings. It could suggest little more than parental failure to inculcate socially acceptable standards in their children; or it could mean that damaging behavioural and psychological patterns were imitated and consequently repeated from one generation to the next, or that such patterns were genetically predetermined. The Women's Group on Public Welfare argued in 1942 that where children were grossly neglected there was ample evidence that one or both parents, usually the mother, suffered from some serious physical or mental defect, although no explicit link was made with congenital malfunction;[12] but more often than not, the assumption was made that much antisocial behaviour was genetically transmitted. In 1946, for example, the Medical Officer of Health (MOH) Elect for Warwickshire appeared to give weight to explicit notions of biological determinism when he claimed that it was a 'common belief that all the parents are borderline mental defectives, that their condition is due to poor inheritance...'.[13] Ten years later, the survey on problem families conducted by the Eugenics Society suggested that the problem family commonly presented five features:

> ... subnormal intelligence in one or both parents, and instability of character distinguishable from subnormal intelligence, intractable ineducability, a squalid home and the presence of neglected and often numerous children.[14]

Such commentators serve to illustrate Alan Walker's argument that in virtually every decade in the twentieth century a concerted attempt has been made in the UK to differentiate between two groups of poor people: those whose poverty is caused by factors largely beyond their control, and those whose behaviour contributes in large measure to their own poverty[15] – a rewording of the traditional distinction between the 'deserving' and the 'undeserving' poor. Walker's analysis rings true when applied to problem families; such families were not just poor, although their poverty was rarely in doubt, but their behaviour also presented real difficulties for those, perhaps equally poor, 'who... are forced to neighbour with [them]'.[16] PSUs, while acknowledging that the family income of their 'cases' was low, believed that chronic ill-health, and mismanagement, characterised their homes.[17] Walker failed to note that during the inter-war period, and well into the post-war years, hereditary weaknesses were believed to play a substantial part in the construct of the poor family which was responsible for its own misfortune. As John Welshman has demonstrated, eugenically inspired explanations for chronically poorly-functioning families were widely accepted during the inter-war period and beyond.[18] Furthermore, the Eugenics Society had a practical impact on policy once the concept of the problem family became embodied in Ministry of Health circulars and in local authority public health provision.[19] Paradoxically, improved environmental conditions which resulted from the provisions of the evolving welfare state, and to some extent remedied factors which were perceived to be beyond the family's control, served to highlight the distinction between the two groups and to contribute to the stigmatisation of those who continued to fail to meet accepted standards. The pessimism associated with assumptions of congenital incapacity meant that many commentators, including the Women's Group on Public Welfare, were less concerned for the disadvantaged than with the threat to social order which they represented, suggesting that the real cause for anxiety was, or should have been, the plight of affected neighbours.

Although a large number of supposedly congenital weaknesses had aroused concern among those influenced by eugenic theories, mental handicap and malfunction were given disproportionate attention. Wartime PSU workers had suggested that some mental incompetence was present in almost all the mothers and half the fathers with whom they worked,[20] and their observations were borne out by other commentators. In his surveys of Hertfordshire S. W. Savage had found what he described as a high incidence of intellectual incapacity,[21] as had the MOH in Luton.[22] These findings were confirmed by research conducted by Dr Querido, the director of the Institute of Mental Hygiene in Amsterdam. In articles which had a ready reception in public health circles in Britain he argued that the incidence of epilepsy, schizophrenia and 'feeble-mindedness' detected in the families he had studied reinforced the view that mental defect alone was sufficient to explain the social condition of some families.[23]

In 1947, the deputy MOH for Liverpool, Dr C. O. Stallybrass, offered his own definition. He averred that problem families were those with 'stone age standards in an age of steel' and that irregular and uncertain meal-times and a failure to pay the rent were among their defining characteristics.[24] Some of his colleagues offered different descriptions. In 1944 the deputy MOH for Rotherham, Dr R. C. Wofinden (who was later to take up a similar appointment in Bristol), produced a description which he repeated in numerous articles during the following years and which became what some commentators have dubbed the 'classical description' of the problem family.[25]

> Almost invariably it is a large family, some of the children being dull and feeble-minded. From their appearance they are strangers to soap and water, toothbrush and comb; the clothing is dirty and torn and the footwear absent or totally inadequate. Often they are verminous and have scabies or impetigo. Their nutrition is surprisingly average – doubtless due to extra feeding in schools. The mother is frequently substandard mentally. The home, if indeed it can be described as such, has usually the most striking characteristic. Nauseating odours assail one's nostrils on entry, and the source is usually located in some urine-sodden faecal-stained mattress in an upstairs room. There are no floor coverings, no decorations on the walls except perhaps the scribbling of the children and bizarre patterns formed by absent plaster. Furniture is of the most primitive, cooking utensils absent, facilities for sleeping hopeless – iron bedsteads furnished with fouled mattresses and no coverings. Upstairs there is flock everywhere, which the mother assures us has come out of a mattress she has unpacked for cleansing. But the flock seems to stay there and the cleansed and recapped mattress never appears. The bathroom is obviously

the least frequented room of the building. There are sometimes faecal accumulations on the floors upstairs and tin baths containing several days' accumulations of faeces and urine are not uncommon. The children, especially the older ones, often seem to be perfectly happy and contented, despite such a shocking environment. They will give a description of how a full sized midday meal has been cooked and eaten in the house on the day of the visit when the absence of cooking utensils gives the lie to their assertion. One can only conclude that such children have never known restful sleep, that the amount of housework done by the mother is negligible and that the standard of hygiene is lower than that of the animal world.[26]

Much of Wofinden's description was not unique and may not have been original. A year earlier, in an appendix to a report produced by the Women's Group on Public Welfare in response to the outcry about the conditions exposed by evacuation, the Superintendent Health Visitor for Durham had written in remarkably similar terms of the characteristics of what she called the 'derelict family'.[27] The Minority Report of the Poor Law Commission as long ago as 1909 had also drawn attention to evidence that had a lot in common with both descriptions.[28] One explanation for the consistency of description may be that the characteristics of the problem family had changed little in 40 years; another might be that investigators asked similar questions, applied similar standards and made similar discoveries. However it originated, Wofinden's description, frequently repeated or referred to in articles written by him and by others from the mid-1940s onwards, suggests the existence of a syndrome with well-recognised elements. It raises questions about how many families he had seen in whom all elements of his definition had been found; it also invites comparison with the descriptions given by his colleagues in other regions who, while agreeing that there was a subsection of the population which exhibited antisocial characteristics, produced different lists of attributes. Unlike Lord Balfour, Wofinden failed to attach importance to the civilising effects of hot water,[29] or to appreciate the difficulty of obtaining such a commodity given the conditions in which some families were forced to live. The failure to consider that poverty rendered such families unable to afford the fuel which made high standards of cleanliness and nutrition possible, and the absence of any comment on the responsibilities of landlords for the condition of their properties, meant that blame was directed towards those who were powerless to alter their situation. As Stephens noted in 1945, most of the families with whom PSU was in contact were badly housed in old and insanitary property (although he pointed an accusing finger at the tenants and argued that the disrepair was partly the consequence of 'wartime difficulties, but equally often to misuse by tenants').[30]

In Wofinden's mind, most of the responsibility for the plight of the problem family lay with the mother.[31] It was in the mother that he detected a 'low mental standard' and 'an almost complete inability to improve'. His preferred remedy was to prevent 'mentally defective' women from producing children, arguing that to allow them to do so was a negation of social progress:

> Sterilisation of mental defectives would reduce the numbers of the defectives in the next generation. If Parliament feels that 'public opinion' would not stand such a measure, then it should ensure that cases of mental deficiency are segregated and prevented from propagating. Leaving aside the relation of mental deficiency and heredity, a mentally deficient mother is not a fit person to make a home for children. If mental defectives were efficiently ascertained and adequately dealt with we should have progressed toward solving the slum problem.[32]

His views would have received a ready acceptance in some Liverpool circles. In 1934, Caradog Jones, whose *Social Survey of Merseyside* was intended as an explication of the relationship between low intelligence and social problems, had suggested voluntary sterilisation for the mentally deficient, sex offenders, criminal recidivists and 'feeble-minded' mothers of illegitimate children.[33] Dr Stallybrass, while stopping short of advocating sterilisation, agreed that women bore considerable responsibility for serious physical health problems in their families. He believed that their failures played a contributory role in the development of a particular sort of peptic ulcer found, so he said, only among men in problem families and caused by the '... illness and discouragement of a wife who has to go out to work, irregular and ill-cooked meals, family dissension'.[34] And in other cases of family dysfunction:

> ... [the] discouragement of the mother is only a step towards the broken family. If the mother is incompetent the neglect of the home may drive the husband to seek solace in alcohol or gambling or may lead him to take his affections elsewhere.[35]

The frequent mention of the mother and her responsibility for domestic 'failure' demonstrates once again the dominant class-based notion of the 'family' which sprang from a middle- and respectable-working-class problematising of aspects of working-class life. The implicit assumption – that the desirable norm was the middle-class model of an employed husband with a capable and home-based wife who catered to all the emotional and physical needs of her family – also demonstrated a profound ignorance of the actual conditions in which some of the poorest British families were trying to survive. It placed the responsibility for family health in all its aspects on the woman, permitting her male partner to abdicate all such responsibility. The ease with which medical personnel and welfare workers – but perhaps most especially the former – labelled as 'problems' families who failed to conform to such norms, and attributed their difficulties to inherited intellectual inadequacy, was to colour the debate for a decade or more.

A significant change in what was believed to constitute good mothering took place in the post-war period. Concern about standards of domestic hygiene gave way to anxiety about the quality of mother love in the wake of the work of Donald Winnicott and John Bowlby, and there was a consequent rejection of the regimented and hygiene-based theories of child-care associated with pre-war experts such as Frederick Truby King. A dirty home had been condemned out of hand by some commentators during and immediately after the war, even though they noticed with some surprise – as did Wofinden – [36] that the children of these homes, if not very clean, were happy, reasonably well nourished and affectionately cared for.[37] By the late 1950s, many workers with families would have thought that slightly grubby but happy children were the product of good mothering, and their contentment proof that their emotional welfare was more important than the cleanliness of their clothes.[38]

Not everybody would have agreed that the mother was entirely responsible for the plight of the problem family. Nevertheless, the imprecise definition of this phenomenon helped to conceal the biologically-based reasoning which was used to justify a social construct that took little account of the economic misfortune which made life at anything other than a basic level an impossibility for some families. Whether its problems were believed to be largely economic or essentially genetic, the term problem family remained in common use, although it was employed without conviction by many social workers and other health and welfare workers. For some, it became increasingly clear that the imprecision of the term rendered it problematic. In the early 1950s, Noel Timms argued for it to be abandoned, or at least applied with greater care. He was convinced that the appellation had begun to lose any meaning which it might have had to those who had first used it a decade earlier.[39] At that time, it was argued that the problem was a biological rather than an economic one, and that it was characterised by a heartbreaking tendency to relapse after some slight behavioural amendment which, so it was argued by the Liverpool deputy MOH, may have been just a '*quid pro quo* for a gift of bedding or other *douceur*'. A similar imprecision was highlighted by Charles Murray when, in 1990, he noted the range of interpretations placed on the term 'underclass', which was used in the late 1980s to describe those poor people who were unable to live up to society's standards of acceptable behaviour.[40] It remains to be seen whether 'socially excluded', the Blair government's euphemism for those who fail to meet society's expectations, eventually invites such a wide variety of interpretations.

PSU/FSU must take a large share of responsibility for the continued popularity of the term problem family; at the very least, the publication of a book bearing that name served to perpetuate the notion that such families could be clearly identified. However, if PSU/FSU must take some blame, the Eugenics Society – which saw PSU/FSU as an ally and invited its contribution to a research programme into problem families in the immediate post-war period[41] – must share in it. Moreover, a belief in biological determinism was not solely the characteristic of fringe groups but was embedded in orthodox thinking about human nature and human abilities. It underpinned such post-war developments as the 1944 Education Act, which assumed that children's abilities were genetically predetermined and that it was possible, therefore, to design an education system which catered for measurable academic or non-academic abilities in every child.[42] A theoretical framework that was deemed to provide an adequate basis for educational selection was considered to be equally appropriate for explaining the characteristics of one section of the working class.

In the 1940s and 1950s, problem families became the social phenomenon which, more than almost any other, occupied the thinking of the welfare and public health professions; their existence posed a challenge to the notion of the 'good home', which had the 'good mother' at its heart and was characterised by order and cleanliness. However, attempts to distinguish between the problem family and the family with problems began to be made.[43] At least one writer on social work in the 1950s remarked on the probable causal link between poverty and the problem family, and noted the latter's relative numerical decline in the face of the increasing provisions of the welfare state,[44] thereby suggesting that the boundary dividing the family with problems from the problem family was defined to some extent by relative degrees of deprivation and was by no means as fixed or inevitable as had once been supposed. The 1956 annual report of the Kensington and Paddington FSU noted that it had very few examples 'of the really bad problem family type' on its books, and its author wondered whether such people were becoming less numerous as a result of the increasing efficiency of the social services.[45] In this way, the biological determinism which had underpinned the definition of the problem family was gradually challenged as the effects of environmental factors, including bad housing and poor health-care, were recognised and remedied. Other commentators, their observations informed by insights which arose from psychiatric social work, began to contest the assumption that problem families suffered from any unitary pathological condition, pointing instead to a range of features – including manifestations of extreme immaturity, depression and schizoid withdrawal[46] – which might reduce the ability of certain families to function at a satisfactory level.

Concern about families at the bottom of the social heap has also to be seen within the wider context of the anxiety about marital and family breakdown which, as Jane Lewis has noted, pervaded the government, the medical profession and the press during the war and the years that followed. Part of this anxiety was directed at the welfare of children, and was expressed in the establishment, by the Ministries of Health and Education, of the Committee on the Care of Children (Curtis committee) in 1946; the passing of the Children Act of 1948; and the appointment by the Women's Group on Public Welfare of the Committee on the Neglected Child and his Family, which reported in 1948. All were informed by the belief that the adequate functioning of the traditional family unit was crucial to national welfare,[47] an ideal given official expression in a Home Office circular in July 1948.[48] Foster rather than institutional care for children who were unable to live in their own homes was explicitly recommended by the Curtis report, and the 1948 Act reinforced the underlying assumption that family life on the traditional model, even if offered by foster rather than natural parents, offered advantages over care in a children's home. This represented a shift in views about child welfare and demonstrated a questioning of 'scientific' child-rearing notions which had dominated the inter-war period, and which had accorded importance to the professional, implying that child-care was too important and too difficult to be left to parents. As Philp and Timms pointed out in 1956, since the early discussions about the problem family there had been a considerable change in views on the desirability of removing children from their own homes, and an acknowledgement of the stress that such separation can cause for small children. Like Wofinden and Stephens before them, they also commented that in spite of inadequate physical care, there was little evidence that children in problem families were necessarily unhappy or that they showed any sign of emotional disturbance.[49]

Nikolas Rose has shown that a number of different factors came into play in what he has called the 'therapeutic familialism' which 'enmeshed conjugal, domestic and parental arrangements in the post-war period'.[50] In addition to the debate about what constituted adequate mothering, there were other concerns about the role of the family in the post-war world. The growing anxiety about the low birth rate, as expressed in Lord Beveridge's fear, if the birth rate continued at its 1942 level, that the 'British race cannot continue', was reinforced three years later by a Mass Observation report which characterised the low birth rate as the dominant problem of western civilisation.[51] The Royal Commission on Population, which reported in 1949, concluded that a series of broad social reforms was necessary if the population was to be prevented from falling below replacement level,[52] although as Denise Riley has pointed out, the Statistics Committee went against the general flow of the Royal Commission by casting doubt on the question of serious deficiency and drawing attention to 'the striking and largely unexpected increase in the number of births which took place in Great Britain after 1941'.[53] The question was not just one of numbers, however; the quality of the population, as demonstrated in its mental and physical health and social values, was also critical. Paradoxically, in spite of anxiety about the nation's low birth rate, part of the fear of the problem family was informed by the perception that its rate of reproduction was high when compared with that of its middle- and respectable-working-class counterpart. Films, radio broadcasts and popular magazines at the end of the war promoted images of heterosexual reunions with, as Wendy Webster has shown, 'their promise of fertility'.[54] They were intended to portray 'a unanimity of aspiration across class boundaries for the reconstruction of British society with its best features intact and its recent economic difficulties and unemployment absent'.[55] The existence of problem families appeared to undermine this emphasis on the healthy family, reunited after lengthy wartime separations and providing the social stability necessary for post-war reconstruction. Problem families had few easily recognisable best features and they continued to suffer severe economic difficulties, frequently caused or exacerbated by unemployment. Pro-natalist pressures, which judged couples with small families to have failed in their duty to the nation, were selective and did not extend to families at the bottom of the social pile. The continued existence of a section of the population which was suspected not only of perpetuating undesirable traits, but also of aggravating the problem by breeding prolifically, was seen to threaten the greatly-to-be-desired ordered society. The supposed fecundity of such families had been much discussed, particularly by eugenicists, towards the end of the Second World War; they concentrated their energies on the solution of the linked problems of feeble-mindedness and high fertility,[56] generally favouring a scheme in which compulsory detention in state institutions and voluntary sterilisation of the 'unfit' worked 'hand in hand'.[57] Other commentators, including Eleanor Rathbone, took a different tack and argued that the rise in family income caused by the provision of family allowances would have the effect of encouraging poor, working-class families to develop greater cultural and material aspirations and, as a result, they would understand that the achievement of these aspirations was closely linked to the reduction of family size.[58]

Anxieties about the effects on normal society of the presence of what was perceived to be an abnormal group were discussed in the national press. *The Times* of June 15 1953, for example, spoke in its leading article of:

> ... the feckless residue beyond the reach of the most comprehensive of welfare states. Incompetent in almost every sense for life in a civilised community, unable to manage their own affairs... unable even to make use of the many services for social casualties... [they] cause the community trouble and expense out of all proportion to their numbers... the characteristic most widely shared among them is a low standard of intelligence, bordering on mental defect, which is inherited rather than caused (though perhaps aggravated) by bad environment.

This was nothing new.

The anxiety provoked by the problem family led to proposals for energetic intervention. Superficially, these appeared to run counter to the traditional notion that the family was essentially private and should be allowed to manage itself, free from state interference. Such interventions as were necessary were thought to be better provided by private or charitable agencies but, as Nikolas Rose has demonstrated, this ideal bore little relation to reality. By the early twentieth century, the family was administered and policed by non-private practices and agencies; many of their powers were legally constructed, they were often publicly funded, and their workers were formally accredited by some form of licensing. In attempts to resolve social problems, 'the autonomy of the poor family was not to be destroyed but re-modelled through enhancing and modifying the family machine' through the efforts of statutorily recognised personnel.[59] The need to intervene in the lives of families and individuals for the greater demographic good and the production of socially and economically active and healthy citizens contributed to the atmosphere in which the advent of FSU was welcomed, and also provided the impulse for a government grant to the National Marriage Guidance Council in 1949.[60] Both organisations, with their emphasis on the importance of the family unit, can be seen as part of the post-war determination to safeguard the traditional family at a time of recovery from severe disruption to all aspects of domestic and social life. Such organisations also represented an attempt to build a stable future on the model of an idealised past. The Family Welfare Association (the new name, from 1946, of the Charity Organisation Society), the Eugenics Society and a number of medical practitioners became involved in the drive towards the secure family. Some individuals, among them the Liverpool deputy MOH, became associated with both marriage guidance work and efforts to rehabilitate problem families.[61]

With the family bearing the hopes of a nation, the term problem family rapidly became part of the vocabulary of social workers, doctors, housing managers and those involved in community medicine. Writing in 1959, Barbara Wootton struck a more positive note than earlier commentators when she indicated that important developments had taken place in the decade or so since the end of the war. She observed that the change in nomenclature applied to those whose difficult relationships and inadequate domestic organisation resulted in lifestyles which were unacceptable to the majority of the population, and high levels of dependence on the welfare services, was significant. As concern shifted from the existence of a social problem group to anxiety about the best method of treating problem families,[62] she saw evidence of the waning influence of eugenic assumptions which, as G. R. Searle has demonstrated, had been particularly influential in the 1930s.[63] Wootton's analysis over-simplified the matter. Her respect for FSU as the agency in the fore-front of practical work with such families failed to take into account the extent to which FSU both influenced, and was influenced by, those in the medical and social administration professions who clung to elements of eugenic teaching. For example, C. P. Blacker of the Eugenics Society had noted that FSU was responsible for encour-aging a more sympathetic attitude to problem families,[64] but his insistence on the maladjustment of such families is indicative of the belief that they suffered from some sort of abnormality. Some slight alleviation of the stigma attached to problem families followed the introduction of the welfare state, the post-war slum clearance, housing programmes, and the consequent improvement in the poor environmental conditions which had weighed heavily on some sections of the population. However, although Wootton may have been correct in arguing that eugenicists and members of other social hygiene movements were less influential in the post-war period than they had been in the 1930s, they had, nevertheless, been responsible for much of the research into that lowest stratum of the population, and the legacy of their influence was pervasive.

Assumptions about the genetic predisposition to criminality and antisocial behaviour were not waning. For example, in 1956 H. C. M. Williams, the MOH for Southampton, refuted the idea that environment was more than a minor factor in the aetiology of the problem family and stressed the importance of biology.[65] John Macnicol has argued that the term problem family was less pessi-mistic than its predecessor, 'the social problem group', because it was generally applied to those whose problems were deemed to be responsive to treatment and who could be trained to achieve socially acceptable standards of behaviour, rather than to those who were doomed to be lifelong victims of their poor genetic endowment. Yet although it may have denoted greater optimism it was, as Macnicol also points out, merely a recasting of an older concept,[66] and the term could be – and was – applied to families suffering a wide range of difficulties which demonstrated no discernible common pattern. Macnicol has argued that determinist notions were implicit in the 'cycle of deprivation' speeches made by Sir Keith Joseph in the

1970s, and were explicit in Joseph's use of personal characteristics – including 'poor genetic endowment' – as an explanation for some social problems.[67] Such assumptions did not end in the 1970s. In the discussion following the conviction of two eleven-year-old boys for the murder of a toddler in Bootle in 1993, similar genetic arguments were advanced. On November 25 1993 the *Guardian* carried a report from a child psychologist at the Tavistock Clinic which claimed that there was an hereditary element in the familial tendency to '...criminality, alcoholism, those kind of things'.

The use of a non-specific blanket term such as problem family also permitted shifts in the sorts of families thus stigmatised. One example of this can be seen in Bristol[68] where the city's department of public health, which was responsible for the supervision of what were euphemistically termed 'special families', noted the local effects of changes over the period 1953–67. These changes suggested that in spite of improvements to the physical environment as a result of slum clearance, and to families' conditions as a result of the provisions of the welfare state, the numbers of those deemed to be in need of special care was increasing. In 1953 the report from the MOH recorded 411 families on the 'special families' register; they were given support and supervision by a team of health visitors aided, on one estate, by a Family Service Unit.[69] In 1965, there were 915 such families and in his report for that year the MOH commented on squalor which 'would not have been tolerated some years ago'.[70] The following year, in spite of the transfer of responsibility for such families from the department of public health to the children's department consequent upon the provisions of the 1963 Children and Young Persons Act, the number of special families on the MOH's register had increased to 933 and he noted that '... new cases are constantly surfacing so that the work of the special team has in no way diminished'.[71] In 1967, the number had risen to 1,000.[72] It seems certain that the nature of the 'special family' as defined by the Bristol department of public health had changed during the period between the early 1950s and 1967. When FSU was first invited to the city in 1952, the problems it encountered were the same as those which were frequently found elsewhere – poor families living in bad accommodation failing to reach what were assumed to be acceptable levels of domestic organisation. In so far as it was possible to categorise them, the families transferred to the children's department in 1964 fell more or less into that group. By the mid-1960s new groups were being stigmatised; immigrant families, whose number had doubled between 1961 and 1965[73] and who were frequently to be found living in sub-standard accommodation in poor areas, accounted for about 15 per cent of the new families added to the register of 'special families'.[74] The 1959 Mental Health Act, which required that people with mental health problems should be absorbed into the community whenever possible, added to the total number of people requiring special supervision who were unlikely to be willingly accepted as neighbours. The increasing pressure to keep children out of care contributed, in the opinion of the MOH, to a general lowering of standards and to an increase in the number of families on the health visitors' books.[75] Working mothers and prosperous adolescents who spent their money unwisely and married too early were also impugned as adding to the steady increase in the number of 'special families'.[76] Bristol's experience demonstrates that, although it may have been given the same label, the late 1960s problem family had little in common with its 1940s counterpart, apart from its poor environment and its lack of appeal to its neighbours.

In the post-war period, the difficulties faced by problem families and the methods of treating those difficulties gave rise to conferences, learned articles and the development of what was perceived to be a new approach to social work in the form of intensive family casework, largely on the PSU/FSU model. The gradual change in FSU's mode of intervention, from one in which personal and domestic hygiene was dominant to one which acknowledged the importance of mental health and psychiatry, began earlier than Wootton had assumed and is evidence of eugenicist influence. That greater optimism detected by Macnicol, which to some extent made the cooperation between the eugenicists and FSU possible, is symptomatic both of the diversity of thinking in eugenicist circles in the 1940s, and of the evolution of a more sophisticated approach to social work with families in difficulty which was to become a function of the post-war welfare state. The change was slow in coming, however, and some medical authorities in the late 1940s were still arguing for an increase in '... colony accommodation for the mentally defective to reduce the number who enter matrimony'.[77]

Although such eugenically informed ideas had influenced social thinking in the inter-war period, the fact that a group of amateurs like the Liverpool PSU should have stumbled across them requires explanation. The initial encounter appears to have taken place in

Liverpool; perhaps this should occasion no surprise, as there was in the city a long history of interest in eugenics. The first provincial branch of the Eugenics Society (which had been founded as the Eugenics Education Society in 1907)[78] was started there in 1909, and boasted representatives of prominent local families among its membership.[79] The branch experienced hard times in the years immediately after the First World War, as did others,[80] but in 1935 it nevertheless had a secretary who was interested in the eugenic possibilities of sterilisation.[81] During the 1930s, members of the society organised lectures and meetings in Liverpool and recruited for the Eugenic Alliance. Their reports to the headquarters of the Eugenics Society suggest a fair amount of local interest, with 50 people and more attending meetings and exhibitions with titles like 'Eugenics',[82] 'Heredity, healthy and unhealthy families',[83] and 'The future of our population: its quality and quantity'.[84]

Direct links between PSU and local eugenicists appear in the first instance to have owed little to such activities, perhaps because many PSU workers were not themselves Liverpudlians but had been sent to the city by the London headquarters of the organisation, either to work as members of the unit or to receive training in casework before being sent to Manchester and Stepney.[85] Relationships appear to have developed as a result of personal contacts with members of the academic staff of the University of Liverpool, where key members of the Eugenics Society were employed.[86] David Caradog Jones, a statistician with an interest in demography whose work on the social composition of Merseyside had a great impact on the PSU,[87] had begun teaching at the university in 1924. Apart from his professional interest in the unit's work with those whom he designated the 'social problem group', Caradog Jones enjoyed other points of contact with them. He was a member of the Society of Friends which offered practical support to the unit, and he shared the pacifist principles in which they believed; during the First World War he had been imprisoned because of his conscientious objection. Caradog Jones was also concerned to develop means for achieving world peace, an ambition which would have found ready acceptance in the PSU community.[88] He was converted to eugenics soon after his appointment as a lecturer at the university,[89] partly through the influence of Professor A. M. Carr Saunders, and his new interest is evidenced by the emphasis on eugenic considerations in his writings and his interest in the social problem group.[90] The *Social Survey of Merseyside*, for which he and his team of researchers had conducted a comprehensive survey of Liverpool and the surrounding areas in the years after 1929, was published in 1934. Its conclusion had much in common with that of the Wood Committee on Mental Deficiency, in that it identified a local manifestation of that 'defective' group which the committee had believed to be an invariable element in any population.[91]

Caradog Jones became an enthusiastic supporter of the Liverpool PSU, and its members came to rely on his analysis of the social problems they encountered.[92] In a letter to the unit in August 1945, Caradog Jones applied his determinism to an analysis of the families encountered during the unit's wartime work, arguing that problem families were characterised either by an inability to 'get through life without more or less help of a friendly kind from some official body, voluntary organisation or private individual', or were those for whom 'the struggle is hopeless and they will always be a heavy drag on the community'.[93] The *Social Survey* reinforced PSU's impressions of a city whose slum districts had borne the brunt of enemy bombing in 1941, leaving already vulnerable inhabitants exposed and homeless. It also helped to inform the conceptual framework within which they worked. Although they were eventually to question the validity of biological determinism, in the early days of their work they had no alternative model to help them make sense of the problems they encountered.

In addition to their contacts with Caradog Jones, PSU also encountered eugenicist influence as a result of the shift in emphasis of their work away from the scrubbing and cleaning which Wootton had identified as characteristic of their approach.[94] Wootton had correctly suggested that, so far as PSU was concerned, the squalor in which some families lived distinguished them as problem families; but by 1943 – influenced by contemporary social work and public health literature, and by their experience of families with problems – PSU members were gaining some insight into the psychological needs of their clients. Indeed, it could be argued that such concern was always an element in their outlook, and that the cleaning and scrubbing in which they engaged was only a part of the 'friendship with a purpose' which they believed to be their mission. Moreover, their attempt at psychological diagnosis – even if it was limited to the observation of a high incidence of 'mental defect' or 'instability' among the families with whom they worked, and the labelling of some of them as 'dull' or 'feeble-minded' (terminology employed in the 1913 Mental Deficiency Act and elaborated on in the 1927 amendment to the Act)[95] – is itself evidence of an effort to deal with more than just the environmental problems presented by these families, and to see both psychological and structural elements in the genesis of these problems. Liverpool PSU casenotes frequently comment on the limited mental ability of the family members, and particularly of the mother. This stress on 'mental defect or instability' is also identified by Stephens in his description of problem families.[96]

An opportunity to extend their understanding of these issues came in October 1943, when links were forged with the Provisional National Council for Mental Health (PNCMH) which had close contacts in eugenicist circles. The PNCMH had a complex history. Three bodies concerned with mental health – the National Council for Mental Hygiene, the Central Association for Mental Welfare, and the Child Guidance Council – had combined in 1939 as the Mental Health Emergency Committee, and had become the PNCMH in 1942. Much of its funding came from the Ministry of Health.[97] The first of its constituent elements had been formed by prominent members of the Royal Medico-Psychological Association with the aim of encouraging the development of the mental sciences and their adoption in medical schools and elsewhere.[98] The Central Association for Mental Welfare had been constituted as a result of the 1913 Mental Deficiency Act, passed in part as a consequence of eugenicist pressure,[99] and was successor to the National Association for the Welfare of the Feebleminded. Its most important work was done through local voluntary committees whose task was to refer to the appropriate authorities those in their areas deemed to be mentally defective and in need of institutionalisation.[100] It also organised courses and conferences on mental deficiency for doctors and trained the first social workers in mental health.[101] Mental health training for social workers appears to have been one of the activities taken on by the PNCMH in 1942, and it was in the exercise of this function that contact was first made with PSU.[102] In October 1943, a representative of the PNCMH visited the Stepney unit after hearing about the work being done there from a representative of the Institute for the Scientific Treatment of Delinquency. There can be little doubt that the offer of training subsequently made to Stepney PSU was motivated in part by the PNCMH's need for help, particularly in providing support for men requiring psychiatric treatment who had been discharged from the forces.[103] In February 1944 the PNCMH, anxious that the work of PSU should continue, suggested through its local representative that the organisation might be able to provide training for Stepney PSU caseworkers.[104] An approach was made to the Manchester unit in March 1944, and subsequently to the Liverpool unit. That all three offers were made in so short a time suggests that, far from representing an attempt by the PNCMH to respond to local situations, the move was centrally orchestrated – although carried out by local agents – and was directed specifically at PSU. The PNCMH's Liverpool representative, a local solicitor, informed the caseworkers that the PNCMH was looking for people '… of the right type, adapted to work done by the Council'.[105] By this time, PSU workers were confident that their form of casework, largely instinctive and untutored though it was, could offer effective support to problem families. Their contacts with local eugenicists in Liverpool, and the nature of the informal tuition they had organised for themselves, must also have helped to satisfy the PNCMH that they were 'of the right type', because by April 1944 a short course had been designed to meet their needs and the first batch of trainees, made up of workers from all three units, were in London to receive training.[106]

The late summer of 1944 saw cooperation between the PNCMH and PSU strengthened to such an extent that PSU workers were being recruited by the PNCMH as part-time workers – clear evidence that they had proved themselves to be 'of the right type' and that the offer of training had not been intended simply to help the new casework agency but also to recruit staff for the PNCMH. The following year saw a discussion of the possibility that the local PNCMH branch might rent rooms in the unit's house in Liverpool,[107] and a few months later the PNCMH organised a series of lectures in Liverpool for the unit.[108] By this time some division had occurred within the Liverpool unit about the function of the PNCMH courses. The end of the war prompted workers to consider both their personal peacetime ambitions and the future of the family casework they had pioneered. Anxious to avoid wasting training opportunities on those who were intending to leave the unit, they had begun to consider the place of the courses in their long-term plans. Finally it was decided that, provided that those who followed the courses intended to remain in some sort of social work, they should be encouraged to continue.[109]

Those PSU caseworkers trained by the PNCMH were at the end of a process which had begun in the early days of their work in

Liverpool and Manchester. Although most lacked formal training in any type of social work, they were anxious to take any available opportunity to extend their knowledge and improve their practice.[110] Their inexperience meant that to a large extent they were working in isolation and without any critical framework by which to evaluate either their own contribution or the literature they read. The pressures of the work they had chosen to do were considerable. They lived together in rented houses and made themselves available to people in need 24 hours a day. When they went into the homes of families, it was often to do strenuous, physical work and to face the hazards of severe infestation by fleas, bugs and other vermin. Although they had managed to forge good relationships with some other welfare agencies, and enjoyed the continued support of their pacifist committee, their work was not always appreciated. In spite of protestations to the contrary, relationships with other social work agencies were not always harmonious; one in particular, the Liverpool Personal Service Society, believed that the PSU was doing more harm than good, and tried to put a stop to its activities.[111]

In 1945, Tom Stephens claimed that members of the unit had endeavoured to keep abreast of current literature on social work.[112] Most Liverpool workers claim to have read the influential textbook on social work by Gordon Hamilton[113] during their time in the local unit.[114] Other works available to them were written by men and women with eugenicist leanings, illustrating the extent to which they had initiated research into the problems of the most deprived section of society. As David Jones has explained, there was little on the subject in the inter-war period which had not been influenced by eugenicists.[115] Eugenics also helped to inform the thinking of largely self-taught caseworkers, who were feeling their way by instinct and common sense in a difficult and demanding area of welfare. Stephens cited Cyril Burt's work which demonstrated that 'sordid homes are responsible for mentally and emotionally backward children'. Although he questioned the notion that this was as a direct result of heredity, he suggested that it was often the least mentally and physically fit who were the most prolific, and that their children were stunted by neglect and handicapped by an atrocious upbringing.[116] Stephens also used John Bagot's work on juvenile delinquency; Bagot's conclusion, which echoed Blacker's link between class and psychology, owed a great deal to eugenic classification, and he argued that psychological factors had an even more potent influence than conditions of environment over the development of delinquency. He claimed that in Liverpool the problem was concentrated in one section of the population, the very poor:

> ... and even within this section minor subnormal groups are responsible for a large proportion of the total number of cases... they are likely to be boys who are mentally backward, unemployed, from large overcrowded families where normal relationships are broken in some way, where discipline is weak and where there is probably already another delinquent.[117]

Stephens also made a distinction between the old notion of the 'submerged tenth' – whose difficulties were largely economic in origin and whose lifestyle improved with social and educational services – and 'problem families', who were unable to profit from the facilities made available to them.[118] He noted that nearly half of the parents described in his book had children who were mentally deficient or educationally backward. He linked these defects to poor school attendance,[119] a failure in the exercise of parental responsibility that, it might be argued, could account for educational backwardness but not for mental deficiency.

In Manchester PSU, where Tom Stephens was fieldwork leader in 1946, the emphasis on eugenics was sometimes explicit. The unit welcomed a visit from Miss Voller of the PNCMH to discuss the 'low mentality group'.[120] Stephens himself proposed a paper on 'Sterilisation, birth control and eugenics' for an inter-unit case conference. The conference was eventually given over to discussion of the social problem group, with special reference to the work of David Caradog Jones expressed in a letter to the units.[121] There is only the merest suggestion that workers should challenge Caradog Jones's views. They were enjoined to increase their knowledge of the social problem group and, if possible, to make a special study of some particular aspect, for instance 'eugenics, mental defect or the influence of environment'.[122]

Similar ideas fed into the new, post-war organisation. At a conference for FSU trainees in 1952 Eryl Roberts, an ex-FSU trainee,[123] in a talk entitled 'Is FSU too optimistic about the possibilities of rehabilitation?', argued that there were a number of factors inhibiting FSU's work, including the poor psychopathology of FSU families. Like other commentators, she noted particularly the importance of the mother whose psychological problems, in many instances, were of more significance than environmental factors. Some mothers were also written off as 'unteachable' because of their low intelligence.[124]

As far as the definition and diagnosis of mental health and

intellectual capacity was concerned, the first generation of PSU/FSU workers apparently accepted aspects of eugenicist teaching without serious question or any attempt at precision of definition. They demonstrated greater independence in the area of contraception, even though the control of fertility was an important part of any eugenically inspired programme. In a city like Liverpool, which had a large Roman Catholic population for whom the church was an important welfare agency offering material as well as spiritual help, it was important that the PSU workers trod carefully, both out of consideration for their clients and in order to ensure that their hard-won credibility was not damaged by antagonistic local clergy.[125] Nevertheless, PSU workers have claimed that they did make their views known and encouraged parents to consider limiting the size of their families, not to prevent the 'unfit' from breeding but in an effort to relieve those problems which resulted from the struggle to support several children on a small income, and to enhance the emotional, medical and financial well-being of the family.[126]

The stirring up of religious opposition was not always avoided. In 1950 in Oldham, another town with a large Roman Catholic population, opposition came from local Catholic councillors who complained to the unit about the contraceptive advice given to clients. The workers protested that they gave information only when requested and that the families concerned were not Roman Catholics, but although the MOH supported the principle of making information available, it was on condition that any advice about contraception was given by health visitors,[127] thus making it clear to FSU workers that this was not an area in which they were credited with expertise.

By the 1950s, the FSU leaders were exhibiting growing ambivalence about the Eugenics Society. Although they wished to distance themselves from elements of eugenicist thinking, they were conscious of their dependence on some members of the Eugenics Society. In 1953 David Jones, then FSU national secretary, advised Alf Strange, leader of the Bristol unit, to use caution in his relationships with Blacker and the Eugenics Society, and especially to avoid criticism of the report on problem families which the society had produced. Care was necessary in part because R. C. Wofinden – deputy MOH for Bristol, a member of the Eugenics Society, a prolific writer on problem families and a contributor to the Eugenics Society report – had engineered the invitation to FSU to set up its work in Bristol. Moreover, his department paid all the unit's costs.[128]

Examination of PSU/FSU methods demonstrates that they consisted of much more than the mop and bucket of Barbara Wootton's description.[129] Even in the earliest days of the agency the obsession with personal and domestic cleanliness, frequently believed to be their trademark, concealed a more reflective and analytical approach to the problems they encountered, but they were inexperienced and, on occasion, confused in their thinking. Tom Stephens, while arguing that the eugenicists' arguments were nonsense, also argued that genetic inheritance played a part in the problem family syndrome.[130] Stephens, who prided himself on his clear thinking, was probably unaware of the confusion. It was a product of youthful idealism, informed by concern for the underdog, and a limited understanding of social problems. There can be little doubt that, whatever their private and semi-formed opinions, their methods met with considerable approval from those, particularly MOHs, whose thinking was consciously informed by eugenic ideas.[131] A number of MOHs, particularly those from Sheffield, Liverpool, Oldham, Bristol and Salford, endorsed and supported PSU/FSU over the next decade.[132] Dr Burn, from Salford, attempted to persuade a PSU worker to join his staff as hygiene officer,[133] and his colleagues in Oldham and Bristol arranged for the full costs of their local unit to be met from departmental funds.[134]

Too close an association with eugenicists may have become unacceptable by the mid-1950s, and the subsequent anxiety of FSU workers to distance themselves from an ideology which had become demonised is understandable. However, it had represented social scientific orthodoxy in the inter-war period and as David Jones, the first national secretary of FSU, has since commented, 'They were the only people who had done any research'.[135] It was hardly surprising that PSU/FSU was influenced by such research – it would have been more remarkable if they had not.

The metaphor changed in the post-war years from a biologically deterministic one to a medical one. The Liverpool FSU annual report of 1954–55 noted that the parents of FSU families must be thought of as sick people who needed help to recover or who might need permanent care.[136] The idea was repeated in a review of the first ten years of the organisation, in the context of widespread unease about the use of the term problem families: '... our clients are ill, some more than others'.[137] The change of metaphor signals a move from stigmatisation to pity and a change of direction from corrective to therapeutic work. It is also a reversion to the terminology used by the Charitable Organisation Society at the end of the nineteenth century, whose Principles of Decision published in 1881 stated that 'Each case of distress is to be considered as that of a sufferer from some malady, of one afflicted in mind, body or estate.'[138]

# NOTES

**1.** T. Stephens, *Problem Families: An experiment in social rehabilitation* (London, 1945), p45.

**2.** M. Rustin, 'Social work and the family', in N. Parry, M. Rustin and C. Satyamurti (eds), *Social Work, Welfare and the State* (London, 1979), p140.

**3.** J. Donzelot, *The Policing of Families* (London, 1979), p4.

**4.** Women's Group on Public Welfare, *Our Towns, a Close Up: A study made during 1939–42 with certain recommendations by the hygiene committee of the Women's Group on Public Welfare* (Oxford, 1943), pxiii.

**5.** A. F. Philp and N. Timms, *The Problem of 'The Problem Family': A critical review of the literature concerning the 'problem family' and its treatment* (London, 1957), ppi and vii. Women's Group on Public Welfare, *Our Towns*, ppxiiiff. It has been suggested that C. P. Blacker, general secretary of the Eugenics Society in the interwar period, used the term, but that he may not have intended it as a technical description.

**6.** Women's Group on Public Welfare, *Our Towns*, pxiii. See also J. Macnicol, 'The effect of the evacuation of schoolchildren on official attitutes to state intervention' in H. L. Smith (ed.), *War and Social Change: British Society in the Second World War* (Manchester, 1986), pp3–31.

**7.** C. Booth, *Life and Labour of the People of London* (reprint, London, 1903), pp18ff. See also W. Booth, *In darkest England and the way out* (London, 1890), pp65–6.

**8.** E. J. Lidbetter, *Heredity and the Social Problem Group* (London, 1933), p18. See also N. Rose, *Governing the Soul: The shaping of the private self* (London, 1989), p136.

**9.** Board of Education and Board of Control, *Report of the Inter-departmental Committee on Mental Deficiency, 1925–29* (Wood report) Cd 3545 (HMSO, 1929), pt III, p.80.

**10.** C. P. Blacker, *A Social Problem Group?* (London, 1937).

**11.** D. Caradog Jones, *A Social Survey of Merseyside* 3 vols, (Liverpool, 1934), vol 3, pp546–7. This explanation for the perceived mental incapacity of some poor families was not limited to the UK, or even Europe. As Molly Ladd Taylor has shown, similar ideas pervaded North American policy making and social work circles. M. Ladd Taylor, '"Fixing mothers": Child welfare and compulsory sterilisation in the American Midwest, 1925–1945', in J. Lawrence and P. Starkey (eds),

*Child Welfare and Social Action From the Nineteenth Century to the Present* (Liverpool, forthcoming).

**12.** Women's Group on Public Welfare, *Our Towns*, Appendix VI, p123.

**13.** S. W. Savage, 'Rehabilitation of problem families', *Journal of the Royal Sanitary Institute*, 66 (August 1946), p337.

**14.** C. P. Blacker, *Problem Families: Five inquiries* (London, 1952), p20.

**15.** A Walker, 'Blaming the victims', in Charles Murray (ed.), *The Emerging British Underclass* (London, 1990), p49.

**16.** Women's Group on Public Welfare, *Our Towns*, pxiii.

**17.** Stephens, *Problem Families*, p3.

**18.** J. Welshman, 'In search of the "problem family": Public health and social work in England and Wales 1940–1970', *Social History of Medicine*, 9 (1996), pp448ff.

**19.** J. Welshman, 'Evacuation and social policy during the Second World War: Myth and reality', *Twentieth Century Social History*, 9 (1998), p50.

**20.** See for example Stephens, *Problem Families*, pp4, 6, 22–5 and 28–31.

**21.** S. W. Savage, 'Intelligence and infant mortality in problem families', *British Medical Journal*, 2 (1946); S. W. Savage, 'Rehabilitation of problem families', *The Medical Officer*, 75 (1946).

**22.** C. C. Tomlinson, *Families in Trouble: An enquiry into families in trouble in Luton* (Luton, 1946).

**23.** Quoted in C. O. Stallybrass, 'Problem families', *Social Work*, 4 (1947), p32. A. Querido, 'The problem family in the Netherlands', *Medical Officer*, 75 (1946), p193.

**24.** Stallybrass, 'Problem families', *Social Work*, p30.

**25.** Philp and Timms, *The Problem of the 'Problem Family'*, pix; C. P. Blacker, *Eugenics: Galton and after* (London, 1952), pp311–4.

**26.** R. C. Wofinden, 'Problem families', *Public Health*, 57 (September, 1944), p137. See also 'Basic facts of problem families', *Medical Officer* (December 1955), p377.

**27.** Women's Group on Public Welfare, *Our Towns*, pp128ff.

**28.** Poor Law Commission, *Minority Report*, Cd 4499 (HMSO, 1909) p752.

**29.** See above, p36.

**30.** Stephens, *Problem Families*, p4.

**31.** See P. Starkey, 'The feckless mother: Women, poverty and social workers in 1940s Britain', *Women's History Review*, 9 (2000), pp593ff.

**32.** R. C. Wofinden, 'Problem families', *Eugenics Review*, 38 (1946–47), pp129 and 131.

**33.** G. Jones, *Social Hygiene in Twentieth-Century Britain* (London, 1986), p90.

**34.** Stallybrass, 'Problem families', *Social Work*, p33.

**35.** Stallybrass, 'Problem families', *Social Work*, p34.

**36.** See above, p51.

**37.** See, for example, the case studies in Stephens, *Problem Families*, pp16 and 21.

**38.** Starkey, 'The feckless mother', p552.

**39.** N. Timms, 'Casework with difficult cases', *Social Work*, 11 (1954), p920.

**40.** C. Murray, 'Underclass', in Murray (ed.), *The Emerging British Underclass* pp1–2; and 'Rejoinder', p68.

**41.** David Jones represented FSU on the Eugenics Society Problem Families

Committee. Minutes of the FSU national executive committee, November 5 1948. ULSCA D495(HQ)M2/2.

**42.** M. Hill, *The Welfare State in Britain: A political history since 1945* (Aldershot, 1993), pp18–9.

**43.** M. Whale, 'Problem families: The case for social casework', *Social Work*, 11 (1954), p81.

**44.** E. Howarth, 'Definition and diagnosis of the social problem family', *Social Work*, 10 (1953), p766.

**45.** Kensington and Paddington FSU, annual report for 1955–56. ULSCA D495(WL)M5/3.

**46.** E. Irvine, 'Research into problem families: A discussion of research methods', *British Journal of Psychiatric Social Work*, 2 (1951–54), p27.

**47.** J. Lewis, D. Clark and D. Morgan, *Whom God Hath Joined Together. The work of marriage guidance* (London, 1992), pp58 and 85. See also W. Webster, *Imagining Home: Gender, 'race' and national identity 1945–1964* (London, 1998), pp1ff; B. Berger, 'The bourgeois family and modern society', in J. Davies (ed.), *The Family: Is it just another lifestyle choice?* (London, 1993), pp8–9.

**48.** Cited in N. Timms, *Social Casework: Principles and practice* (London, 1964), p154.

**49.** Philp and Timms, *Problem of 'The Problem Family'*, p13.

**50.** Rose, *Governing the Soul*, p157.

**51.** See also H. Hendrick, *Child Welfare: England 1872–1989* (London, 1994), p220.

**52.** *Royal Commission on Population Report*, Cmnd 7695 (HMSO, 1949).

**53.** *Report and Selected Papers of the Statistics Committee of the Royal Commission on Population*, Papers of the Royal Commission on Population (HMSO, 1950), vol 11, p2. Quoted in D. Riley, *War in the Nursery: Theories of the child and mother* (London, 1983), p157.

**54.** Webster, *Imagining Home*, p5; Rose, *Governing the Soul*, p157.

**55.** Webster, *Imagining Home*, pp3–5.

**56.** See for example Lidbetter, *Heredity and the Social Problem Group*; Blacker, *A Social Problem Group?*; D. Caradog Jones, *The Social Problem Group* (Cambridge, 1945); D. Caradog Jones, 'The social problem group: poverty and sub-normality of intelligence', *Canadian Bar Review*, 28 (March, 1945); cf. Rose, *Governing the Soul*, pp136ff.

**57.** Letter from the President of the Eugenics Society to the Secretary of the Central Association for Mental Welfare, October 1930. The Wellcome Institute for the History of Medicine (hereafter, Wellcome), CMAC:SA/EUG/D53. The psychologist, Cyril Burt, a member of the Eugenics Society, also argued that if a tendency to crime is hereditary, little or nothing could be done apart from segregating or sterilising all those who openly manifested criminal tendencies. He also noted that the provisions of the Mental Deficiency Act allowed for the segregation of mental defectives during the period of procreation. C. Burt, *The Young Delinquent* ( London, 1944), pp60, 331 and 316.

**58.** E. Rathbone, *The Disinherited Family: A plea for the endowment of the family* (reprint, Bristol, 1986), passim.

**59.** Rose, *Governing the Soul*, pp125ff; Rustin, 'Social work, welfare and the family', p140; C. Jones, 'Social work education, 1900–1970' in Parry, Rustin and Satyamurti (eds), *Social Work, Welfare and the State*, p82.

**60.** As Jane Lewis has noted, anxiety about problem families, as well as about juvenile delinquency, neglected children and married women's employment, were reflected in *Marriage Guidance,* the journal of the National Marriage Guidance Council. Lewis et al, *Whom God Hath Joined Together*, p95.

**61.** As well as writing a number of articles about problem families, Stallybrass initiated a marriage guidance committee within the Liverpool Personal Service Society. Lewis et al, *Whom God Hath Joined Together*, p95.

**62.** B. Wootton, *Social Science and Social Pathology* (London, 1959), p55.

**63.** G. R. Searle, 'Eugenics and politics in Britain in the 1930s', *Annals of Science*, 36 (1979), pp159–69.

**64.** Blacker, *Problem Families*, p12.

**65.** H. C. M. Williams, 'Problem families in Southampton', *Eugenics Review*, 47 (1956), p222.

**66.** J. Macnicol, 'In pursuit of the underclass', *Journal of Social Policy*, 16 (1987), p297.

**67.** J. Macnicol, 'In pursuit of the underclass', pp293ff.

**68.** A fuller account of Bristol FSU can be found in P. Starkey, 'The Medical Officer of Health, the social worker and the problem family: Family Service Units, 1943–1968', *Social History of Medicine*, 11 (1998), pp430ff.

**69.** *Report of the Medical Officer of Health for 1953*, B24. Bristol Record Office (hereafter BRO), 33416 (27)b.

**70.** *Report of the Medical Officer of Health for 1965*, p49. BRO, 33416(31)a.

**71.** *Report of the Medical Officer of Health for 1966*, p38. BRO, 33416(31)a.

**72.** *Report of the Medical Officer of Health for 1967*, p52. BRO, 33416 (31)a.

**73.** *Report of the Medical Officer of Health for 1965*, p10. BRO, 33416 (31)a.

**74.** *Report of the Medical Officer of Health for 1961*, p16. BRO, 33416(29)d.

**75.** *Report of the Medical Officer of Health for 1965*, p49. BRO 33416(31)a.

**76.** *Report of the Medical Officer of Health for 1967*, p.52. BRO, 33416 (31)a. See Starkey, 'The Medical Officer of Health, the social worker and the problem family', pp430ff.

**77.** Stallybrass, 'Problem families', *Social Work*, p38.

**78.** G. R. Searle, *Eugenics and Politics in Britain, 1900–1914* (Leyden, 1976), p10.

**79.** Searle, *Eugenics and Politics in Britain*, p11; Jones, *Social Hygiene in Twentieth-century Britain*, pp19–20, 23 and n34.

**80.** Searle, *Eugenics and Politics in Britain*, p163.

**81.** Report on lectures and meetings in Liverpool. Wellcome, CMAC:SA/EUG/ G8.

**82.** Lectures given to pupils of the Day Trade School for Girls at Wavertree Technical Institute in March 1937. Wellcome, CMAC:SA/EUG/G8.

**83.** Given to the Mothers' Association Monthly Meeting at Fonthill Road Council School, 1937. Wellcome, CMAC:SA/EUG/G8.

**84.** Given to the Liverpool Wives' Fellowship, 1937. Talks were also given during the same year to the university settlement and the local Trained Midwives' Board. Wellcome, CMAC:SA/EUG/G8.

**85.** Minutes of the PSU national committee, passim. ULSCA D495(HQ)PSU/1.

**86.** J. G. Adami, Vice-Chancellor of the University of Liverpool from 1919 to 1926, published and lectured on eugenics. See J. G. Adami, *Medical Contributions to the Study of Evolution* (London, 1918), and *The True Aristocracy: an address to the International Eugenics Congress, New York, 1921* (London, 1922). Cyril Burt, the psychologist, had taught there from 1908 to 1913. The demographer A. M. Carr Saunders had been holder of the Charles Booth Chair of Social Science in the School of Social Sciences and Administration from 1923 to 1937.

**87.** Caradog Jones's work is listed, along with that of Blacker, in an undated PSU document as essential study material. ULSCA D495(LI)M5/3.

**88.** See his unpublished autobiography. ULSCA D48/2 (i).

**89.** Macnicol, 'In pursuit of the underclass', p310.

**90.** See for example D. Caradog Jones, 'Mental deficiency on Merseyside: Its connection with the social problem group', *Eugenics Review*, 24 (1932); 'Differential class fertility', *Eugenics Review*, 24 (1932); 'Eugenics and the decline in population', *Eugenics Review*, 28 (1936); 'Eugenic aspects of the Merseyside survey', *Eugenics Review*, 28 (1936–37).

**91.** Caradog Jones, *Social Survey of Merseyside*, vol 3, pp447–89.

**92.** Personal communication from David Jones, January 1993.

**93.** Letter from David Caradog Jones to members of the Liverpool unit, August 5 1945. ULSCA D495(LI)M1/6. See also minutes of the Liverpool PSU committee, August 9 1945. ULSCA D495(LI)M1/5.

**94.** Wootton, *Social Science*, p55.

**95.** According to the 1927 amendment to the Mental Deficiency Act, mental deficiency was 'a condition of arrested or incomplete development of mind'. There were three subdivisions: the feebleminded, the imbecile and the idiot. 'Legally normal' children were also classified in three ways as normal, dull or backward. See Blacker, *A Social Problem Group*, p17.

**96.** See Stephens, *Problem Families*, pp9–37.

**97.** Jones, *Social Hygiene*, p137; Rose, *Governing the Soul*, p159.

**98.** Jones, *Social Hygiene*, pp82–3.

**99.** Jones, *Social Hygiene*, pp31–3. See also, Searle, *Eugenics and Politics in Britain*, chapter 9; Jones, *Social Hygiene*, p88; P. Mazumdar, *Eugenics, Human Genetics and Human Failings: The Eugenics Society, its sources and critics in Britain* (London, 1992), pp23–4.

**100.** The Central Association for Mental Health had a branch in Liverpool at 14 Castle Street, and the Liverpool Ladies' Association for the Training of Girls and the West Derby Board of Guardians had been members of the Association in the late 1920s. Wellcome, CMAC:SA/EUG/D53.

**101.** Jones, *Social Hygiene*, p27.

**102.** The initial contact may or may not have come from PSU; the official record appears to differ from the recollections of one of the members. A. Cohen, *The Revolution in Post-war Family Casework. The Story of Pacifist Service Units and Family Service Units, 1940–1959* (Lancaster, 1998), p32.

**103.** Minutes of the Manchester PSU committee, March 25 1944. ULSCA D495(MA)M1/1; Cohen, *Revolution in Post-war Family Casework*, p32.

**104.** Cohen, *Revolution in Post-war Family Casework*, p32.

**105.** Casework report, Liverpool PSU. ULSCA D495(LI)M5/1.

**106.** Minutes of the Liverpool PSU, April 19 1944. ULSCA D495(LI)M1/5.

**107.** Minutes of the Liverpool PSU, February 7 1945. ULSCA D495(LI)/M1/5.

**108.** Minutes of the Liverpool PSU, October 1945. ULSCA D495(LI)M5/1.

**109.** Minutes of the Liverpool PSU, April 11 1945. ULSCA D495(LI)/M1/5.

**110.** Some appear to have attended lectures given to other groups, for example the lecture on psychopathic behaviour given to the Liverpool Child Guidance Clinic in February 1945 and attended by Elwyn Thomas. Minutes of the Liverpool PSU committee, February 22 1945. ULSCA D495(HQ)M1/5.

**111.** See above, pp29–30.

**112.** Stephens, *Problem Families*, p72.

**113.** G. Hamilton, *Theory and Practice of Social Casework* (New York, 1940).

**114.** Cohen, *Revolution in Post-war Family Casework*, p31.

**115.** Personal communication from David Jones, February 1993.

**116.** Stephens, *Problem Families*, p6.

**117.** J. H. Bagot, *Juvenile Delinquency* (London, 1941), pp85–6; Stephens, *Problem Families*, p6. Bagot was Reader in Social Statistics at the University of Liverpool and a colleague of Caradog Jones.

**118.** Stephens, *Problem Families*, p2.

**119.** Stephens, *Problem Families*, p5.

**120.** Minutes of the Manchester PSU unit meeting, May 10 1945. ULSCA D495(MA)M2/1.

**121.** Minutes of the Manchester PSU committee, March 12 1946. ULSCA D495(MA)M1/1.

**122.** Minutes of the Manchester PSU unit meeting, February 19 1946. ULSCA D495(MA)M2/1.

**123.** See minutes of the Liverpool FSU committee, September 7 1949. ULSCA D495(LI)M2/1.

**124.** Minutes of Manchester FSU unit meeting, March 9 1948. ULSCA D495(MA)M2/1. Papers given at a conference for FSU trainees held in Liverpool, April 1952. ULSCA D495(HQ)M3/5.

**125.** Stephens, *Problem Families*, p18; personal communication from David Jones, January 1993.

**126.** Minutes of the Manchester PSU unit meeting, July 16 1946. ULSCA D495(MA)M2/1. Personal communication from David Jones, February 1993. See the discussion about the link between family size and the incidence of the problem family in Blacker, *Problem Families*, p20.

**127.** Minutes of the Manchester FSU casework sub-committee, November 2 1950. ULSCA D495(MA)M3/1. Starkey, 'The Medical Officer of Health', p 431.

**128.** Letter from David Jones to Alf Strange, August 27 1953. ULSCA D495(BL)M2.

**129.** But see J. Lewis, *The Voluntary Sector, the State and Social Work in Britain* (London, 1995), p111.

**130.** Cohen, *Revolution in Post-war Family Casework*, p33.

**131.** See J. Welshman, 'The social history of social work: The issue of the "problem family", 1940–1970', *British Journal of Social Work*, 29 (1999), pp465–6.

**132.** Minutes of the Liverpool FSU committee, December 2 1952. ULSCA D495 (LI)M2/1. Minutes of the Manchester and Salford FSU casework sub-committee,

November 2 1950. ULSCA D495(MA)M3/1. Minutes of the Sheffield FSU committee, November 20 1950. ULSCA D495(SH)M1/1. Minutes of the FSU national executive committee, February 2 1951. ULSCA D495(HQ)M2/1. See also Starkey, 'The Medical Officer of Health', pp425–6.

**133.** Minutes of the Manchester PSU unit meeting, July 16 1946, July 30 1946. ULSCA D495(MA)M1/3.

**134.** Minutes of the Manchester and Salford FSU casework sub-committee, September 26 1949; November 24 1950. ULSCA D495(MA)M3/1. *Report of the Medical Officer of Health for 1953,* B21, BRO 33416(27)b. See Starkey, 'The Medical Officer of Health', p433.

**135.** Personal communication from David Jones, February 1993.

**136.** Liverpool FSU, annual report for 1954–55 ULSCA D495(LI)M11/8.

**137.** Liverpool FSU 1948–1958 ULSCA D495(LI)M2.

**138.** Quoted in N. Timms, *Social Casework: Principles and practice* (London, 1964), p77.

## 3

# The Growth of a Social Work Agency

The late 1940s saw the Manchester and Liverpool FSUs, together with a branch of the organisation which had opened in West London and was known as the Kensington and Paddington unit, becoming firmly established in their peacetime mode. In addition, plans were being laid for more new units throughout the country. For a brief period the Liverpool unit had functioned as the head office of the embryonic agency, with David Jones, the fieldwork organiser, working from there as national secretary.[1] In October 1948 he moved to London, established the national office at the Kensington and Paddington unit, and again took on the dual roles of local fieldwork organiser and national secretary. After a short interval during which two other ex-PSU workers, Bert Wood and John Williams, jointly managed the unit,[2] Jones was replaced in Liverpool by Fred Philp, who had also been a member of the wartime team and had recently returned from reconstruction work with the Friends Relief Service in Europe.[3]

The establishment of a national office in London meant that the organisation's administrative centre shifted to the capital, and control of national events was removed from those key members of the Liverpool committee who had both steered and supported the work during the war and played a vital part in setting up the peacetime organisation. It was a development destined to have long-term consequences. Tension between Liverpool and London, centring largely on a lack of clarity about the division between local and national responsibility, was to colour organisational relationships for the next 20 years.[4] The tension may be traced in part to this move and to the perception that the north-western units which had been responsible for the lion's share of the pioneering work were to become no more than branches of a London-based organisation.

The fact that the first two national secretaries had themselves been important members of the Liverpool unit during the war may have helped to mask the worst of the resentment and have ensured that the unit believed itself to have a close personal link with headquarters, but on occasion it may also have exacerbated a difficult situation by allowing accusations of personal animosity to be made.[5]

At the same time that the national organisation launched itself into the unknown waters of peacetime Britain, Stepney, the third in the trio of wartime caseworking units, had steered itself into a backwater. Its workers' commitment to pacifism and to the special contribution they believed that pacifists could make to the solution of social problems had led them to resolve to retain their independent identity, to resist joining FSU in 1948 and to continue to operate under the auspices of the Peace Pledge Union.[6] But the times were against them. Like those of their contemporaries who had been members of the armed forces, most PSU workers and other conscientious objectors were attempting to resume careers which had been interrupted by war and to adopt ordinary lifestyles. Few were prepared to continue to live in financial insecurity, committed to an organisation and an ideal which appeared to be on the wane. The scale of the Allied victory held the promise that war might become no more than a memory, and so the humanitarian ideals which had informed the pacifist cause became diverted from war-resistance to the care of the poor and other social casualties. Stepney PSU was determined to remain true to pacifism and was convinced that it had a particular contribution to make to the post-war world, but as the recruitment of caseworkers slowed, so standards of work began to drop and requests for help by or on behalf of needy families had to be turned down. In 1949, when six new members offered their services, the unit experienced a brief respite from the downward spiral and hopes were raised locally that the unit might survive. This prompted a review of the work so far undertaken together with an assessment of the future needs of the area,[7] but the revival was short-lived. In 1953 the Stepney PSU, more recently known as the Stepney Family Rehabilitation Unit, finally abandoned its independence and joined FSU.[8]

FSU had enjoyed considerable acclaim since its inception as a permanent peacetime organisation in 1948. It had helped to bring to public attention the existence of those who had been labelled problem families, and offered a way of working with them which seemed to promise an alleviation of their difficulties. It had contributed to public discussions on the difficulties facing the problem family; such discussions were themselves prompted by a more general concern about the state of marriage and family life which preoccupied social workers, public health doctors and churchmen in the post-war period. As divorce rates increased rapidly (there was a five-fold increase in the period 1946–50 when compared with the figures for 1936–40),[9] the creation of the working-class-oriented FSU and the largely middle-class-oriented National Marriage Guidance Council was a feature of 1940s society whose significance was not lost on contemporary commentators.[10] As Noel Timms has argued, concern for the health of the family focused on its role as the foundation of a stable society and on its twin tasks of socialising children and maintaining the achieved socialisation of adults;[11] it was compounded by the fear that many families were failing to fulfil these roles. The message which the PSU/FSU had preached about poor, antisocial families had fallen on receptive soil and prompted praise for the organisation's success in helping those thought to be incapable of achieving socialisation unaided, and in protecting the rest of the population from what were assumed to be the unpleasant effects of living in close proximity to them.

In addition to the praise heaped on its work by local authorities and other public bodies, FSU was soon to secure royal patronage. The Honourable David Bowes-Lyon, brother to Queen Elizabeth (who was to become the Queen Mother), had been recruited by Lord Balfour to serve as chairman of the FSU national committee in 1947[12] and had become president in 1954,[13] which suggests that the Queen Mother may not have been entirely ignorant of the organisation's growth and activity. In 1955, she became its patron.[14] Such recognition is noteworthy. Royal approval was thereby given to an organisation which had originated in the work of a group of conscientious objectors who had taken pride in their refusal to contribute to the war effort, and which numbered among its members some whose pacifist stance had resulted in criminal convictions. In many minds FSU must have been tainted with a lack of patriotism. In its favour was the reputation it had gained for its wartime social work, which happened to fit the pattern of the Queen Mother's patronage; even before the war, she had specialised in supporting causes relating to women and children. Its size may also have made it an attractive proposition. The Queen Mother had already demonstrated interest in the work of small charities, and so her support for FSU was a continuation of her earlier interests. In the post-war climate of anxiety about the state of the family, it was also an act of patronage which served to place the royal family in the mainstream of contemporary public concern. Moreover, the Queen Mother's patronage of FSU helped to establish her in the new-style voluntary sector at a time when royal patronage was having to be reshaped, as the creation of the new National Health Service and other parts of the welfare state rendered support for some charitable institutions redundant. A small organisation working with families suffering the worst effects of urban poverty seems almost to have been tailor-made for a senior member of the royal family, whose pattern of philanthropy had been dealt a sharp blow by the encroachment of state provision. For FSU, anxious to increase its public support, such royal approbation was invaluable. As Frank Prochaska has pointed out, Queen Elizabeth the Queen Mother proved to be 'one of the best patronage players the royal family ever produced'.[15]

Wider recognition of the potential of FSU's rehabilitation work came through the discussion of the problem family in the pages of a range of professional journals, from the *Lancet* to *The Housing Manager*, from *The Medical Officer* to *Social Work*. Articles on the work of PSU/FSU appeared in *The Nursing Times*, *The School Child*, *Juvenile Worker*, *The World's Children* and in popular publications like *Reveille*, *John Bull*, *Reynolds News*,[16] *Manchester Evening News*, *Peace News*, *Evening News* and *Manchester Evening Chronicle*.[17] Even the *Farmers Weekly* carried an article.[18] All concentrated on the squalor in which such families were thought to live, stressed the need for urgent, rehabilitative help and applauded the work of FSU.

FSU's success was explained in a variety of ways; the families' unacceptable lifestyles were often believed to be a consequence of their failure to achieve normal levels of maturity, and FSU was credited with helping them to grow up. One social work commentator believed that PSU/FSU owed its achievements to the ways in which it had tailored its methods to the infantile, dependent needs of problem families.[19] These techniques, Elizabeth Irvine argued, allowed social workers to play the part of uncritical, permissive and supporting parents and thereby to counteract the bad parenting which, it was assumed, many parents had themselves experienced; the clients were allowed to enjoy the attention of a parental figure who was more understanding, less demanding and more patient than most parents can be once the infant phase is completed.[20] Irvine's analysis gave credence to the descriptions of problem families circulated by public health doctors such as R. C. Wofinden in Bristol and C. O. Stallybrass in Liverpool, and explained the antisocial features of life in some households by equating them with those which could be expected from a young child left without adult guidance.

Although some FSU members believed Irvine's comments to be an incomplete explanation of the reasons for their success, there can be little doubt that they appreciated that her comments were founded in a sense of admiration for their work. Expressions of approval came from other quarters, too. An article in the *Methodist Recorder* remarked on the notable work being done by FSU, particularly in Liverpool. Like other commentators, the *Methodist Recorder* focused on what it perceived to be the failings of mothers, on whom responsibility for their families' plight was seen to fall. Their 'lack of ability in the home', exemplified by their inability to plan their housework and their ignorance of what were generally accepted to be ordinary household tasks, was noted.[21] In attempting to describe the typical problem family, journalists – like MOHs – frequently fell into the trap of thinking that such a family exhibited invariable and easily recognisable symptoms. Specific weaknesses were described by the paper as though symptomatic of identifiable disease; they included the failure to manage money and the tendency to use the coal supply as soon as it was delivered, so that there was not enough to last until the next consignment. Women were also condemned for breaking up doors and furniture to burn as fuel. Accounts of sexual irregularity were employed to illustrate the degree of deviance believed to characterise the problem family; the *Methodist Recorder* produced a case study of one family with five illegitimate children, the offspring of their mother's stepfather.[22] Illustrative material of this sort was frequently used to highlight the fecklessness, immorality and poor management of the woman concerned and to hint that her behaviour was typical of other women in her situation. It was rarely used to prompt an examination of the financial and social circumstances which might have contributed to her plight. Other journalistic comments demonstrated the prevalence of notions of inherited intellectual inadequacy, and were an indication of the influence of eugenicist-inspired explanations for human failure. Reference to FSU's activities in *The Times* in 1953 evinced the persistence of notions of mental instability which had informed social commentators in the inter-war period, as it stressed the prevalence of '... inherent personal deficiencies such as backwardness, incapability, weakness of character, instability or marital disharmony'. It urged that 'In an environment of bad housing, poverty and lack of home equipment, they must be tackled vigorously and quickly with such practical help as each family may require.'[23] Little guidance was given as to how, in such poorly equipped conditions, practical help could be given, nor is it clear whether the underlying problems for which practical help was necessary were assumed to be personal deficiency or poverty. Although some acknowledgement is given to the part played by environmental factors, greater stress is placed on mental incapacity, the need for external assistance and the implied inability of the family to act on its own behalf. As has been shown, to a considerable extent such observations chimed with assessments made by FSU personnel.[24] The failure of the mother was presumed to be central to family difficulties, and bad housing and overcrowding were dismissed as being relatively unimportant.[25] As well as illustrating the assumption that women were entirely responsible for financial management, domestic cleanliness, emotional health and child-care, this also demonstrated that the tendency of social workers to make the mother the target of their professional visits and to limit themselves to conversations with her tended to limit their understanding of the situation. It also increased the burden on the woman, reinforcing the assumption that all family matters were primarily her concern while tacitly absolving the man of the family from any responsibility.

The perceived ubiquity of such incapable families, mothered by incapable women, was fostered by the public health, welfare and housing departments of local authorities who were facing the task of reconstructing towns and cities damaged by bombing; this helped to reinforce the view that there was a national problem. Their concerns also prompted mechanisms for dealing with such families. Although there was some uncertainty as to the most effective methods to employ, FSU was seen as the organisation best placed to provide assistance, and the publicity it attracted resulted in a considerable number of requests to set up new units in urban areas around Britain. Plans for a Sheffield unit were first mooted in July 1949, when work with problem families in the area began under the auspices of an interim committee and with the help of a local authority grant;[26] the unit made a successful application to join FSU in June 1950. Like other units, Sheffield experienced severe financial difficulties in its early days; in January 1955 it noted its inability to support the number of workers allocated to it and discussed the prospect of allowing one of them to transfer to another unit.[27] 1949 saw interest from York, too. The local MOH first made enquiries about the possibility of setting up a unit in May that year,[28] and work with problem families started in the city a few months later under the auspices of the York Community Council, with the support of the local authority.[29] FSU provided training for the York workers from March 1950,[30] and the unit was invited to join FSU formally in June that year.[31] The Manchester unit, meanwhile, had spawned a daughter unit in Oldham, funded by the local authority. The work there began in 1949 at the instigation of the MOH Dr Keddie, who arranged with the Manchester FSU for workers to be employed in his area for an experimental period of two years. Four local authority committees contributed to the grant of £500: the welfare services committee, the children's committee, the public health committee and the housing committee. Most of the families referred to the unit came from the caseload of the department of public health.[32] Requests for FSU's expertise had also been received from local authority officials in Birmingham,[33] Leicester, Swansea, Devon, Nottingham,[34] Wolverhampton, Cornwall, Kent, Sussex[35] and Bradford.[36]

There was interest from the north-east, too, although there was little immediate prospect of FSU being able to set up a branch there. The personal welfare organiser of the Northumberland and Tyneside Council of Social Service attempted to persuade FSU to train caseworkers to work in his area in 1953. That it was five years before his attempts achieved success[37] was not his fault but a function of FSU's severely strained resources. In the same year Frank Rumball, a wartime PSU worker who had since become the children's officer in Tynemouth, wrote to David Jones to tell him that the children's officer in Newcastle was interested in exploring the idea of establishing a unit there.[38] In that case, too, FSU was unable immediately to offer help; it was more than a decade before sufficient staff and finance were to become available. However, in spite of the difficulties attendant upon setting up new units, 12 had been established by 1958.[39]

The organisation's inability to train suitable workers quickly enough to establish and staff the units that local authorities were requesting was not the consequence of a shortage of applicants; many more applied than were able to meet FSU's high standards of selection and then complete the training satisfactorily. Sometimes as many as half of those who wished to become FSU caseworkers were rejected, and it was not unknown for those who had been accepted to be asked to withdraw before the training period was complete because they had proved to be unsuitable. The organisation even rejected some of those who had been key players during the war. Ken Richardson, who had energetically pioneered work in the Liverpool shelters and dispersal rest centres, had his application for a peacetime position rejected.[40] Michael Lee, another Liverpool pioneer and someone to whom the agency was indebted both for the organisation of the unit's activities and for publicity about its work, also discovered that '... the time for people like [Ken] and me was past... we'd started things, but it was now for other people to carry on'.[41]

Although the employment of strict criteria in its choice of trainees was a major cause of its shortage of staff, the constraints imposed by a precarious financial position exacerbated the situation. Local authorities may not have been aware of FSU's difficulties, but they were attracted by the likelihood that FSU could and would employ practical measures to aid families who were living in poor environments and who demonstrated 'inherent personal deficiencies'. The agency's mop-and-bucket reputation, earned by wartime activities which had included practical assistance with homes and children, had been reinforced by photographs in PSU publicity showing workers whitewashing walls, or cycling through Liverpool and Manchester streets with items of cleaning equipment balanced across their handlebars. This willingness to tackle the mess in which some families lived appeared to offer assistance with post-war urban reconstruction and the work of remedying some of the ills exposed by evacuation and bombing. FSU had gained a reputation for teaching parents how to keep their houses clean and make their children socially acceptable. Local authorities, anxious to limit the difficulties which they feared might be caused by the presence of antisocial families in some neighbourhoods, were keen to enlist the agency's services.

Furthermore, FSU sold itself as an agency which could enable the public authorities to save money. In its annual report for 1954–55, the Kensington and Paddington unit noted that the cost of providing institutional care for a family with nine children which was currently on its books would be roughly £10,280 a year. FSU claimed that it was supporting that family in its own home for a fraction of the cost. Two years later, the same unit justified its work with 20 families with whom it had been working for more than two years by drawing attention to the cost to the taxpayer had FSU not offered support –

the implication being that without such long-term help the children would have been taken into care and have become a drain on the public purse.[42] Such observations would not have fallen on stony ground. The rising costs of the new children's departments, formed in 1948, were giving cause for concern; the numbers of children taken into care had climbed steeply from 55,000 in 1949 to 64,500 in 1952.[43] Moreover, one effect of the 1948 Children Act had been to give local authorities greater powers and responsibilities towards children in care; where boarding out with substitute parents was not practicable, local authorities were required to maintain children either in their own institutions or in those of a voluntary agency. Many local authorities elected to provide their own children's homes, with the result that the number of children in voluntary institutions declined while those in direct local authority care increased.[44] Rising maintenance costs stimulated an awareness of the savings that could be made through preventive work designed to keep the family intact. As Jean Packman has noted, the House of Commons Select Committee on Estimates (1951–52) recorded its view that:

> Much frustration and suffering [would be] avoided if more attention were directed towards the means whereby situations that end in domestic upheaval and disaster might be dealt with and remedied before the actual breakdown of the home occurs.[45]

FSU's track record of successful preventive work had demonstrated its ability to forestall situations of 'domestic upheaval and disaster', and this ability had been widely recognised. The Liverpool unit's annual report for 1954–55 drew attention to the plaudits that the organisation had attracted since 1948. The Society of Women Managers had commented in January 1955 that the only type of organisation which could really help the problem family was something like FSU, while in April 1955 the Scottish Standing Committee of the National Council of Women had stated its belief that FSUs should be established in all towns with a population of 40,000 or more.[46]

The message that preventive work with families could facilitate the achievement of an acceptable level of functioning, and avoid the separation of parents and children with the resultant call on public finances, was one that received ready acceptance among some senior local authority officials. Those newly appointed children's officers who had taken on board some of the lessons of the PSU/FSU experiment, although stopping short of inviting the agency to work in their areas, found that by employing family casework methods they could avoid excessive expenditure and provide a high level of care. Barbara Kahan, who had been appointed children's officer in Dudley in 1949, deliberately employed an ex-PSU worker, Frank Rumball, to do preventive work,[47] and she continued the practice when she left the authority a couple of years later. As children's officer for Oxfordshire County Council, she calculated that George Harnor, the PSU-trained preventive worker she engaged in 1952, had helped to keep 50 children from 13 families out of care. Her experiment was watched with interest by other children's officers, with the result that a family caseworker post was created by the neighbouring Oxford City Council in 1953 and posts for two preventive workers were shortly afterwards established by the London County Council (LCC).[48] The LCC workers were sent to the Kensington and Paddington FSU for training in casework methods, a further reinforcement of the organisation's reputation.[49]

It was not the methods employed by FSU that attracted local authorities so much as the type of client with whom they worked; the problem family was at the forefront of the minds of local councillors and social workers. Some local authorities considered a range of remedies for such families. The Bristol department of public health examined the possibility of setting up remedial institutions on the Netherlands model. These were situated in areas far from the cities in which the families had lived and were designed as rehabilitation centres in which basic housewifery and child-care could be taught.[50] Examples of similar centres were to be found in Britain; Dr Barnardo's ran a family rehabilitation unit in Essex[51] and the Brentwood Home in Lancashire and the Mayflower Home for Neglectful Mothers, run by the Salvation Army in Plymouth, provided similar service. FSU was aware of the work of Brentwood and the Mayflower; the Manchester unit had sent some of its families to Brentwood.[52] There was, however, no unanimity of opinion about their usefulness, and some workers expressed doubts about their value. While some believed that the 'jolt of compulsion' might have helped families to raise their standards,[53] others expressed ambivalence about places in which women and children were separated from their home environment and their partners. Although some sections of FSU had made use of such institutions, other workers believed that where families exhibiting antisocial behaviour were brought together in large groups and separated from their friends, family and neighbourhood, the community spirit that developed was 'of such a nature as to be socially undesirable',[54] and tended to undermine the lessons that the workers hoped to instil. Other disadvantages included the difficulties of managing and staffing the centres; the likelihood that they would excite political and public opposition; the recognition that some communities might object to having such institutions in their neighbourhood; and the fear that families selected for treatment might face ostracism when they were eventually rehoused. All these disadvantages centred on the inconveniences and difficulties envisaged for neighbours and staff. No discussion appears to have taken place about the effects on family life of separation from husbands and fathers, or the potentially damaging effects of the regimes that were sometimes imposed. Women at the Mayflower in the 1950s, for example, were subjected to a regimen that entailed regular scrutiny of all their domestic and child-care duties; their standard of bedmaking was observed and the state of cleanliness of the children constantly monitored. That the women might have to return to a house considerably less well-equipped than the Mayflower does not seem to have been taken into consideration. The women were allowed only one telephone call home a week, and if husbands visited their wives and families, they were forced to stay at the local public house.[55] As well as reinforcing the suspicion that the family 'failure' was entirely the fault of the mother, who needed to be incarcerated in an institution in order to be trained to perform her duties responsibly and perhaps even to be punished for her past inadequacy, the effects of the separation that such a scheme imposed might also be criticised; the strains on the marital relationship which could ensue might have had long-term and harmful results for the whole family.

The Bristol department of public health, which considered introducing such a scheme in the early 1950s, eventually decided against it. As the housing situation in Bristol was not as serious as in Rotterdam – the city it had used as a guide – the health committee resolved to accept the advice offered by FSU and to examine alternative schemes. One, the suggestion of the deputy MOH R. C. Wofinden, involved dispersing problem families throughout the city, using reconditioned property made available by the housing department and caseworkers attached to welfare services.[56] Another idea was to ask FSU to work with selected families in cooperation with other services. The second proposal was eventually accepted, and in 1952 the Bristol department of public health formally invited

FSU to open a unit in the Southmead area of the city. The unit started work in April 1953, with an ex-Liverpool PSU worker Alf Strange as fieldwork organiser.[57]

Local authority departments were not alone in their admiration of FSU's work. From the Association of Housing Managers came further expressions of approbation for the agency and its methods of work with families who failed to conform to social expectations and to respond to the efforts of 'normal social services'.[58] Although the association's comment about families' failure to respond to general exhortations to raise their standards said as much about the 'normal social services' as it did about the families and FSU, it may to some extent have been based on a misunderstanding, or perhaps a partial understanding, of FSU's ways of working. In many cases the emphasis in expressions of appreciation of the organisation's activities was on the improvement it was thought to bring about in standards of domestic organisation and cleanliness. As has already been shown, PSU/FSU had been influenced by theories of relative mental incapacity early in its history and, even before it gratefully received training from the PNCMH, had pursued an approach to work with some of its clients which, although largely untutored, had much in common both in practice and in concept with that of mental health workers. His time with the Provisional National Council in 1944 had prompted one of their number to write in his report:

> ... I realise how little I knew of the behaviour problems arising from mental aberration and I know that I am better equipped already to deal with many of the problems arising in PSU work... I believe that undoubtedly in PSU we have been approaching the casework problems from the standpoint of the psychiatric social worker, but of course within the limits of our knowledge and experience... the problems we are encountering [on a PNCMH placement] are closely related to the problems we have met in the last three years, sometimes even of a comparable degree... often closely resembling the type of case we have been handling so nearly that names spring to one's mind spontaneously... already I am sure that we have obtained a refreshingly new outlook on problems of mental deficiency neuroses and psychoses which appear so regularly in PSU casework.[59]

With many of the problems faced by their wartime clients so clearly perceived to lie within the general area of psychiatric disorder, it can be no coincidence that when PSU workers wished to undertake formal training in the years after the war, they frequently chose to enrol on psychiatric social work or mental health courses. It was but a short step from perceiving problem families as mentally defective, to seeing them as of normal, or nearly normal, mental capacity but with psychological and emotional problems. As another PSU worker on the same Provisional National Council course reported:

> Most of our problem families are in their present plight as a result of the interaction of many factors, from weak heredity to long-standing bad environment... all human problems and difficulties are bound up with mental attitudes at some point.[60]

As has already been shown, FSU appeared to offer hope that the antisocial behaviour of some particularly needy families could be improved as the result of long-term, intensive work. 'Intensive family casework' became the agency's trademark, even though its negligible use of professional casework methods had given rise to some comment.[61] The fact that its approach was perceived to differ from that of traditional caseworkers enhanced its reputation. The methods employed by the Charity Organisation Society, which presumably was what was meant by 'professional casework methods', had sometimes been rigidly applied and had necessitated a degree of dehumanising, perhaps most clearly seen in the readiness of caseworkers to invade the privacy of the family by making enquiries of friends and neighbours in order to establish its eligibility for help. As well as being considered old-fashioned in the post-war period, this practice was becoming increasingly unacceptable. Moreover, it was wasteful of time and effort. As Jane Lewis has noted, the Charity Organisation Society/Family Welfare Association had been criticised for spending too much time on 'ponderous investigation for the performance of small services'.[62] Family casework, FSU-style, fitted more easily into the climate which both informed and was informed by the emerging welfare state. It was characterised by a more sympathetic attitude towards the individual and a more generous interpretation of 'welfare'. Furthermore, although the workers used the descriptive title 'family casework', and ran the risk of their approach being confused with earlier brands of family casework practice, it is unlikely that they consciously modelled their methods on those of any other agency; rather, they believed that their 'friendship with a purpose' represented an entirely new approach to an old problem.

The context in which they were increasingly having to work had been profoundly influenced by other developments, both structural (such as the extension of the personal social services as a result of the post-war arrangements) and theoretical (advances in psychology and psychiatry, and the growth of specialities such as psychiatric social work). That this emphasis on mental health and the methods associated with psychiatric social work was continuing to influence FSU's own methods and training can be seen from the records of student placements and trainee conferences. At a conference held in Liverpool in 1952, the use of relationship in casework was discussed, emphasising the use of the worker's own relationship in the resolution of conflict; but far from giving a picture of one easily identifiable FSU method, the conference demonstrated the wide range of perceptions among workers about both the problems some families faced and the techniques for helping them. The topics chosen by speakers in 1952 ranged widely, from concern with material standards and the condition of the goods given to alleviate need, to the role of statutory officials and the effects of recent legislation. Taken together they portray an organisation anxious to understand the context within which it worked, experimental in its methods and prepared to employ a variety of techniques.[63] As will be shown, this was not always understood and the tendency to assume that the intensive family casework for which FSU became known was the only method its workers employed coloured its reputation for years to come.

Some of FSU's methods came in for criticism and the underlying motives of its workers were challenged. The tendency to offer material aid too easily had attracted censure during the war, when the Liverpool Personal Service Society (LPSS) had thought that a better method would have been to persuade the family to save for what it needed rather than allow it to accept gifts.[64] The tension between FSU and LPSS over this episode was reflective of emerging schools of thought among social workers, with some committed to encouraging self-sufficiency and independence while others believed that the relief of need, as an integral part of a total casework process, provided an experience of generous parenting to those who had never experienced it. For one commentator, FSU represented a method of providing goods which communicated 'the right spirit' and enabled the casework process to progress.[65] Other social workers would be more critical, and in failing to appreciate some of the theoretical underpinning to family casework as practised by organisations like FSU, would consider that giving money or goods to needy families demonstrated a paternalistic attitude and was evidence of superficiality of approach. According to such reasoning, granting material aid could be criticised as failing to consider the underlying cause of the family's distress.[66] This approach assumed that deeper causes (that is, emotional and psychological factors) necessarily underlay material need. It would be challenged by the radical social workers of the 1970s.

As well as their concern to bring about physical improvement, many FSU workers also wished to explore the reasons for family and personal failure. Like those in other agencies, they were influenced by developments in the US where psychoanalytic teaching about unconscious motivation and the influence of early experience on personality development had begun to take hold in the inter-war period. In the aftermath of the Second World War, psychiatric social work began to assume a greater importance in Britain and to some extent left other branches of social work behind. By the late 1950s agencies were increasingly turning to psychiatric social workers and to the insights afforded by psychoanalytical techniques for guidance during case discussions, in attempts to deepen and extend their understanding. FSU had employed, albeit in inchoate form, psychodynamic methods from the mid-1940s in addition to offering considerable practical and material help.

Such methods demanded confidence in the worker's ability to see beneath the surface of her client's problems, even, perhaps, to disregard the client's self-knowledge and interpretation of events. As one writer on social affairs noted, in judging what the client 'really' wants the caseworker does not rely exclusively on what the client says but also on what is communicated by other means.[67] Caseworkers also used concepts such as transference, generally taken to mean the projection by the client on to the worker of his/her feelings about a person who had been influential in the past and who, perhaps, had played a significant part in the client's present dilemma. The social worker's task was ultimately to encourage the client to achieve equilibrium through adjustment between the inner and outer world.[68] In practice the adjustments were largely one-way, assuming the maladjustment to be located within the personality of the client and aimed at enabling him or her to accommodate to the demands of the social environment. The Family Welfare Association's aims and policy committee statement argued, for example, that the worker should be able to use his or her understanding of human behaviour and knowledge of social resources in order to build up the client's inner capacity 'by releasing the feelings and anxieties that hindered adjustment'.[69] Throughout the 1950s, the treatment method of choice became based on such methods. The PSU worker who in the

1940s had argued for a connection between material need and psychological health[70] had anticipated what was to become the dominant strand in social work thinking and practice. A highly respected textbook of the period, emphasising the importance of using the worker's personality in the process of helping the client to come to terms with difficulties, argued that every problem – even an explicit request for some form of material assistance – had an emotional component.[71]

Reports from trainees who spent some time with FSU as part of their courses reveal some scepticism on their part about the effectiveness of a method which relied so heavily on the use of the worker's personality. For example, a University of Liverpool student, studying for a Certificate in Social Science in 1960, started his placement at the local unit by expressing doubts about the method and wondering, aloud, whether caseworkers were just taking credit for having helped in situations that had (or could have) cured themselves with the passage of time and natural maturation. But he was soon to discover that he was wrong:

> In his reading of a good many records, however, he found more evidence of development than could be accounted for in this way and his own contacts with clients... gave him some experience of how the caseworker can use his personality to help the client improve his situation.[72]

At least, that is how the student's supervisor in the unit chose to assess the student's experience.

This concentration on the client's psyche did not receive universal approval. In her well-known broadside against social casework in 1959, Barbara Wootton lampooned the ambitions of caseworkers who used psychoanalytical techniques, arguing that the intention to meet emotional need could only be realised if the caseworker married his or her client.[73] FSU workers did not marry their clients, but they gave them time and attention which far exceeded normal casework practice. The intensity of its visiting programmes distinguished FSU from other agencies, whether voluntary or statutory. It was a legacy of the wartime practice in the Liverpool and Manchester PSUs. Regular calls were made to their clients, their frequency determined both by the family's difficulties and the extent to which the workers believed themselves capable of helping to resolve them. It may also have been a function of youthful inexperience and anxiety which led workers to see themselves and their contribution as an indispensable ingredient in the family's recovery. Weekly visits were normal, while daily or even twice daily visits were not unusual, as part of a programme of re-education and training in acceptable standards of domestic organisation. Such intensive work with families continued in the post-war organisation. An indication of the importance attached to this is to be found in the careful keeping of statistics about the numbers of visits made and their publication in annual reports, a practice common to all units. For example, in the year 1953–54, the Kensington and Paddington unit, with a staff of one fieldwork organiser and six caseworkers and a caseload of 87 families, paid 5,370 visits to families and 4,833 other visits (usually to local authority departments) on the families' behalf. In the year ending in March 1961, with a staff of just one fieldwork organiser and two caseworkers, 2,901 contacts were made with families by York FSU and 1,107 official contacts were made on behalf of their clients.[74] Visits were scrupulously counted at the Bristol unit, too; during 1960, 41 families received between them 3,657 visits (averaging nearly 90 per family over the course of a year) from a staff consisting of a fieldwork organiser and two caseworkers. In addition, a further 1,437 contacts were made with other bodies on the families' behalf.[75] The following year, 35 families received 4,029 visits, averaging 115 visits each.[76] The dependence which such close contact inevitably encouraged was later to be criticised, but in the early years of preventive work, such close supervision of families deemed to be causing social nuisance was welcomed by some local authorities and justified by FSU workers as a realistic way to offer support and encourage change.

Although the agency's reputation had tended to concentrate the public's mind on the importance of therapeutic intervention in the lives of families, FSU's intention was more far-reaching than the simple containment of antisocial behaviour; it stressed the importance of preventing the break up of families and the charge on the public purse which would follow the reception of children into care. If the extent to which local authorities clamoured for units to be set up in their neighbourhoods was anything to go by, FSU had touched a sensitive nerve. Even on the eve of the 1963 Children and Young Persons Act, which stressed the promotion of preventive work and appeared to hold some threat for parts of the voluntary sector, FSU's acute national shortage of workers was still making it impossible for the organisation to accede to the requests for more units in various parts of the country.[77] From a pacifist endeavour, motivated largely by humanitarian convictions and a rejection of the mores of wartime society, FSU had become a well-established social work agency with an unrivalled reputation. It had become respectable, and its methods both influenced and were influenced by the growth of social work as a profession.

# NOTES

**1.** Minutes of the PSU executive committee, September 8 1946. ULSCA D495(MA)PSU/1.

**2.** Minutes of the Liverpool FSU committee, October 18 1948. ULSCA D495(LI)M2/1.

**3.** Minutes of the Liverpool FSU committee, January 4 1950. ULSCA D495 (LI)M2/1; A. Cohen, *The Revolution in Post-war Family Casework: The Story of Pacifist Service Units and Family Service Units, 1940–1959* (Lancaster, 1998), p52.

**4.** See A. Penn, 'The Management of Voluntary Organisations in the Post-war Period' (unpublished DPhil thesis, University of Sussex, 1992) for further discussion of the effect that such an arrangement can have on organisations.

**5.** See below, p217.

**6.** See above, p37.

**7.** Stepney PSU annual report for 1949. ULSCA D495(EL)M7/2.

**8.** Report to Liverpool FSU executive committee, November 1953. ULSCA D495(LI)M12/2.

**9.** O. McGregor, *Divorce in England: A centenary study* (London, 1957), p6.

**10.** E. Howarth, 'The present dilemma of social casework', *Social Work*, 8 (1951), p528. See also J. Lewis, *The Voluntary Sector, the State and Social Work in Britain* (Aldershot, 1995), pp107–9; J. Lewis, D. Clark and D. Morgan, *Whom God Hath Joined Together: The work of marriage guidance* (London, 1992), pp71ff.

**11.** N. Timms, *Social Casework: Principles and Practice* (London, 1964), p185; N. Rose, *Governing the Soul: The shaping of the private self* (London, 1989), pp154–5.

**12.** Minutes of the FSU national committee, January 10 1947. ULSCA D495 (HQ)M2/1.

**13.** Minutes of the FSU national committee, March 12. ULSCA D495 (HQ)M2/3.

**14.** Minutes of the FSU national executive committee, April 6 1955. ULSCA D495(HQ)M2/2.

**15.** F. Prochaska, *Royal Bounty: The making of a welfare monarchy* (London, 1995), pp192 and 216.

**16.** Cohen, *Revolution in Post-war Family Casework*, p40.

**17.** Minutes of the Manchester FSU executive committee, February 5 1948. ULSCA D495(MA)M1/2.

**18.** A. Hartup, 'Families on the mend', *Farmers Weekly*, September 28 1951.

19. E. Irvine, 'The hard-to-like family', *Case Conference*, 14 (1967), p97.

20. Irvine, 'The hard-to-like family', p99.

21. *Methodist Recorder*, April 26 1951.

22. *Methodist Recorder*, April 26 1951.

23. *The Times*, June 15 1953.

24. See above, p21.

25. FSU trainee conference held in Liverpool, April 1952. ULSCA D495 (HQ)M3/5.

26. FSU annual report, June 1949. ULSCA D495(HQ)M2/12; Cohen, *Revolution in Post-war Family Casework*, pp40 and 53.

27. Minutes of Sheffield FSU committee, January 1 1955. ULSCA D495 (SH)M1/1.

28. Minutes of the FSU national executive committee, May 27 1949. ULSCA D495(HQ)M2/2.

29. Minutes of the FSU national committee, November 18 1949. ULSCA D495(HQ)M2/2.

30. Minutes of the FSU national executive committee, March 7 1950. ULSCA D495(HQ)M2/2.

31. Minutes of the FSU national executive committee, June 12 1950. ULSCA D495(HQ)M2/2.

32. Minutes of the FSU national committee, November 24 1950. ULSCA D495(HQ)M2/2. See also report compiled by Bert Wood for the inter-units conference, November 1950. ULSCA D495(HQ)M3/3.

33. Minutes of the FSU national executive committee, November 24 1950. ULSCA D495(HQ)M2/2.

34. Minutes of the FSU national executive committee, January 17 1951, February 28 1951. ULSCA D495(HQ)M2/2.

35. Report compiled by Bert Wood for the inter-units conference, November 1950. ULSCA D495(HQ)M3/3.

36. Minutes of the FSU national executive committee, April 19 1951. ULSCA D495(HQ)M2/2.

37. Report of Liverpool FSU executive committee, July to September 1958. ULSCA D495(LI)M12/3.

38. Letter from Frank Rumball to David Jones, January 26 1953. ULSCA D495(HQ)M2/3.

39. These were in Liverpool, Manchester, Birmingham, Bradford, Bristol, Leicester, Oldham, Sheffield, York, West London, Islington and East London. Liverpool FSU, *Report on the Years 1948–1958*, ULSCA D495(LI)M2.

40. Cohen, *Revolution in Post-war Family Casework*, p53.

41. Cohen, *Revolution in Post-war Family Casework*, p53.

42. Kensington and Paddington FSU annual report for 1956–57. ULSCA (WL)M5/4.

43. Local authorities' returns of children in care, quoted in J. Packman, *The Child's Generation* (Oxford, 1981), p54.

44. Packman, *The Child's Generation*, p54.

45. Packman, *The Child's Generation*, p54.

46. Liverpool FSU annual report for 1954–55. ULSCA D495(LI)M11/8.

47. Interview with Barbara Kahan, May 1990.

48. Packman, *The Child's Generation*, p56.

49. Kensington and Paddington FSU annual report for 1957–58. ULSCA D495 (WL)M5/5.

50. Document about Dutch scheme for isolating problem families for rehabilitation, no date. ULSCA D495(HQ)M3/16–18.

51. E. G. Collins, 'Family rehabilitation at Barkingside', in D. Lambert (ed.), *Change and the Child in Care* (Harpenden, 1965), p87.

52. A. Price, 'School for mothers', *Child Care: The Quarterly Review of the National Council of Associated Children's Homes*, 28 (April, 1954), pp57–9.

53. Minutes of the Manchester PSU unit meeting, February 8 1946. ULSCA D495(MA)M2/1. Minutes of the Manchester FSU unit meeting, December 14 1948. ULSCA D495(HQ)M1/2. Document about Dutch scheme. ULSCA D495(HQ) M3/16–18.

54. Report compiled by Bert Wood for the inter-units conference, November 1950. ULSCA D495(HQ)M3/3.

55. Price, 'School for mothers', pp57–9. See also document about Dutch scheme ULSCA D495(HQ)M3/16-18

56. 'Basic facts on problem families', *The Medical Officer*, 94 (December 1955), p377. See also letter from Alf Strange to David Jones, July 2 1953. ULSCA D495 (BL)M2.

57. Report to health committee (nursing services sub-committee), January 8 1953. ULSCA D495(BL)M4; P. Starkey, 'The Medical Officer of Health, the social worker and the problem family, 1943–68: The case of Family Service Units', *Social History of Medicine*, 11 (1998), pp421–41.

58. Anonymous article, 'Unsatisfactory tenants and applicants', *Society of Housing Managers Quarterly Bulletin*, 17 (1955).

59. Brief report on work and presumed prospects with Provisional National Council for Mental Health, June 19 1944. ULSCA D495(HQ)PSU/7.

60. PNCMH prospects, July 1944. ULSCA D495(HQ)PSU/7.

61. Howarth, 'The present dilemma of social casework', p528. See above, p27.

62. The criticism was made by an almoner, Cherry Morris. See Lewis, *The Voluntary Sector, the State and Social Work*, p103.

63. FSU trainee conference held in Liverpool, April 1952. ULSCA D495(HQ) M3/5.

64. See above, p30.

65. Irvine, 'The hard-to-like family', p105.

66. Timms, *Social Casework*, p198.

67. Timms, *Social Casework*, p61.

68. Timms, *Social Casework*, p67; Lewis, *The Voluntary Sector, the State and Social Work*, p105.

69. Timms, *Social Casework*, p67; Lewis, *The Voluntary Sector, the State and Social Work*, p105.

70. See above, pp88–9.

71. F. P. Biestek, *The Casework Relationship* (London, 1957), p36.

72. University of Liverpool, Department of Sociology, Social Policy and Social Work Studies. Student records, 1960.

73. B. Wootton, *Social Science and Social Pathology* (London, 1959), p273.

74. York FSU annual report for 1960–61. ULSCA (YK)M1/8.

75. Bristol FSU, report to the MOH for 1960. ULSCA (BL)M4.

76. Bristol FSU, report to the MOH for 1961. ULSCA (BL)M4; *Report of the Medical Officer of Health for 1961*, B18, BRO 33416(29)d; Starkey, 'The Medical Officer of Health', p435.

77. Minutes of the South London FSU committee, September 18 1962. ULSCA D495(SL)M1/2.

# 4

# Changes and Adjustments

The approbation and endorsement which the agency had attracted during the 1940s and 1950s continued into the following decade and beyond. In spite of debates about the relative merits of different forms of intervention within both the social work profession generally and the organisation itself, FSU remained associated with intensive family casework. By stressing the importance of the whole family group, and of the child within the family, FSU even influenced the work of the voluntary agencies which had traditionally been associated with child rescue and the institutional care of children from families in which their well-being was thought to be threatened. For instance, it formed the basis of small-scale experiments like First Aid for Families, practised by National Children's Homes and explicitly based on FSU's example.[1]

FSU was also singled out for praise by a Home Office Committee on Children and Young Persons which had been set up in 1956 under the chairmanship of Viscount Ingleby,[2] and which reported in 1961. One commentator claimed that the report contained a 'plea for a rationalised and huge extension of the pioneer work done by Family Service Units'.[3] He was in a position to know; as a magistrate and a former chairman of the London County Council Children's Committee, Donald Ford had been a member of the Ingleby committee. However, his exultant comment appears to have been based on slim evidence and a partial reading of the report. The committee's terms of reference had been to inquire into the working of the law in England and Wales, specifically the juvenile court system and its jurisdiction and procedures, together with the remand home and approved school systems.[4] The greater part of the report, therefore, is concerned with the prevention and treatment of juvenile delinquency, which was reported to have increased by 47 per cent since 1954.[5] While the sort of family rehabilitation in which FSUs were involved had some bearing on the incidence of delinquency, it requires a good deal of imagination to see in the 125 Ingleby recommendations an encouragement to extend its work considerably. The committee was also required to inquire into, and make recommendations on, local authorities' powers and duties in order to prevent or forestall the suffering of children through neglect in their own homes, but it was secondary to the main purpose of the report. It was, as David Donnison argued at the time, 'respectable and cautious, lacking all sense of urgency and offering no vision of the future structure of the social services – in fact, conservative'.[6] Not surprisingly, its publication was greeted with a sense of disappointment by those most closely involved with child-care services.[7]

Ingleby may not have accorded FSU quite the sort of attention that Ford had imagined, but FSU's origins owed much to the same climate of anxiety about the family that had given rise to fears of an increase in antisocial behaviour. Ingleby had located the cause of delinquency within the family and its relationships, noting that 'It is often the parents as much as the child who need to alter their ways...', so that it was with family problems that any preventive measures would be largely concerned.[8] FSU claimed considerable expertise in dealing with family relationships. Although he may have exaggerated, Ford was not mistaken in his claim that Ingleby was impressed by accounts of FSU's work. In a section outlining statutory and voluntary provision, the report devoted a substantial paragraph to the work of FSU and the esteem in which it was held. A much shorter paragraph mentioned the work of the National Society for the Prevention of Cruelty to Children (NSPCC), noting merely that its work was well known but that few of its staff were trained social workers. The suggestion that the NSPCC's statutory powers be reduced was later vigorously contested by the society and its supporters and was eventually dropped.[9] The work of the Family Welfare Association was described in two lines, and a number of other voluntary organisations whose functions impinged on family welfare were grouped together in a couple of sentences. Little distinction was made between the methods adopted by FWA and FSU; both were described as being involved in casework, although FSU's more intensive practice was noted. It is possible to say, therefore, that FSU was given greater notice than any other voluntary organisation in the published report, but that is not saying much.

Although the sorts of changes suggested by Ford are hard to find in the substance of the report, his conviction that the organisation could play a valuable role in family rehabilitation was echoed in both Houses of Parliament during the debates prior to the passing of the 1963 Children and Young Persons Act, and served to reinforce the view that FSU was employing effective methods of working with families in difficulty. The FSU's annual report for 1962–63 proudly noted that the MPs for Edgbaston (Dame Edith Pitt), Widnes (James McColl) and Salford West (Charles Royle) had all commented on the achievements of the agency. In his speech the member for Oldham East (Charles Mapp) had urged that the aims of the new Act be furthered by the award of monetary assistance to FSU in recognition of the contribution that its experience of preventive work could make to the education of the workers who would be necessary for the implementation of the legislation:

> The FSU is the vital area of training for caseworkers. Whichever way one looks at it – either the FSU alone or in conjunction with the universities – this is the body which must have some financial grant if we are to write the meaning of Clause 1 into the areas that are concerned.[10]

This was not a short-lived recognition. A few years later, the achievements and methods of the organisation were noted with approval by Lord Beaumont of Whitley[11] and Lord Donaldson of Kingsbridge[12] during a House of Lords debate on poverty in the UK.

Public plaudits like these, which understandably delighted FSU, suggest that there was an identifiable FSU method and that it was the only organisation working in what was perceived to be a particularly valuable and appropriate way. Both assumptions were inaccurate. PSU/FSU may have pioneered a particular approach to intervention in the lives of problem families, but by the early 1960s it no longer had a monopoly on family casework, and the process of extending the practice to other agencies was already well underway before the Ingleby committee reported. It is not surprising that those who had experience of implementing it were quick to draw attention to the fact. Barbara Kahan, a long-time supporter of PSU/FSU-inspired methods of intensive work with families, pointed out in response to Ingleby that such methods were no longer a relatively unknown experiment.[13] She had employed PSU-trained caseworkers to do preventive work during her time as children's officer, first in Dudley from 1948 and then in Oxfordshire from 1951.[14] In neither Dudley nor Oxfordshire did Kahan advocate the establishment of an FSU, but instead demonstrated that the methods originally associated with FSU could be transferred easily and effectively into a statutory agency. She argued that by keeping one family with three children out of care, a family caseworker would save the children's committee the cost of his annual salary and justify his employment.[15] Although she was not hostile to voluntary agencies, Kahan believed that good local authority services were fundamental to the solution of family problems, and in 1961 urged that the '... door on which all can knock, knowing that their knock will be answered by people with the knowledge and capacity and with the willingness to help them' which Ingleby had advocated should have children's department written on it.[16] The City of Oxford children's department and the London County Council (LCC) department of dealth had followed Kahan's example and had appointed family caseworkers in the 1950s,[17] something that did not go unnoticed by FSU.[18] The organisation's sense of its worth was further enhanced when those recruited to work with the LCC were sent for training in casework methods to the Kensington and Paddington unit.[19] Central government endorsement of the method had come in 1954 with the Ministry of Health circular 'Prevention and break-up of families', which suggested that local authorities might find it necessary to employ trained social caseworkers to meet the needs of some families.[20]

Voluntary, as well as statutory, agencies had also developed the preventive side of their work.[21] Some, for example the Church of England Children's Society, had been employing methods which aimed to alleviate acute financial problems and keep children at home with their families since before the Second World War.[22] The NCH First Aid for Families, which has already been mentioned, was also designed to keep children out of care. The Family Welfare Association, whose methods differed from the inquisitorial and rigid ones associated with its predecessor the Charity Organisation Society,[23] was actively fostering the practice of more sympathetic casework methods in the 1950s. FWA preferred to think of itself as dealing with families with problems rather than with problem families – a distinction made by Ingleby[24] and one whose implications were to become clear when FWA and FSU worked together for a short time in Hackney[25] – but however they classified the types of families with whom they worked, both FWA and FSU attached high importance to the integrity of the family and to efforts to prevent children being taken into care. Jane Lewis's assertion that FSU gained more public support for its work than FWA because the former was concerned solely with offering practical care does not stand up to scrutiny, at least so far as the work of some units was concerned, although it may reflect the inaccuracies of public perception. It was also a function of the division that had grown up between those social workers who advocated practical services and material help, and those who wanted to allow the development of a relationship in which the client felt it possible to express emotions such as anger, fear or anxiety. The latter tended to think that the provision of practical help would distract both the client's and the worker's attention from the 'real' problem. As has already been demonstrated, from early in its history PSU/FSU had absorbed and used psychodynamic methods in its work with families. Even if the lessons had been imperfectly learned, and knowledge of psychiatric social work was limited, the notion that FSU was concerned only to improve domestic hygiene and offer other practical assistance is erroneous.

If the FSU method of family casework was not unique to the organisation, neither was FSU limited in its approach. Casework was only one of a range of interventions it employed. The organisation's management structure, which gave considerable autonomy to local units, also enabled the development of a great deal of variation between them. In addition, FSU's culture encouraged experiment and innovation. By the early 1960s, the value of the intensive family casework which had attracted the members of the Ingleby committee was being questioned, and in some cases modified, by FSU – which had, of course, been its original proponent. If Ford assumed that the ensuing Act would usher in a period during which both voluntary and statutory agencies would begin to practise intensive family casework on the FSU model, he was wide of the mark. Although the 1963 Children and Young Persons Act promoted the value of preventive work, the methods employed by many social workers, even by those working with FSU, were already wider and based on more varied principles than those utilised by FSU 20 years earlier.[26]

That FSU had begun to question, and often to modify, its traditional ways of working is not surprising. The agency's origins in the activities of independent and strong-minded individualists had ensured that a questioning, experimental attitude was a constant characteristic of their approach, and the leadership had constantly urged workers to engage in action research and to publish accounts of their activities. As a consequence, FSU continued to attract workers who found the prospect of experiment, innovation and critical analysis exciting. By the early 1960s, although some units retained the traditional emphasis on intensive family casework, others were actively exploring the possibilities of a variety of methods of assistance for disadvantaged families. Traditional patterns were modified and group work and community work were considered as methods of intervention in line with new thinking.[27] In addition, units cooperated with other voluntary agencies and entered into, or strengthened, working relationships with statutory agencies.

The desirability of greater cooperation between agencies had already been underlined in the 1959 *Report of the Working Party on Social Workers in the Local Authority Health and Welfare Services* (Younghusband report), which had recommended the provision of a comprehensive service for those families whose range of problems was currently being dealt with by a number of separate organisations.[28] In the same year, an experiment in East London designed to rationalise the local provision of family casework was suggested by Sir Donald Allen, Clerk to the Trustees of the City Parochial Foundation (CPF), which set £60,000 aside to support it.[29] A preliminary meeting was attended by Eileen Younghusband and Sir Donald Allen as well as by representatives of the National Association for Mental Health, the Home Office, the National Council for the Unmarried Mother and her Child, the Invalid Children's Aid Association (ICAA), St Thomas's Hospital, the Middlesex Hospital, the Moral Welfare Council, the Family Welfare Association, the Probation Service, LCC and FSU.[30] The resultant Combined Casework Unit in Hackney was intended to explore the potential of cooperative activity between the FWA, the ICAA and FSU. This was to be achieved by employing a composite casework team operating from a central office under a single director.[31] Its stated objectives were to demonstrate the value of a coordinated family casework service and thereby to reduce any overlap in provision between the agencies; to act as a local focus for family casework; to reduce overhead expenses by enabling separate organisations to share buildings and administration; and to improve the quality of care to clients by providing a number of specialist services under one roof.[32] Its success, Allen believed, would result in a comprehensive service to families at a considerably lower cost than if the agencies had operated independently from their own premises. However, because a formal union offered no advantage to any of them, it was agreed by the directors of the collaborating agencies that each should retain its own identity, and work within its own management structures.[33]

Work in the Combined Casework Unit (CCU) started in October 1962, with a staff of caseworkers seconded from each of the three organisations. The director of the unit, Maria Boselli, saw the different identities of the agencies reflected in the caseworkers' styles of work and their use of office accommodation. FWA clients turned up at the CCU for pre-arranged weekly or fortnightly interviews and its staff preferred to work from individual offices. FSU clients tended to call at the unit more frequently than those of the other agencies, although they were also visited in their own homes, and their workers liked to share offices. ICAA workers preferred to have individual offices, but used them only for office work and conferences, because almost all their casework was carried out in the clients' homes.[34] While reflecting the origins and traditions of the parent organisations, such different patterns of working were also informed by a debate about home visiting which had been taking place among caseworkers for several years. The value of the home visit was not universally acknowledged. Some workers believed it allowed essential information about the family's relationships and domestic circumstances to be gathered. Others, perhaps most especially those who looked for the seeds of the client's problems within his or her own personality, admitted that it could help to check the caseworker's first impressions or act as a gesture of goodwill, but believed that it might have negative effects if it helped the client to avoid his or her problems, or neutralised hostility which might be more easily expressed within the more impersonal atmosphere of the office.[35] The director's exploration of the differences between the workers led her to comment that they revealed attitudes and largely class-based preconceptions which affected the workers' relationships with their clients. She noted, for example, that the FSU workers, accustomed to disorganised and almost invariably working-class families, found it difficult to work with young, professional women bringing up children who, in other circumstances, might have been referred to the FWA. The ICAA workers, who were used to focusing on the needs created in a family by the presence of disabled children, did not know what to do about the permanently broken windows which appeared to characterise the homes of some of the families they were required to add to their caseloads.[36]

Their differences, if occasionally puzzling, had some advantages. Each participating agency contributed its own expertise to the CCU.

FSU shared knowledge about ways of reducing the isolation of families who were unpopular with their neighbours, while the FWA was able to exercise its traditional skill in differentiating between clients who needed a lot of support and those who were capable of taking a greater degree of personal responsibility. The ICAA contributed theoretical knowledge about the feelings and experiences of parents with handicapped children. For the clients, the main advantages were assumed to lie in the elimination of the duplication of investigation, a more comprehensive service and an increase in the caseworkers' skills.[37]

The professional development of the caseworker was clearly valuable and may have been a successful feature of the project, but given the very different types of clients found on the caseloads of the agencies, it is difficult to see how the CCU could have reduced duplication. On occasion, a problem family with a handicapped child might have been on the books of more than one agency, but the workers' own accounts of the experience of combining caseloads suggest that on the whole there had been little overlap.

Even if the original aims of the unit had not wholly been achieved, the workers professed enthusiasm for the experiment, and expressed disappointment when the grant from the City Parochial Foundation ran out. The views of the workers were not generally shared by the senior management of the agencies. Communication between the parent organisations, the management committee, the director and the workers had proved difficult.[38] That the work of the CCU seldom featured in the annual reports of the parent bodies implies a reluctance to take public ownership of the work that was being done in Hackney,[39] and may have informed the initial insistence that all three agencies should retain their own identities while working cooperatively. From the CCU's earliest days it was clear that David Jones, FSU's national secretary in 1960, had grave misgivings about the project[40] and that these were shared by Fred Philp, who succeeded him in 1962.[41] While this unease may reflect a degree of inter-agency rivalry as well as a managerial reluctance to associate with other agencies too closely, it also threw into relief the relationship between benefactors and the organisations that profited from their generosity. If the 1967 report on the CCU by Fred Philp[42] was representative of the views of the FWA and the ICAA, then there was a sense of having been pushed reluctantly into an experiment out of a sense of duty to a generous donor:[43]

I felt that FSU with its clients was in danger of allowing itself to be used to prove an administrative point about which Sir Donald had already made up his mind... I considered that FSU could not afford to appear uncooperative or reluctant to consider new ideas.[44]

It is also questionable whether the CCU had much impact in the area. When the CPF funding ran out, Hackney Borough Council declined to take over responsibility on the grounds that the services the unit had offered could be provided by the statutory authority. The parent organisations brought the CCU to an end in 1967,[45] and the building was taken over by the FWA.[46]

Although they professed disappointment when the CCU closed, the workers also expressed reservations which suggested that they were becoming uneasy about the narrow, caseworking basis of the agency and that they hoped, were further funding to become available, that any new service would widen its approach to intervention and concentrate on community development and group work '... as casework by itself and divorced from other aspects of social work has latterly come in for a good deal of scrutiny and criticism'.[47]

Much of the scrutiny and criticism had been directed at the practice of psychodynamic forms of casework. The Ingleby committee had noted in 1960 that there had been a 'certain reaction against the indiscriminate application of intensive or deep case work for family or personal difficulties' and had recommended that attention should first be given to the 'simple forms of social aid'.[48] While casework and the use of the social worker's own personality to help to effect change in the individual client was a technique which was still employed, an emphasis on the person as a social being was adding a significant dimension. Methods of social work intervention had already been widened by the inclusion of group work and community work, as the importance of the wider environment to the client's experience became recognised – as did the fact that it was impossible for the social worker or anyone else to detach clients from their environment.[49] Social work had not been the only caring profession to adopt these methods. In the 1950s and 1960s the nurse–patient relationship was considered instrumental in the resolution of patients' problems, particularly those categorised as psychosocial, and it became incorporated into the professional definition of nursing.[50] Nursing, like social work, was attempting to identify the unique theoretical perspective in its practice and to define its own professional role in the context of respect for the integrity of the client's, or the patient's, life – in contrast to the other social welfare agencies such as departments of housing or public health, which concentrated on the relief of physical needs. While holistic notions had wide currency, it was the psychiatric social work profession, with its roots in the child guidance movement, which accepted without question that the social worker had the right to intervene in the emotional lives of families, and had the confidence to assert that its intervention was relevant to the families' problems and likely to help in their resolution.[51]

By the early 1970s, the process of reassessing the usefulness of psychodynamic casework, which had been criticised in robust style by Barbara Wootton in 1959,[52] was well underway. The belief that all social casework should have a psychological or mental hygiene aspect had been an essential element in social work in the US during the inter-war period, and had influenced casework developments in the UK, but it had been subjected to critical reappraisal by social work commentators. Reservations about a form of intervention which appeared to ignore the social and economic dimensions to clients' problems were expressed by T. S. Simey, Professor of Social Science at the University of Liverpool, and Richard Titmuss, his counterpart in the Department of Social Science and Social Administration at the London School of Economics. Both believed that by focusing on the internal world of the client, intensive psychodynamic casework was in danger of 'ignoring both wider social problems and administrative realities'.[53] That academics like Wootton, Simey and Titmuss, concerned mainly with social policy and social administration, should be critical of an approach which stressed personal and psychological factors at the expense of environmental ones is understandable, but social workers shared some of their misgivings. Although the employment of psychodynamic methods and language had enabled social work to develop its own scientific vocabulary in place of the explicitly moral categories of the pre-war social worker,[54] as Noel Timms pointed out certain sorts of casework tempted their practitioners 'towards rhapsody, mysticism and, at times, a triumphant vagueness'.[55] Behind all these comments lay the fear that some types of casework depended too heavily on the personal interaction between worker and client and too little on intellectual rigour; too heavily on individual emotional and psychological difficulties and too little on the implications of social policy.

Their research in the late 1960s had led John Mayer and Noel

Timms to believe that FWA's clients, subjected to casework on the psychodynamic model, were more likely to be dissatisfied with the service they received than were those whose difficulties were dealt with more straightforwardly, perhaps with the addition of some form of material assistance.[56] The absence of any such research in the preparation of its report had been one of the criticisms levelled at the Younghusband committee when it presented its findings in 1959. Although it pleaded lack of time, key members of the committee also entertained reservations about the usefulness of asking clients about their experience of poorly developed social work in the health and social services, when they had no standard by which to measure it. Low levels of expectation on the part of clients, as measured by those who thought they knew what clients ought to have wanted, might have damaged the case for improved services as defined by experts. As Younghusband commented, the Committee on Local Authority and Allied Personal Services (the Seebohm committee), reporting in 1968, faced the same criticism and gave the same explanation.[57] Eric Sainsbury's survey, published in 1975, appeared not to be dogged by such doubts, and attached importance to clients' observations. His findings reinforced those of Mayer and Timms and revealed that FSU's clients, who often received some practical aid in addition to help with relationships, experienced a greater level of satisfaction than those who were offered no material assistance.[58] Nevertheless, client satisfaction was only one measure of effectiveness, which reflected merely a personal, local and short-term understanding of any one problem and neglected a consideration of wider issues.

While claims were being made by at least one of the original Liverpool workers that the broad pattern of FSU work had been established by 1945 and that later developments had been based on that wartime experience,[59] some workers were recognising the disadvantages of its method of working. Writing from the perspective of his experience as a psychiatric social worker, Stan Ambrose, who was employed in the Liverpool unit, noted the agency's tendency to encourage dependency in its clients. He contested the value of a way of working that used dependence as a therapeutic tool, as well as the mythology that underlay some casework methods; and he questioned a method which, by its insistence that problem families needed a substitute parental figure, justified what he believed to be infantilisation.[60] Some of his colleagues would have disagreed. In the Bristol unit, workers noted without any sense of regret the tendency for some families to accept the service as a more or less permanent and continuing factor in their lives,[61] and the Bradford unit produced an account of work with a women's group where the workers consciously adopted a parental role towards the clients.[62] The account, and the method employed, attracted considerable praise from Elizabeth Irvine, one of the leading authorities in social work in the 1960s, who represented those social workers who saw in the problem family syndrome proof of immaturity.[63] Ambrose, though, argued for a more assertive form of casework and stressed the need to resist the manipulative and overdemanding behaviour which he believed to characterise some clients.[64] His was not a lone voice. Another Liverpool worker commented that the acceptance of regression through extreme dependence was detrimental to the well-being of families, as was the adoption of a permanent parental role towards those who seemed to be unable to achieve minimal standards without constant support.[65] At about the same time, the West London unit made reference to one family which had been on its books for 20 years,[66] thus providing an illustration of the sort of dependence that was being questioned, if not condemned. When he conducted his survey of FSU families in Sheffield in 1972–73, Sainsbury noted the tendency for some FSU social work to settle into 'a wholly undynamic friendliness'.[67]

If the work in Hackney provides one example of FSU's cooperation with other voluntary agencies, the Kensington and Paddington unit, which believed itself to be closely related to the welfare state and to have grown alongside it, illustrates one unit's relationship with statutory bodies. It took pride in the close links it had fostered over the years with the school care committees, the maternity and child welfare service, local housing departments and the children's department,[68] but close cooperation did not preclude criticism. In 1954 its interest in the effects of environmental pressures on families and its commitment to 'political' activity on their behalf had prompted the unit to conduct a small research project into housing in its area. Workers discovered that it was quite normal to find families with ten children living in two rooms, with no bathroom, no hot water and no proper kitchen. Many had little prospect of being moved into more suitable accommodation because of the length of the housing waiting list and the shortage of suitable dwellings.[69] The unit's criticisms led the housing department to complain that it was being unjustly judged,[70] but housing continued to be a serious problem for families in the Kensington and Paddington area and most of the problems on which legal advice was sought were concerned with relations between landlords and tenants.[71] FSU's continued interest in this area led to its involvement with other voluntary agencies, and in the early 1960s to cooperation with another local housing survey. This time workers followed up advertisements in local papers and newsagents' windows in an attempt to discover how much reasonably priced rented accommodation was available in the private sector. They were able to find only one letting under £6 a week. With the income of poorer families in the order of £10–£12 a week, a rent of £6 was impossibly high. Reports of their research were sent to the Minister of Housing and Local Government and to all London MPs, and were widely reported in the press.[72] The unit also gave evidence to the Milner-Holland committee, set up to investigate the serious housing shortage in greater London.[73]

The Kensington and Paddington unit was not alone in drawing attention to structural problems. However, the pattern of activity within FSU was very varied, and the external perception of the organisation reflected a lack of knowledge about the range of interventions it used and the changes which had taken place or were in progress. The Sheffield unit was more than a little taken aback by being asked by the West Riding of Yorkshire authority in 1967 to help with house cleaning and decorating for some families – work which FSU would gladly have undertaken two decades earlier in order to further its campaign of educational and preventive work with families, but which now seemed inappropriate.[74]

In 1977, the pressure to consider social policy issues was formally recognised by FSU with the establishment by the national council of a social policy group.[75] This was both a reflection of and reaction to activities already taking place within the units. The change of approach did not always meet with the approval of local management committees, which were often more conservative in their understanding of social work method than the unit workers they managed. In July 1975, the Newcastle unit had proposed expanding its methods in order to become a multifunctional social work service in a limited geographical area, using casework, community work and group work in complementary ways to meet the needs of a socially deprived locale. The rationale behind the proposal recognised that FSU's traditional emphasis on the personal rather than the socio-political aspects of its work failed to address the fact that the problems facing the unit's families in Newcastle were both emotional and socioeconomic and, thus, quasi-political.[76] The practical out-working of this conviction was greeted with some anxiety by the management committee. It promised basic support to a worker whose task was to encourage local initiative and leadership and facilitate communication between communities and branches of the local authority, but expressly warned against the danger of mis-leading a community into 'demanding more than was realistic'.[77] Reservations about the new approach in Newcastle were also expressed at the FSU national office, although they were countered by the unit organiser who argued that the interests of the families would best be served by a wider service and a more overtly political stance; in his view, FSU should be more vocal than it traditionally had been in championing the needs of the underprivileged.[78] This explicit shift in the focus of the work gave a clear message that families' problems were in part the result of poor housing, poverty and other environmental factors which it was beyond their power to influence, at least as individuals. In spite of the reservations expressed locally and nationally, the Newcastle unit began to join with other agencies in advocacy on behalf of disadvantaged families. For example, a meeting with the assistant regional controller of the Supplementary Benefits Commission, called to express disquiet about the unsympathetic treatment clients received in benefit offices, included representatives from the NSPCC, the Probation Service, the Anglican Diocese of Newcastle, FSU and Age Concern, as well as a local community project. The initiative was not welcomed by the chairman of the Supplementary Benefits Commission, David Donni-son, who believed that the agencies were more interested in attacking the DHSS staff than in helping the people for whom they were all responsible.[79] However, endorsement for Newcastle's stand in this instance came from FSU's national office, which supported the unit in its refusal to pass to the Supplementary Benefits Commission the names of those clients who had complained about their treatment.[80] That the Newcastle clients' experience was not unusual was borne out by Sainsbury's 1975 survey of 27 FSU families, which found that 10 contacts with the supplementary benefits offices were rated as helpful while 13 were thought to have been unhelpful.[81] Local councillors in Newcastle, though, were not convinced. They were anxious that the unit's new form of intervention was 'stirring up people deliberately', a reference to FSU support for a local group wanting to set up a tenants' association.[82] The unit's continued support for and active involvement in tenants' associations led to the resignation of one local councillor from the Newcastle FSU committee because she disapproved of the new emphasis in the unit's work.[83] While her position as both an elected representative and a committee member might have engendered a degree of conflict and an uncertainty about where her loyalties should lie, she was not alone in feeling anxious about FSU's departure from its traditional ways of working, which, whatever their inadequacies so far as the clients were concerned, had not tended to rock the political boat. On the contrary, these methods had enabled FSU families and their needs to remain invisible to some local authorities, as their antisocial behaviour was controlled by FSU's intervention.[84] Invisibility was no longer acceptable to social workers or their clients.

A related discussion among social workers hinged on the issue of social control in social work and asked fundamental questions about the nature of the encounter between client and worker. Was the social worker society's instrument for the control or elimination of inconvenient behaviour, or an advocate for the disadvantaged and misunderstood – or both, and if so in what measure? While commentators a few years later were to insist that an element of social control was inherent in many social work tasks,[85] in the 1970s the suggestion raised anxieties in the minds of some social workers. An agency like FSU, with a tradition of offering very long-term and labour-intensive support to families and of failing to face the issues that such close supervision might suggest, was in danger of looking both expensive and backward. Widespread dissatisfaction was expressed with the central premise of psychiatrically inspired casework – that is, the notion that clients' difficulties must always be located in their personal and intimate relationships – and social work thinking began to move towards the encouragement of greater self-help through the medium of the client's local social environment.[86]

The doubts about the efficacy of intensive family casework which had been expressed by FSU workers became common currency during the 1970s among social workers in a number of agencies, both statutory and voluntary. In 1973, Younghusband reflected on the process of change; she noted the innocent arrogance with which, in the process of progressing from the implementation of Charity Organisation Society principles to employing psychoanalytic theory in the wake of the setting up of the first mental health course at the

London School of Economics in 1929, caseworkers had claimed to be able to make significant intervention in almost every form of social problem.[87] The claims could not be substantiated. By the end of the 1970s intensely personal casework had come under attack from both radical left-wing social work theorists who located personal problems within a socio-political framework, and their right-wing counterparts who argued that there was no evidence that psychodynamic social work did any good.[88] Nevertheless, the position was not uniform and some local authorities still wanted to buy a casework service when they funded FSUs, though whether they were necessarily able to say what sort of casework they wanted to buy is not clear. A social worker from the Leicester unit, writing in 1977, noted that the caseworkers there were funded by the local authority social services department and were on permanent contracts, whereas those workers who were involved in group work or advocacy were supported by the Urban Aid Fund. Such workers were always on short term contracts, less secure in their employment than their caseworker colleagues and aware that their work was seen as being less important because it involved projects that were frequently organised on a temporary, one-off basis.[89] More than 20 years later, a report commissioned by the National Council for Voluntary Organisations was to identify the still-present dangers of the short-term funding of workers and projects. Together with the reduced sense of worth attached to short-term funding, there was a risk that staff time would be taken up by securing the next grant, or applying for the next job, as much as by providing a service.[90]

The tensions generated by the introduction of community work activities into an agency which had hitherto stressed the importance of casework were noted by the authors of a 1978 report on the development of FSU. They commented on the care necessary at the local level to avoid certain problems; for example, families who were given the undivided attention of a social worker might be envied by other families whose problems were tackled through more structural community approaches. As another writer pointed out, serious difficulties might be produced if families receiving casework-style help were given access to an activity like a unit-organised bonfire party, while the under-resourced neighbourhood community association struggled to finance and arrange one of its own.[91] The unavoidable lesson seemed to be that if a unit attempted to operate at more than one level using different theoretical bases for different methods of intervention, it ran the risk of being seriously misunderstood by its client group.[92]

Other difficulties envisaged by the working party arose from the activities of community groups and workers whose funding came primarily from local authorities; if they criticised the activities of their funders they might put any future grants at risk. While acknowledging that no community work projects in FSU had been designed to produce conflict with the statutory authorities, it also noted that in some cases strategies which resulted in a challenge to official policy or practice were legitimate. Somewhat naively, it believed that FSU projects were concerned with creating new resources, improving communications and encouraging self-help schemes and were, therefore, unlikely to tread on local authority toes.[93] If problems arose, then resolution had to be sought, in the working party's view, in separate funding for those projects which might be seen to challenge any one local authority's policies or in an agreement with the funding body about the legitimate scope of community work.[94] The tension created by FSU's dependence on local authority funding, and the possible limits that such dependence put on its activities, had already been noted in 1973 by Patrick Goldring. Although the Seebohm committee had commented on the desirability of a 'certain level of mutual criticism' between local authority and voluntary organisations in 1968, this was a stance that FSU could ill afford to adopt.

> ... any criticism of the local authority or of the government by FSU has to be tempered by the consideration that the former is an essential source of money for operating expenses and the latter a valued provider of research and training finance. By going actively into politics FSU would jeopardise both these sources of funds and thus sharply reduce its ability to help families in need.[95]

As Goldring showed, some members of FSU had found a solution to the dilemma in the formation of the Child Poverty Action Group, which had its origins in the activities of Fred Philp and Geoffrey Rankin (one-time unit organiser in Islington)[96] and was based at FSU's headquarters.[97] The 1978 report noted the separation of activities which '... allowed FSU to concentrate on the personal work with families while individual workers campaigned through other agencies for social, economic or administrative changes'.[98]

In the quest for new approaches to problems experienced by families in deprived areas, the Bishop Auckland unit made a deliberate effort during the 1970s to integrate a number of methods of intervention.[99] Working with families referred to them from other agencies, the small team at first employed a range of casework and group work methods, each of which had the family and its individual members as its main focus. They originated in two different traditions: the individualistic perspective of social work, which had given rise to casework based on psychodynamic models, and community work which aimed at tackling problems within a community rather than looking at political and economic forces affecting the community from outside.[100] By 1974, the team had modified its approach in the light of the conviction that it should be serving the whole community, thus moving away from what many saw as being the traditional FSU approach of intensive casework with individual families. Influenced by the systems theory of Pincus and Minahan and attaching importance to the interactions between people and social systems,[101] the Bishop Auckland team began to consider where to locate the responsibility for any one family's distress. It resisted the notion that any family could be studied and helped as a discrete entity and argued that an appreciation of its social situation was vital, eventually coming to the conclusion that it was important to understand the different levels of interaction between the local council, the family and the immediate environment. Because of the complexity of the relationships, any work of value had to take account of all three systems.[102] When it came to consider this unitary approach, the FSU working party on development stopped short of wholehearted endorsement; it commented in a cautious way on the effectiveness of integrated methods of social work delivery and recommended action research.[103] While this may be seen as an attempt to placate those who were committed to experiment while ensuring that no firm commitment was made by the organisation as a whole, it may also reflect a response to the uncomfortable questions that an integrated approach raised for traditionally oriented agencies, noted by Ron Baker a few years later.[104] Nevertheless, experienced and influential voices within the profession were advocating the serious consideration of integrated methods of working.[105]

If the Bishop Auckland unit represented a part of FSU which was experimental and innovative in its methods, the more conservative wing was exemplified by Oldham which in 1974 found itself defensively protesting the value of its traditional casework stance; but there was a price to pay. The unit felt its position within the national organisation to be increasingly marginalised, perhaps indicating the extent to which FSU as a whole had moved on. A document recording the visit of one of the assistant directors in 1974 noted that the unit organiser felt that the work at Oldham was undervalued because it concentrated on casework, while at national unit organisers' meetings discussion appeared to focus on subjects other than the 'central core of FSU work'.[106]

The FSU tradition of offering support that lasted for many years but may have achieved little was challenged by the working party on development in 1978. One explanation it offered – that in FSU's early days there were no 'acceptable alternative work models' – was hardly credible by the late 1970s. Moreover, as the authors commented, the tendency to encourage relationships which created mutual dependency between client and worker gave no incentive for change; rather the reverse. It also puzzled recruits; newly trained social workers, encouraged by tutors on their training courses to consider a variety of forms of intervention and discouraged from using dependence as a tool, found that the practice had little to commend it. The convention of giving 10, 15 or even 20 years' service to relatively few families was bound to be viewed critically by workers whose own term of employment within the agency spanned only three or four years. It was difficult for them to maintain belief in a process which seemed never to be completed.[107]

Yet as has been shown, few units remained totally committed to the ideal of intensive family casework. By the late 1970s, the national organisation was able to claim that it offered a wide range of services and had shifted decisively from long-term supportive work to short-term interventions focused on attainable objectives.[108] Workers and clients in some units found the use of contracts helpful in the process of achieving client participation and in reducing what one commentator called 'the compulsive care-giving that characterises much of social work', which was impugned as tending 'to reduce the client's autonomy' and engender dependency and hostility.[109] John Corden, a lecturer in social work at the University of Leeds, used US social work literature as a basis for his discussion about the use of contracts in social work in 1980,[110] and when he moved to Leeds FSU as unit organiser he and a colleague engaged in correspondence with Chris Rojek and Stewart Collins through the pages of the *British Journal of Social Work* about the underlying theoretical concepts. In his original article, Corden had argued that the justification for the contractual model must be grounded in values rather than in claims about its therapeutic effects. The fundamental value on which contract work should be based was that of reciprocity, which required that each party recognise the different needs and goals of the other and aimed to enable the achievement of agreed objectives.[111] Such an assertion represented a considerable move from a tradition which had tended towards direction, however skilfully concealed, by the worker. As Rojek and Collins showed, it also raised questions about the nature of reciprocity, highlighted the inequality of the relationship between client and worker and failed to address the effect on both of any contractual arrangement.[112] Nevertheless, agreements drawn up between social workers and their clients which set out realisable short-term objectives were extensively used – whether or not they were technically contracts – and appear to have proved effective in a number of cases.

In the quest for more effective forms of intervention social workers also began to explore ways of cooperating with other services, particularly schools and education departments. In the wake of the failure to implement the recommendations of the Seebohm committee for a closer relationship between education and social work services, the Association of Directors of Social Services, meeting in 1978, tried to revive the principle and reiterated the need for much closer cooperation.[113] Such cooperation had already been anticipated in FSU experiments based in the Islington unit. In 1972, it sought to address the difficulties that some schoolchildren experienced in the classroom, such as their tendency to be disruptive and to underachieve. The unit, in partnership with the Inner London Education Authority (ILEA), opened a full-time educational centre – the Cromartie Centre – which was physically separate from any local school, and was intended for a group of about 15 children of secondary school age who had a history of truanting. This intermediate treatment centre was staffed by two teachers and two social workers. By 1982, although it was still an integral part of Islington FSU's work,[114] the balance of funding had changed. The centre was now jointly funded by ILEA, which paid for two teachers, and Inner-City Partnership, which supported the other two workers, one of whom was a qualified social worker.[115]

The experience of organising an off-site centre for a group of children disenchanted with mainstream schools was both frustrating and stimulating. Reflecting on the first years of the project in the late 1970s one of the original workers recorded a mixture of failures and successes. He argued that the Cromartie Centre had provided a cheaper and more effective method of giving help to truants than had previously been on offer within the welfare services. To prove his point, he claimed that it cost just over £1,000 per year per child in 1974–75 to teach a child at the Cromartie Centre while he/she was living at home; this compared favourably with the cost of taking that child into the care of the social services (about £2,500) or of sending him/her to an approved school (approximately £5,000). Yet the scheme enjoyed limited success; although attendance levels were high and the children appeared to enjoy the experiences that Cromartie gave them, few children, however academically able, had been able to break out of the traps of social and economic deprivation or to clear conventional academic hurdles.[116]

In 1975, convinced that in many cases help would have been more effective had it begun earlier, the Islington FSU set up an off-site unit for younger children, again in partnership with ILEA. Initially known as a Junior Intermediate Treatment Centre, later as the Pakeman Unit, it had places for 10 children exhibiting severe difficulties ranging from an inability to make relationships with their peers and teachers to educational underachievement and behavioural and health problems. All the children came from the same junior school, and the Pakeman Unit was staffed by a teacher from the school and two FSU workers.[117] So that contact was not lost with the normal school routine and the children's classmates, those selected spent the mornings in the unit and the rest of the day in their normal classroom. The aims were broad, from the reduction of the attainment gap between the unit children and their peers to the fostering of positive relationships with adults and other children. Behaviour modification techniques, such as the use of limited contracts between staff and children, were used; for example, achievable targets of improved behaviour were set by child and worker and a simple written agreement made. The approaches adopted necessitated close cooperation with classroom teachers which demonstrated to the pupils the unity of purpose between the unit and the school. For example, teachers would occasionally exercise discipline on behalf of the unit by keeping a child in school when the rest of the unit were going on an expedition if the child had behaved badly on a previous outing.[118]

An internal report on the work of the unit in 1983 noted the advantages of its unusual bidisciplinary approach. These included bringing together the two main agencies dealing with the children and their parents, the fundamental importance of parental involvement, and the firm and direct links with the school.[119] By the time that an account of the experiment was written in 1984, 56 children had attended for periods ranging from one week to nine terms, with an average length of stay of about four or five terms.

The Pakeman project lasted until 1987, by which time it is clear that the high level of confidence in what the workers were doing and the way in which they were doing it had begun to evaporate. Moreover, the enthusiastic report in 1983 had told only part of the story; that same year it had also been noted that although the unit appeared to have clearly defined objectives, and that there was agreement about the specific aims relating to educational and social work input, there was, nevertheless, some mistrust and misunderstanding on the part of the teachers in the school. Some believed the project to be indulging naughty children by giving them treats, and argued that children referred there were not necessarily the most needy, just the most demanding and disruptive.[120] A second report on what became known as Pakeman Unit phase two, in February 1987, also noted that in 1983 ILEA had reported a lack of clear aims, with the attendant dangers of high expectations and consequent disappointment when difficulties were experienced back in the classroom.[121]

Assessment of the work of both the Cromartie Centre and the Pakeman Unit was mixed. It is clear from its response to working parties set up by ILEA in the mid-1980s that FSU was beginning to feel that its efforts were not fully appreciated, and that the ideals it had espoused had not been understood. In the 1985 Hargreaves Report on the curriculum and organisation of ILEA schools as they affected underachievers and absentees, Islington FSU found some vindication of the work that had been in progress at the Cromartie Centre for 14 years, but FSU was critical of the terminology used and the solutions proposed by ILEA. These included reintegrating children with problems and, if that failed, searching for an alternative on the lines, FSU suspected, of an older ILEA scheme for disruptive children. FSU noted particularly the labelling of children who did not fit into secondary schools as 'problems'; the lack of a mandatory requirement to consult parents; and the failure to address career development issues for staff. It also expressed concern that some off-site solutions organised by education authorities could become little more than dumping grounds for difficult children, reducing the disruption they might cause at a conventional school but giving them restricted access to the curriculum. The report's recommendations for the establishment of such complementary centres by the local authority attracted criticism from FSU on three principal grounds: such centres did not appear to be very different from school; there was no mention of cooperation with voluntary agencies; and there was no exploration of more community-based methods of education.[122] ILEA's failure, as it was perceived, to appreciate the skills and achievements of voluntary agencies led FSU to respond angrily to the report of the Metcalf working party, set up by ILEA to give further consideration to the provision of off-site centres. It claimed that Metcalf's assumption that truancy rates were falling was contradicted both by the Hargreaves Report and the current figures for Islington; that Metcalf had not examined the philosophical and methodological bases for FSU's success; and that it gave a totally inadequate account of FSU's role and contribution over 14 years.[123]

Units outside London also tried to influence and improve the educational experience of children from families referred to FSU. In Leeds the unit believed that its responsibility to disadvantaged families included a consideration of the failure of the education system to meet the needs of those children, and it resolved to widen the social workers' skills and knowledge. A pre-school worker had been appointed in 1973, the same year in which the educational aspects of family life had been explored at FSU's national conference. The following year an application to the Urban Aid Fund for a grant to pay for the addition of two teachers to the unit's staff was submitted. The unit had several aims in mind: developing the educational aspects of the unit's group work programme; building up liaison between parents of families on the unit's caseload and the schools attended by their children; creating working arrangements with schools in respect of particularly difficult children from families on the unit's caseload; and helping with some educational needs, particularly literacy, of parents on the unit's caseload. In 1976 a major programme was started, with weekly after-school sessions for children in the unit house.[124] By trying to assess the effects of unhelpful school responses to the learning difficulties and behaviour problems that some children exhibited, FSU hoped to challenge the accuracy of the premise that all problems experienced by children in school had their origins within the family. This process was made possible by the addition of teachers to the unit's staff. Their professional insights helped social workers to understand the life of the classroom and also facilitated cooperation with local schools, with the subsidiary aims of changing attitudes among some teachers, as well as some parents and children. Like the unit at Bishop Auckland, Leeds FSU found theoretical justification for its methods in the systems theory of Pincus and Minahan; their concept of a target system, at which efforts to bring about change should be directed, legitimated attempts to bring about change in schools. The notion of a contract between the unit workers and families was also extended for use in a more informal way with schools.[125] By the end of the project, educational work had come to be a vital and distinctive part of the unit's work. By setting up an advisory group – which included staff from the community education and advisory sections of the local education authority, head teachers, and a representative from the unit's management committee – the unit believed that it was developing mechanisms which would enable deprived families to gain increased advantage from education services.[126]

Brent FSU, too, had embarked on educational support work and had two education workers on its staff, responsible for holiday play schemes, individual work with children with behavioural problems, cooperation with schools in trying to alleviate non-attendance, and the running of courses on topics such as group work and sex education.[127] In Sheffield, the Firth Park Children's Project set out to work with a local middle school with the support of a research group based at the University of Sheffield. The project worker helped with reading and language development, and enlisted the support of parents and pupils from the local comprehensive school.[128]

The 1980s saw a spate of FSU publications describing education projects in which units had become involved. Individual initiatives in Edinburgh,[129] Sheffield,[130] and Thurrock were described,[131] and a more general booklet about educational work within the organisation was put together by a group consisting of members from the South London, Thamesmead, East Birmingham, Islington, Brent, Rochdale, Sheffield and Newcastle units. Together these demonstrated the importance that the organisation attached to links between schools, families and social workers, and the need to improve relationships between school and home in order to enhance the educational opportunities of children from unit families.[132]

The South London unit became involved in work which aimed specifically to improve black children's chances at school. In one of the thousands of projects established nationally with the aid of grants from the Urban Aid programme,[133] Lil Bickley was appointed in 1975 to a community work post, with responsibility for forging links between home and school. She was the first black worker to be employed in the unit and one of the first in the whole organisation.[134] Throughout the first three years of the project, she was the only community worker based at the South London unit; throughout its lifetime she was the only black worker. Her work was funded through the section of the Urban Aid Fund devoted to encouraging projects in areas with 'a high proportion of immigrants', and was specifically drafted to meet the special needs of Ugandan Asians who had recently arrived in the UK. Urban Aid Circular 12, under which the application for funding was submitted, also included schemes which aimed to develop links between parents and schools.[135] The South London FSU proposal fitted both criteria. It was based on an estate where a large number of black families were living and where three quarters of the children in the schools included in the project were deemed to be underachieving.[136]

The project lasted for seven years, during which time Lil Bickley was instrumental in encouraging local initiatives and enabling local people to take leading parts in the life of their neighbourhood.[137] However, in some aspects it was not as successful as FSU might have hoped. Teachers, perhaps understandably defending their own professional territory, resisted the community worker's attempts to encourage them to allow parents to help in the classrooms. The worker believed that she detected racist attitudes underlying a reluctance to consider the provision of teaching materials that took account of children's ethnic backgrounds, a reluctance which was to change radically in the aftermath of the 1981 Brixton riots and the subsequent multi-ethnic initiatives taken by ILEA.[138] Although ILEA was a sponsor of the original Urban Aid application,[139] its officers did not make any attempt to support or appraise the project, nor was it invited by FSU to participate in the consultations that took place while it was in progress.[140] If the local authority disappointed her by offering little in the way of support, FSU also seems to have provided Lil Bickley with cause for complaint. She believed that her appointment had implications for the organisation which had not been properly thought through. Little consideration, if any, had been given to the provision of suitable premises.[141] Although part of the local unit team, she had felt that her work was separate. The estate was distant from the unit house and, as the only community worker in a team which consisted mainly of caseworkers, Lil Bickley found it difficult to talk about her work with her colleagues; their more person-centred focus meant that she was constantly forced to defend community work. However, the underlying and pervading difficulty was that of being a black worker in a white organisation.[142]

Lil Bickley highlighted an aspect of FSU's work which was to change significantly in future years. From its early days the organis-ation had been uneasy about issues to do with race. Even in Liverpool, a city with a well-established black population, many of whom lived near the unit, the infant unit had been chary about engaging with black issues and reluctant to work with black families.[143] In February 1943, the Liverpool PSU committee discussed for the first time the problems faced by black people in the city. By then, unit members had met a local black Christian minister, the leader of the African Churches Mission. Pastor Daniels Ekarte is a shadowy figure. As the author of a recent book about him notes, he was subject to police surveillance and all his personal papers have disappeared.[144] His political activities may have given rise to unwelcome attention. Before the war, he had challenged the wages policy of one of the major shipping companies operating from the port of Liverpool. Elder Dempster paid higher wages to white seamen than to local black seamen, and the lowest wages of all were paid to seamen engaged from African countries, mainly Sierra Leone and Nigeria. As Marika Sherwood has noted, even when the government had assumed responsibility for all shipping the discriminatory rates continued to apply. Moreover, the War Risk Bonus was higher for white than for black seamen. When some of the African crew on two of Elder Dempster's ships went on strike in 1940, and Pastor Ekarte supported their move, the shipping company is alleged to have tried to get MI5 to investigate the matter. Liverpool PSU workers appear to have known that some of Pastor Ekarte's activities were politically motivated, although the records suggest that they did not know exactly what he was doing.[145] They were, however, suspicious of him and felt it wise to avoid becoming too closely involved. Although they were aware of other welfare agencies working with black people in the city, they did not work closely with them.[146]

The distance that the unit maintained from the black community in Liverpool reflects an attitude which extended to the employment of black workers. In 1952, the Manchester unit's casework committee reported that David Jones had forwarded the application of a 'coloured lady' for the post of caseworker. This had clearly placed the Manchester unit workers in some difficulty. They were unwilling to engage her themselves and referred the application to their colleagues in Liverpool, on the assumption that theirs was probably the only unit where it might be considered;[147] she was not given a post there either. Other units exhibited similar responses when faced with the prospect of black colleagues. The request from the Council of Social Service that Bristol FSU take a 'coloured' student in 1956 led to a rejoinder based on the assumption that only white workers could work with white families, and that a black worker – even one who already had some social work experience, as did the student in question – would be underemployed because the unit would not be able to find her anything to do.[148] The position was complicated because the Bristol fieldwork organiser admitted in the same letter that there were a number of Jamaican families in need of help on the estate. If the underlying reason for his reluctance to allow her a placement in the unit was an unwillingness to ask white families to accept a black worker, why could a black worker not be permitted to work with black families? It has to be admitted that a racist attitude underpinned the decision not to allow her to undertake a placement in Bristol; it was assumed that she could not have the skills necessary to be a social worker, or the ability to acquire them.

This was not just a local attitude. When advice about Bristol's dilemma was sought from elsewhere in the agency, the Kensington and Paddington fieldwork organiser noted that no other unit had had 'coloured' workers or students. Had she worn a uniform and done a routine job such as health visiting or district nursing, that would have been acceptable; it would have been '... obvious to neighbours who she is and what she is doing... [otherwise she is] likely to arouse neighbours' curiosity and cause gossip'.[149] The fieldwork organiser did not elaborate on what this gossip might be, or why a uniformed black district nurse should be more acceptable than a non-uniformed black social worker. From the East London unit came the advice that it was inadvisable to take a 'coloured' student.[150]

It is clear that for FSU, as for other agencies in the 1950s, black people generally were categorised as potential clients, not potential workers. As Wendy Webster has pointed out there was a class as well as a racial dimension to this view; in the 1950s white people rarely perceived black people to be middle class, regardless of their occupation or educational experience.[151] Attitudes, however, were beginning to change. A steering committee to explore the implications of the family problems faced by 'coloured' people was financed for three years by the City Parochial Foundation and organised by the Family Welfare Association in the mid-1950s. Although a minor contributor to the discussions, FSU was also represented. The committee employed three West Indian workers: one was allocated to a Citizens Advice Bureau, one to an FWA office, and the third was a peripatetic worker available to other FWA offices.[152] Its report, *The West Indian Comes to England*, was published in 1960. In Sheffield in the 1960s, a Nigerian student was accepted on placement with FSU, although it was thought necessary to choose carefully the families with whom he worked so 'that there should be no colour prejudice'.[153] While inherently racist, such a protective attitude may also be understood as having been motivated by personal concern. Interest in understanding West Indian customs which had been prompted by the numbers of West Indian families on their caseloads led to discussions about the needs of black clients at the Combined Casework Unit in Hackney in 1964,[154] but a comment by Philp that same year reveals a considerable degree of uncertainty about the connection between skin colour and social deviancy:

> Of six complete families, in at least three of them the parents are of different racial/cultural backgrounds... all the women are immigrants and the men are coloured immigrants in two of the families. There are illegitimate children in at least four of these families. These cases may not be at all representative of the Centre's total caseload, but I was interested to see that looking at *family composition only* [original emphasis] probably every one of these cases was unusual for an English community. It makes one wonder![155]

Other units in areas with increasing black populations began to consider the special difficulties faced by such communities. The Islington unit noted in 1967 that very few 'coloured' families with problems were referred to them, and gave a student responsibility for investigating their difficulties.[156] There is no record of the results of her investigation.

By the early 1980s, FSU's timidity about tackling issues of race had been replaced by a determination to address them. Some units had begun energetically to pursue anti-racist as well as anti-sexist policies. In this they were more advanced than the decision-making centre of the organisation, which tended to react to local initiatives rather than offer a clear lead. The issue had been addressed in a vague way by the working party on development which suggested that units in areas with 'significant groups from ethnic minorities should debate whether new approaches may be needed to provide an appropriate service for families within these groups'.[157] Meanwhile the Brent unit deliberately recruited black people to serve on its management committee,[158] and other units had anticipated the national organisation's concern more adequately to meet the needs of black and ethnic minority communities. The Newcastle unit had initiated race awareness training in 1982, and a special anti-racism edition of its bimonthly report, which included an article about the training, was circulated to all units as an example of good practice.[159] All aspects of its work were considered in the light of anti-racism, which resulted in care being taken when making choices about toys and equipment as well as attempts to implement non-racist working practices and equal opportunities in employment. The Asian/Chinese counselling service run by the Camden unit also started in 1982. Organised by two FSU workers aided by a number of suitably trained volunteers, its purpose was to provide counselling services for Chinese and Asian people facing serious marital, family or personal problems.[160] In its first two years of work it provided a service for more than 60 families through direct counselling and the support of women's groups, working in a range of languages including Cantonese, Hakka, Bengali, Gujerati, Punjabi, Urdu and Hindi. From 1982 onwards the unit's annual report began to appear in locally spoken non-English languages.[161]

In 1983, the East London unit deliberately switched from providing services mainly to white clients to developing work with a strongly multi-racial emphasis. During 1984 it was able to appoint an Asian social worker and a part-time youth worker funded by ILEA in order to forge links with the local Bengali population.[162] In 1987, the annual report was able to note that the social work team comprised three white and three Asian members.[163]

In the national sphere, the issue of racism and the need for anti-racist strategies was put on the agenda for the unit organisers' meeting and was raised at the union meeting.[164] The national director, Tim Cook, agreed to set up a working party on ethnic minorities, drawing on the experience of units like Newcastle.[165] The organisation as a whole endorsed the move to anti-racism. As discussions continued the Newcastle unit drew attention to the poor, inaccessible and inappropriate services for black people in some areas, and urged recognition of the need to ensure that black people receive services on an equal and equitable par with whites.[166] It gave practical expression to its commitment by sending a volunteer who was able to speak Urdu and Hindi to contribute to the activities of an Asian women's group attached to the Newcastle unit; the aim was to improve the women's experience of childbirth and to enable them to make better use of the hospital system.[167]

In the mid-1980s, an advertisement for a caseworker in the Islington unit notes a number of developments: the formation of anti-racist strategy in FSU; its concern to work positively with women and girls; and its wish to assert the rights of clients and to improve the choices open to them. The local unit was seriously considering the implications of its role as a largely white agency working in a multi-ethnic area and wished to develop concerted anti-racist practice.[168] Other units were beginning to consider the desirability of race awareness training, and black workers' groups were organised both locally and nationally. After a slow start, during the 1980s FSU as a national organisation began to play a key part in developments aimed at combating racism. In October 1983, it adopted an equal opportunities policy. This was little more than an expression of an ideal because FSU lacked both the in-house expertise to put such a policy into practice and the ability to raise the consciousness of its staff or to implement appropriate training. It also lacked the necessary finance.

The solution to the organisation's dilemma came with an exercise in cooperation with other voluntary agencies. Discussions between representatives of FSU, the Voluntary Service Unit at the Home Office and the Department of Health and Social Security (DHSS) led to the creation of an anti-racist consortium which included the Downs Syndrome Association, the National Council for One-Parent Families, the Maternity Alliance and FSU. Applications to the DHSS resulted in grants totalling £65,000 between 1984 and 1988. The aims of the consortium were ambitious; it hoped to enable the participating organisations to challenge and tackle racism and to raise awareness of its effects on both black and white people. By improving the education of workers within the member organisations so far as the requirements, advantages, duties and responsibilities of living in a multi-ethnic society were concerned, it hoped to promote good practice and the achievement of anti-racist ideals.[169]

FSU was the largest of the four organisations, employing over 300 people in 23 units. It was also the most committed;[170] this was,

though, still an on-paper commitment. In December 1984 a monitoring exercise designed to discover the ethnic origins of FSU staff
elicited an 84 per cent staff response, and found that 92 per cent of
the respondents were white. Others were African, Chinese, Guyanese
or Afro-Caribbean. Only 9 out of the 23 units had black or ethnic
minority members of staff; 9 of these were administrative or secre-
tarial workers and 17 were social or community workers, 11 of whom
were funded by FSU while the other 6 were employed on grant-aided
short-term contracts. At senior levels in the organisation there was a
very low representation of non-white staff; FSU had only one black
unit organiser. Of its 300 local and national committee members in
1985, 97 per cent were white. The staff profile was more in line with
the ethnic balance of the general population than that of the committees, although in many cases it did not reflect the racial composition
of the areas in which the units were situated, reinforcing the notion of
white professionals working with black clients. The *FSU Quarterly
Review* of November 1985 devoted a whole edition to race, exam-
ining such controversial issues as trans-racial adoption and race
awareness training. It also tackled FSU's own employment record
and found it seriously wanting. The issue was not just numerical
representation, but also the nature of the work done by black social
workers. It was suggested that black workers within FSU were on the
fringes of the organisation and that their contribution was not valued.
The disquiet continued over the ensuing months; in the March 1986
edition of the *FSU Quarterly Review* the issue of power was addressed,
an extension of the theme at that year's annual conference. Black
workers within the organisation called attention to the failure of the
conference to address policy issues raised by the equal opportunities
and anti-racist strategies which had been embraced by both the
national organisation and local units, and accused the organisation of
institutionalised racism.

The lessons were taken to heart and a positive attempt made to
recruit more black workers to senior positions. By 1987 FSU had two
black assistant directors. When the audit was repeated in summer
1988, it attracted an 85 per cent response rate and revealed significant changes; 82.4 per cent of respondents were white and only one
unit had no black or ethnic minority staff. By 1989 the number of
black assistant directors had increased to 3; in addition, 3 unit
organisers out of a total of 22 were black.[171] The changes in the
organisation's profile reflected the attention that had been paid to

FSU's recruitment policy, as well as to day-to-day unit practice and the development of training activities that fostered anti-racist practices. The membership of management committees had also been considered in order that they should reflect more closely the ethnic composition of the areas in which FSU worked.[172]

Quasi-political activity was a far cry from the intensely person-centred approach of FSU in the 1940s and 1950s, and it was not just focused on issues of racism. In 1977 the West London unit had become actively involved in community projects, specifically in the Powis Square area, prompted by an awareness of the poor conditions in which many families were living. The project there had the double, but potentially contradictory, aims of getting the council to perform necessary repairs and enabling tenants to act on their own behalf.[173] The unit's involvement in the area, in which there was a high incidence of prostitution and drug abuse,[174] led to cooperation with the local Law Centre, the Housing Action Centre, Colville Nursery Centre and the Powis Play Hut.[175] A further project, financed by Campden Charities which paid for one social worker, concentrated on a small geographical area and was attached to a general practitioner's surgery, particularly to the health visitor employed there. Together the social worker and health visitor worked with young families in the area, in part by offering a regular developmental assessment for all children under five registered with the practice. A group for young mothers was run in combination with the neighbourhood worker.[176] The unit, which had for some years engaged in the debates about housing provision in the capital, also became involved in further activity which could be construed as 'political' when it mounted a campaign against electricity disconnections in 1980.[177]

If some units' community involvement had evolved during the course of the previous 20 years, that of the South Birmingham unit owed its origins to the ideas about social and community work which characterised the late 1960s and 1970s, when the image of the social worker as therapist was being replaced by the social worker as radical community worker.[178] Underlying the change was the conviction that social work must confront the structural factors, such as poor housing and inadequate income, which contributed to social problems and family distress. The unit was influenced by community action and radical social work, particularly in so far as it involved local residents in setting up and controlling community resources and in campaigning for improved conditions and resources.[179] The Thamesmead unit, over much the same period of time, ran a project funded by the King Edward's Hospital Fund for London, the London Borough of Greenwich and the Tudor Trust.[180] Based in a house on the large Greater London estate, the Bridge Project aimed to tackle aspects of the isolation experienced by tenants who had been moved there from all over London. The aim was to encourage a number of self-help groups, including a single-parent network and groups for agoraphobics, mothers and babies, black women and ex-psychiatric patients. The project also included some professionally run quasi-medical groups, including one for tenants suffering from anxiety; a post-natal group was set up for first-time parents, as was a sleep disorder group and a group for those coping with separation and divorce.[181] In addition to such formally organised groups, a number of other local organisations also used the project's premises as a meeting place.

The attitudes illustrated by such developments would have been applauded by Younghusband and Wootton as a step forward from the historically paternalistic attitude of social work agencies towards their clients.[182] Projects which enabled FSU clients to achieve a level of adequate functioning and to make use of educational and other resources within the local community fostered a sense of confidence and self-reliance rather than dependence. They marked a change from the previous perception of the client as helpless to the acknowledgement of his or her potential as a help giver, problem solver and person with skills that could be shared,[183] but the division between the professional and the client remained a real one and, however well-intentioned, much intervention was still directive. In Leicester during the early 1980s, for example, a drop-in centre was opened in a council house in order to support young parents in a community in which children were known to be below average in skills when they went to school.[184] The unit also employed short-term behaviour modification techniques with families in difficulty. Such task-centred methods were based on the premise that clients asked for help with particular problems and that their definition of the problems should be accepted by the worker. The worker, however, was not bound to accept any solution suggested by the client, nor was he or she bound to explain the methods of intervention; he or she took direct responsibility for the intervention and its processes.[185]

Changes in patterns of working were reflected in the terminology

used to describe those who availed themselves of FSU's services. On
the surface it reveals a dramatic change in attitude. The 'case' of the
1940s gave way to the 'client' of the 1960s. The latter terminology is
more personal; it reflects a change in attitude on the part of the
worker and an acknowledgement of the person behind the problem,
and suggests some degree of choice and agency on the part of the
'client'. The truth of this is questionable. It might just be, as Wootton
had observed in 1959, that the post-war decades saw a great
improvement in the standards of courtesy which social workers
observed in their dealings with their clients.[186] Suggestions that
'consumer' or 'citizen' might be more appropriate were offered in the
early 1980s.[187] The 'service user' of more recent times further
emphasises ideas of choice and even participation, though how much
choice a user who is under a court order has to control his or her
situation is questionable. Nor does a change of name necessarily
remove stigma. As Patrick Goldring argued in 1973, none of the
replacements for the label 'problem family' has demonstrated any
great improvement in either clarity or social acceptability.[188]

The status of the client and her or his relationship to the unit and
to the services offered there was explored by a worker at the Leeds
unit in 1985. The survey revealed mixed feelings among families
about the services they were being offered, and about how far unit
policy on particular aspects of practice – for example the keeping of
open records – was of any interest to them.[189] As with Sainsbury's
1975 survey, it raised questions about the importance attached to an
encounter with social workers, and suggested that the client's
perception of his or her problems and the extent to which they were
'solved' by social workers were often of more significance than esoteric
matters of policy.

FSU has changed its methods of working more than some of its
supporters care to admit. It became known for family casework of a
particular kind in the 1940s and 1950s, and even in the mid-1980s
some committee members were urging a return to what they believed
to have been a proven method of effecting change in families.[190] By
then, many units recognised that the high level of dependence caused
by FSU's traditional methods had the potential for creating self-
perpetuating caseloads and limiting opportunities for taking on new
work. Such a situation was damaging for clients' self-esteem and
could also threaten the agency's financial base.[191] In 1977, the
retiring chairperson of the Rochdale Family Service Unit argued that

intensive family casework should be FSU's prime task, and that community work or other activity should be subordinate;[192] but FSU could not hold itself apart from general social work practice. The latest ideas and the newest theories were propounded in the colleges and universities in which social workers were trained, and discussed in the professional journals. FSU social workers could not isolate themselves from the ferment of ideas about work with families which characterised the second half of the century. Sometimes branches of the organisation were perceived to be in the forefront of progress, while others were deemed by their local authorities – and even by their own members[193] – to be cosy and old-fashioned; in an organisation which placed so much importance on the local dimension, the influence of a particular mix of social workers in a particular place was more important than it would have been in a more centrally managed organisation.

# NOTES

**1.** Minutes of a meeting of National Children's Homes executives, governors and sisters in charge, February 5 1954. ULSCA D541/F1/2. See also 'Interesting developments of a non-residential kind', February 23 1970. ULSCA D541/C2/2. I am grateful to Julie Grier for these references.

**2.** *Report of the Committee on Children and Young Persons* (chair The Rt Hon The Viscount Ingleby), Cmnd 1191 (HMSO, 1960), p14. Tom Stephens, chairman of FSU, and David Jones, national secretary, gave evidence to the Ingleby committee. Secretary's report March 27 1958 to May 5 1958. ULSCA D495(HQ)M1/4.

**3.** D. Ford, 'Introduction to the [Ingleby] report', *Social Work*, 18 (1961), p5.

**4.** H. Hendrick, *Child Welfare: England 1872–1989* (London, 1994), pp223 and 237.

**5.** J. Packman, *The Child's Generation* (Oxford, 1981), p65; Hendrick, *Child Welfare*, p224.

**6.** D. Donnison, 'Social services for the family', *Fabian Research Series*, 231 (1962), quoted in Packman, *The Child's Generation*, p64. See Hendrick, *Child Welfare*, p223.

**7.** Hendrick, *Child Welfare*, p223.

**8.** Ingleby report, pp7ff; Packman, *The Child's Generation*, p65; Hendrick, *Child Welfare*, pp223ff.

**9.** C. Sherrington, 'The NSPCC in Transition 1884–1983: A study of organisational survival' (unpublished PhD thesis, University of London, 1984), p398. The Home Office had strongly discouraged the plan of several local authorities to subsidise the NSPCC's expansion into preventive work in the 1950s. See S. Mencher,

'Factors affecting the relationship of the voluntary and statutory child-care services in England', *Social Service Review*, 32 (1958), p26.

10. Quoted in FSU annual report for 1962–63. ULSCA D495(HQ)M1/12.

11. House of Lords Debates, *Hansard*, December 4 1968, vol 298, no 16, col 176.

12. House of Lords Debates, *Hansard*, December 4 1968, vol 298, no 16, col 245.

13. B. Kahan, 'Preventive work by Children's Departments, Part II', *Social Work*, 18 (1961), pp19–22.

14. See above, p86. Personal communication from Barbara Kahan, May 1990. See also E. Irvine, 'The hard-to-like family', *Case Conference*, 14 (1967), p97; Packman, *The Child's Generation*, p56.

15. Quoted in Packman, *The Child's Generation*, p55.

16. Ingleby report, p9; B. Kahan, 'Prevention and rehabilitation', *Approved Schools Gazette*, 55 (December 1961). See also Packman, *The Child's Generation*, p66.

17. Packman, *The Child's Generation*, p56.

18. Kensington and Paddington FSU annual report for 1954–55. ULSCA D495 (WL)M5/2.

19. Kensington and Paddington FSU annual report for 1957–58. ULSCA D495 (WL)M5/5.

20. Quoted in P. Hall, *The Social Services of Modern England* (London, 1963), p166.

21. D. M. Smith, *Families and Groups: A unit at work* (London, 1974), p14.

22. Church of England Waifs and Strays Society, annual report for 1948.

23. J. Lewis, *The Voluntary Sector, the State and Social Work in Britain* (Aldershot, 1995), p105.

24. Ingleby report, p9.

25. See below, pp104–5.

26. E. Irvine, 'The needs of client groups with special problems', in E. Irvine (ed.), *Social Work and Human Problems* (Oxford, 1979), p91.

27. FSU working party on development, *The Development of FSU* (London, 1978), pp27–8.

28. Ministry of Health, Department of Health for Scotland, *Report of the Working Party on Social Workers in the Local Authority Health and Welfare Services* (Younghusband report) (HMSO, 1959), p321; Younghusband, *Social Work in Britain: 1950–1975*, vol 1, pp208–9 and 284ff.

29. *Report of a Committee Appointed to Explore the Possibility of Setting Up a Combined Family Casework Unit* no date, ULSCA D495(HQ)B3/1; V. Belcher, *The City Parochial Foundation, 1891–1991: A trust for the poor of London* (Aldershot, 1991), p290.

30. Notes of a meeting to discuss the possibility of setting up a combined family casework unit, January 27 1959. ULSCA D495(HQ)B3/1.

31. Notes of meeting on proposed combined casework unit, February 10 1959. ULSCA D495(HQ)B3/1.

32. Notes of meeting on proposed combined casework unit, February 25 1959. ULSCA D495(HQ)B3/1

33. Notes of meeting on proposed combined casework unit, November 13 1959. ULSCA D495(HQ)B3/1.

**34.** M. Boselli, *Report on the development of the Combined Casework Unit from January 1963 to March 1965.* ULSCA D495(HQ)B3/1. cf. Boselli, 'The Family Centre of Hackney II', *The British Journal of Social Work*, 1 (1971), pp423ff.

**35.** N. Timms, *Social Casework* (London, 1964), p195; Younghusband, *Social Work in Britain: 1950-1975*, vol 2, p108.

**36.** Boselli, 'The Family Centre of Hackney, II', p428.

**37.** Boselli, 'The Family Centre of Hackney, II', pp425ff.

**38.** K. Lloyd, 'The Family Centre of Hackney, I', *The British Journal of Social Work*, 1, (1971), pp411ff; Boselli, 'The Family Centre of Hackney, II', pp425ff.

**39.** It may not be without significance that in her work on the FWA, Jane Lewis makes no mention of its work with FSU and ICAA. She does refer in passing to the Family Centre at Hackney, but only after FSU and ICAA had pulled out. Lewis, *The Voluntary Sector, the State and Social Work*, p131. It is also interesting that the unit organiser from the East London FSU, who went on to become an assistant director of FSU in the 1970s, denied all knowledge of FSU's involvement in work in Hackney. Interview with Janet Williams, June 1997.

**40.** See, for example, a cautious letter from David Jones to John Burt (national secretary of the FWA), December 15 1960, suggesting that FSU was under great pressure to provide staff for new units throughout the country and would not object if ICAA and FWA were to proceed with the Hackney project without it. ULSCA D495(HQ)B3/1. Minutes of the Advisory Group December 13 1962; January 24 1963. ULSCA D495(HQ)B3/4.

**41.** Minutes of Combined Casework Unit management committee, January 6 1966. ULSCA D495(HQ)B3/2.

**42.** Philp, who had worked at the national office since 1959 as training and publicity officer, replaced David Jones as national secretary in 1962. Minutes of the FSU national executive committee, July 21 1959 and March 16 1960; July 12 1962. ULSCA D495(HQ)M2/4.

**43.** There was a history of substantial grants from the City Parochial Foundation to FSU. These ranged from help with the original establishment of the organisation to the setting up of the South London and Islington units. Belcher, *The City Parochial Foundation*, pp284, 290 and 304.

**44.** A. F. Philp, report to FSU national committee on the Combined Casework Unit (1967). ULSCA D495(HQ)B3/6.

**45.** Lloyd, 'The Family Centre of Hackney, I', p420. Philp, report to FSU national committee on the Combined Casework Unit. ULSCA D495(HQ)B3/6.

**46.** Belcher, *The City Parochial Foundation*, p290.

**47.** Lloyd, 'The Family Centre of Hackney, I', p421.

**48.** Ingleby report, p17.

**49.** M. James, 'Common basic concepts to casework and groupwork', *Social Work*, 14 (1957), p378; Younghusband, *Social Work in Britain*, vol 2, p112.

**50.** G. Boschma, 'Ambivalence about nursing's expertise: the role of a gendered holistic ideology in nursing, 1890–1990', in A. M. Rafferty, J. Robinson and R. Elkan (eds), *Nursing History and the Politics of Welfare* (London, 1997), p170. See also Ministry of Health, Department of Health for Scotland, Ministry of Education, *An Inquiry into Health Visiting: Report of a working party on the field of work, training and recruitment of health visitors* (HMSO, 1956), p134.

**51.** E. Irvine (ed.), *Social Work and Human Problems: Casework, consultation and other topics* (Oxford, 1979), pp244ff; cf C. Jones, 'Social work education, 1900-1970', in N. Parry, M. Rustin and C. Satyamurti (eds), *Social Work, Welfare and the State* (London, 1979), p79.

**52.** B. Wootton, *Social Science and Social Pathology* (London, 1959), pp268ff.

**53.** See Lewis, *The Voluntary Sector, the State and Social Work*, p117.

**54.** Jones, 'Social work education, 1900–1970', p85.

**55.** N. Timms, *Social Casework: Principles and practice* (London, 1964), p89.

**56.** J. Mayer and N. Timms, *The Client Speaks: Working class impressions of casework* (London, 1970), pp136ff.

**57.** Younghusband, *Social Work in Britain*, vol 2, p129.

**58.** E. Sainsbury, *Social Work with Families: Perceptions of social casework among clients of a Family Service Unit* (London, 1975), pp26ff; Lewis, *The Voluntary Sector, the State and Social Work*, pp137–8; FSU working party on development, *The Development of FSU*, p25.

**59.** D. Jones, 'Some notes on measuring the results of family casework with problem families', *Social Work*, 21 (1964), pp3–4.

**60.** S. Ambrose, 'From psychiatric social worker to family caseworker', *Social Work*, 24 (1966), p22.

**61.** Bristol FSU, report to the Medical Officer of Health, 1961. ULSCA D495(BL)M4. See also Sainsbury, *Social Work with Families*, p76.

**62.** L. Walker, 'Groupwork with the inarticulate', FSU discussion paper, no date but probably mid-1960s, reprinted in Irvine (ed.), *Social Work and Human Problems*, pp107–34; Irvine, 'The hard-to-like family', in Irvine (ed.), *Social Work and Human Problems*, pp95ff; Irvine, 'Helping the immature to grow up', in Irvine (ed.), *Social Work and Human Problems*, pp135ff.

**63.** Jones, 'Social work education', p86.

**64.** Ambrose, 'From psychiatric social worker to family caseworker', p22.

**65.** A. Davies, 'From psychiatric social worker to family caseworker', *Social Work*, 24 (1966), pp18–19.

**66.** West London FSU annual report for 1968–69. ULSCA D495(WL)M5/16.

**67.** Sainsbury, *Social Work with Families*, p7.

**68.** Kensington and Paddington FSU annual report for 1963–64. ULSCA D495 (WL)M5/11.

**69.** Kensington and Paddington FSU annual report for 1954–55. ULSCA D495 (WL)M5/2.

**70.** Minutes of the Kensington and Paddington FSU committee, April 25 1956. ULSCA D495(WL)M1/2.

**71.** Minutes of the Kensington and Paddington FSU committee, February 9 1961. ULSCA D495(WL)M1/2.

**72.** Kensington and Paddington FSU annual report for 1962–63. ULSCA D495 (WL)M5/10.

**73.** Kensington and Paddington FSU annual report for 1964–65. ULSCA D495 (WL)M5/12. *Report of the Committee on Housing in Greater London* (Milner Holland committee), Cmnd 2605 (HMSO, 1965).

**74.** Minutes of the Sheffield FSU committee, November 16 1967. ULSCA D495(SH)M1/1.

**75.** FSU working party, *The Development of FSU*, p8.

**76.** Minutes of Newcastle FSU committee, July 17 1975. ULSCA D495(NE) M1/1.

**77.** Minutes of a special joint meeting of the Newcastle FSU committee and staff, February 3 1976. ULSCA D495(NE)M1/1.

**78.** Letter from Brian Harrison (unit organiser, Newcastle FSU) to Rex Halliwell (FSU director), December 10 1975. See also letter from Rex Halliwell to Brian Harrison, December 12 1975. ULSCA D495(NE)M1/1.

**79.** Letter from David Donnison to Tom Stephens (chairman of FSU), March 10 1977. ULSCA D495(NE)M1/1.

**80.** Letter from Tom Stephens to David Donnison, March 30 1977. ULSCA D495(HQ)M1/1.

**81.** E. Sainsbury, 'A national survey of FSU families', *FSU Quarterly*, 8 (1975), pp20ff. ULSCA D495(HQ)M9. See also P. Phillimore, *Families Speaking: A study of fifty-one families' views of social work* (London, 1981), p29.

**82.** Letter from Brian Todd to Ruth Popplestone, January 14 1977. ULSCA D495(NE)M1/1.

**83.** Letter from Ruth Popplestone to Councillor Connie Lewcock, September 8 1977. ULSCA D495(NE)M1/1. See also Notes on Tenants' Associations. ULSCA D495(NE)M15-17. By 1981, explicit acknowledgement that social problems should not be seen as just family pathology formed part of FSU's submission to the National Institute of Social Work's committee of enquiry into social work. ULSCA unlisted.

**84.** Notes on the development plan by chairman, secretary and member of Newcastle committee, September 30 1977. ULSCA D495(NE)M1/1; R. Baker, 'Is there a future for integrated practice? Obstacles to its development in practice and education', *Issues in Social Work Education*, 3 (1983), p5.

**85.** Z. Butrym, O. Stevenson and R. Harris, 'The role and tasks of social workers', *Issues in Social Work Education*, 1 (1981), p13.

**86.** M. Clarke, 'The limits of radical social work', *The British Journal of Social Work*, 6 (1976), p504.

**87.** E. Younghusband, 'The future of social work', *Social Work Today*, 4 (1973–74), p33. Cf P. Leonard, 'The place of scientific method in social work education', in E. Younghusband (ed.), *Education for Social Work* (London, 1964), pp65ff.

**88.** Mayer and Timms, *The Client Speaks*, p143. See also Lewis, *The Voluntary Sector, the State and Social Work*, p138.

**89.** Letter from Dick Harding to Mike Wardle, February 16 1977. ULSCA unlisted.

**90.** National Council for Voluntary Organisations, *Meeting the Challenge of Change: Voluntary action into the twenty-first century* (London, 1996), p102.

**91.** *Community Work within FSU*, no date but after January 1976. ULSCA unlisted.

**92.** FSU working party, *The Development of FSU*, p28.

**93.** FSU working party, *The Development of FSU*, p28.

**94.** FSU working party, *The Development of FSU*, p28.

**95.** P. Goldring, *Friend of the Family: The Work of Family Service Units* (Newton Abbott, 1973), p165. See below, chapter 6.

**96.** Goldring, *Friend of the Family*, p166.

**97.** Minutes of the FSU national executive committee, January 12 1966. ULSCA D495(HQ)M2/5.

**98.** FSU working party, *The Development of FSU*, p47.

**99.** An account of the work at Bishop Auckland is found in D. Holder and M. Wardle, *Teamwork and the Development of a Unitary Approach* (London, 1981). See also Baker, 'Is there a future?', pp3ff.

**100.** Holder and Wardle, *Teamwork and the Development of a Unitary Approach*, p23.

**101.** A. Pincus and A. Minahan, *Social Work Practice: Model and method* (Illinois, 1973).

**102.** Holder and Wardle, *Teamwork and the Development of a Unitary Approach*, p168.

**103.** FSU working party, *The Development of FSU*, p31.

**104.** Baker, 'Is there a future?', p4.

**105.** Butrym, Stevenson and Harris, 'The role and tasks of social workers', p4.

**106.** Unsigned document, April 30 1974. ULSCA D495(HQ)B11/13.

**107.** FSU working party, *The Development of FSU*, p27.

**108.** FSU working party, *The Development of FSU*, p5.

**109.** J. M. Hutten, 'Short-term contracts: A rationale for brief focal intervention by social workers', *Social Work Today*, 4 (February, 1974), p709. See also A. N. Maluccio and W. D. Marlow, 'The case for the contract', *Social Work (USA)*, 19 (1974), pp28ff; FSU working party, *The Development of FSU*, p5.

**110.** J. Corden, 'Contracts in social work practice', *British Journal of Social Work*, 10 (1980), pp143–61.

**111.** Corden, 'Contracts in social work practice', p160.

**112.** C Rojek and S. A. Collins, 'Contract or con trick?', *British Journal of Social Work*, 17 (1987), pp199–211.

**113.** E. Harbridge, 'Filling a gap in the arm of care', *Community Care* (February 5 1981), pp18ff.

**114.** An account of the first years of the project is found in R. Grunsell, *Born to be Invisible* (Basingstoke, 1978).

**115.** ILEA had created a number of off-site centres; 37 were operating by April 1979, and 12 more were planned. A number of these centres were organised in partnership with voluntary organisations. Notes of FSU training conference, March 29 1982. ULSCA D495(HQ)B29.

**116.** Grunsell, *Born to be Invisible*, p110.

**117.** D. Reay, M. Lowe and C. Bowker, *Before It's too Late: An account of the Pakeman School Unit* (London, 1984), pp19–20.

**118.** Reay, Lowe and Bowker, *Before It's too Late*, p11.

**119.** H. Logan, 'The role and function of a primary school off-site unit' (unpublished FSU document), p21. ULSCA D495(HQ)B28/1.

**120.** Junior Intermediate Treatment Centre termly consultative meeting, Summer 1982. ULSCA D495(HQ)B29.

**121.** *Second Report: Pakeman Unit Phase 2*, February 1987. ULSCA D495(HQ)B29.

**122.** A. Grumsell and P. Gurney, 'Commentary on recent ILEA documentation on the subject of off-site provision and the implications for Islington Family Service unit of proposed changes, May 1985'. ULSCA D495(HQ)B29.

123. FSU response to Metcalf Working Party, January 1985. ULSCA D495(HQ)B29.

124. R. Jennens and H. Dawe, *Our Teacher's Not from School* (London, 1984), pp20ff.

125. Jennens and Dawe, *Our Teacher's Not from School*, pp52–64 and 95.

126. Jennens and Dawe, *Our Teacher's Not from School*, pp88 and 95.

127. Notes on on FSU training conference, March 29 1982. ULSCA D495 (HQ)B29.

128. Notes on on FSU training conference, March 29 1982. ULSCA D495 (HQ)B29.

129. FSU, *The Homework Project: An account of the inter school social education project, West Pilton, Edinburgh* (Edinburgh, no date but after 1982).

130. FSU, *Fox Hill Reading Workshop* (London, 1982).

131. FSU (ed.), *Bridges to Learning* (London, 1987).

132. FSU's work with schools is described in the FSU discussion paper 'Schools and families and social workers' (London, 1982).

133. The purpose (although never precisely formulated) of the Urban Aid Programme which began in 1968 was to provide financial assistance to local authorities, and through them to voluntary agencies, to set up projects aimed at alleviating some of the problems that were becoming increasingly manifest in the inner areas of many British cities. See J. Edwards, Foreword to C. McCreadie, *Home School Liaison: Report of an experimental project in community work* (London, 1985).

134. McCreadie, *Home School Liaison*, p1.

135. McCreadie, *Home School Liaison*, p2.

136. McCreadie, *Home School Liaison*, p9.

137. McCreadie, *Home School Liaison*, p56.

138. McCreadie, *Home School Liaison*, p52.

139. The South London FSU requested the sponsorship of ILEA for the application to the Urban Aid Fund because, as an experimental project, it could not be financed through the local authority's social services budget. McCreadie, *Home School Liaison*, p2.

140. McCreadie, *Home School Liaison*, p54.

141. McCreadie, *Home School Liaison*.

142. McCreadie, *Home School Liaison*, p53.

143. Minutes of the Liverpool PSU committee meeting, January 27 1943; March 10 1943. ULSCA D495(LI)M1/3. August 4 1943. ULSCA D495(LI)M1/4.

144. M. Sherwood, *Pastor Daniels Ekarte and the African Churches Mission* (London, 1994), pp23ff.

145. Sherwood, *Pastor Daniels Ekarte*. See, for example, minutes of the Liverpool PSU committee, February 10 1943. ULSCA D495(LI)M1/3.

146. See for example minutes of the Liverpool PSU committee, February 10 1943, March 3 1943, March 10 1943. ULSCA D495(LI)M1/3. September 16 1943. ULSCA D495(LI)M1/4. May 17 1944, June 7 1944, June 14 1944, June 21 1944, October 18 1944, January 10 1945, January 31 1945. ULSCA D495(LI)M1/5.

147. Minutes of the Manchester FSU casework sub-committee, January 7 1952. ULSCA D495(MA)M3/1.

148. Letter to David Jones from Alf Strange, July 30 1956. ULSCA D495 (BL)M2.

**149.** Letter to Alf Strange from FSU national office (in David Jones's absence), July 31 1956. ULSCA D495(BL)M2.

**150.** Letter to Alf Strange from FSU national office (in David Jones's absence), July 31 1956. ULSCA D495(BL)M2.

**151.** W. Webster, *Imagining Home: Gender, 'race' and national identity, 1945–64* (London, 1998), p118.

**152.** Belcher, *The City Parochial Foundation*, p286. *Sleeptite Flash* (January/February 1955) ULSCA D495(HQ)M7.

**153.** Minutes of Sheffield FSU committee, March 18 1965. ULSCA D495 (SH)M1/1.

**154.** Minutes of the Combined Casework Unit committee, July 7 1964. ULSCA D495(HQ)B3/1.

**155.** Letter commenting on 10 case summaries from Fred Philp to Maria Boselli, director of the Combined Casework Unit, February 27 1964. ULSCA D495 (HQ)B3/1.

**156.** Minutes of Islington FSU committee, October 18 1967. ULSCA unlisted.

**157.** FSU working party, *The Development of FSU*, p36.

**158.** Personal communication from Margaret Jones, February 1996.

**159.** Minutes of the Newcastle FSU committee, March 17 1982; Newcastle bimonthly report, November 1982. ULSCA D495(NE)M1/1.

**160.** Camden FSU, annual report for 1982–83. ULSCA D495(CA)M4/9.

**161.** Camden FSU, annual report for 1984–85. ULSCA D495(CA)M4/10.

**162.** East London FSU, annual report for 1984–85. ULSCA D495(EL)M7/37.

**163.** East London FSU, annual report for 1987–88. ULSCA D495(EL)M7/38.

**164.** Minutes of Newcastle FSU committee, November 17 1982. ULSCA D495 (NE)M1/1.

**165.** Minutes of the Newcastle FSU committee, January 19 1983. ULSCA D495(HQ)M1/1.

**166.** 'Community care plan response: The service providers and the black community' January 31 1992 (Newcastle). ULSCA D495(NE)M15/3.

**167.** Minutes of Newcastle FSU Birthday Group, May 13 1983. ULSCA D495 (NE)M7/2.

**168.** Job description for social worker in Pakeman unit (no date but probably after November 1985). ULSCA unlisted.

**169.** A. Sedley, *The Challenge of Anti-racism: Lessons from a voluntary organisation* (London, 1989), pp1ff.

**170.** Sedley, *The Challenge of Anti-racism*, p29.

**171.** Sedley, *The Challenge of Anti-racism*, p29.

**172.** Sedley, *The Challenge of Anti-racism*, p31.

**173.** The minutes recording a meeting between social workers and the local committee are dated just March 24, but internal evidence suggests that this was 1977. ULSCA D495(WL)M10.

**174.** Minutes of the West London FSU committee, 'Report on Powis Square area', March 1977. ULSCA D495(WL)M10.

**175.** Minutes of the West London FSU committee, July 6 1977. ULSCA D495 (WL)M1.

**176.** *Report on Campden Project 1976*. ULSCA D495(WL)M8/2.

**177.** West London FSU, annual report for 1980–81. ULSCA D495(WL)M5/ 26.

**178.** G. Rankin, 'Professional social work and the campaign against poverty', *Social Work Today*, 1 (1971), p20.

**179.** P. Dobson, 'An Exercise in Consultation: Residents decide the future of a social and community work agency' (unpublished MSocSci thesis, University of Birmingham, 1987), p1. Cf Coopers and Lybrand, *Organising for a Purpose: Roles and relationships* (London, 1988), pp10–11.

**180.** M. Ruddock, *The Bridge Project, Thamesmead FSU: An interim report* (Thamesmead, 1985), p2.

**181.** Ruddock, *The Bridge Project*, passim.

**182.** Younghusband, 'The future of social work', p35; Wootton, *Social Science*, pp291ff.

**183.** Proposal submitted to the DHSS by FSU for two pilot projects, July 1981. ULSCA D495(HQ)B11/13. See Younghusband, *Social Work in Britain*, vol 2, p39.

**184.** F. O'Malloy, 'Leicester FSU "drop-in centre" for parents with young children', *Social Work Service*, 29 (1982), pp9-11.

**185.** FSU, *Solving Family Problems: A statement of theory and practice* (no date but probably 1980), p72.

**186.** Wootton, *Social Science*, p271.

**187.** *Social Workers, their Role and Tasks*; the report of a working party set up by the National Institute for Social Work, chaired by Peter Barclay (London, 1982); British Association of Social Workers, *Clients are fellow citizens* (Birmingham, 1980).

**188.** Goldring, *Friend of the Family*, p176.

**189.** M. Preston-Shoot, 'An evaluation of a policy of family involvement in one Family Service Unit from families' perspectives', *FSU Quarterly*, 36 (1985), pp52–64. ULSCA D495(HQ)M9.

**190.** Minutes of the Liverpool FSU committee, February 6 1985. Minutes of the Knowsley FSU committee, February 27 1985. ULSCA D495(LI)M2/5.

**191.** G. Smith and J. Corden, 'The introduction of contracts in a Family Service Unit', *British Journal of Social Work*, 11 (1981), p290.

**192.** Minutes of the Rochdale FSU committee, October 28 1977. ULSCA D495(HQ)M1.

**193.** Geoffrey Rankin, one-time unit organiser of the Islington unit, believed working in the organisation to be something of a soft option, offering 'good pay, small caseloads and cosy work conditions'. Quoted in Goldring, *Friend of the Family*, p175.

# 5
# Training and Professional Development

FSU's infancy coincided with a period of significant and far-reaching changes in social work. These changes, driven by a growing sense of professional identity, in turn prompted improved opportunities for training. To some extent the process was also informed by concern over social problems that were not new but that had, to a greater or lesser extent, been uncovered by the experience of war between 1939 and 1945. Such problems were exemplified by the poor living conditions revealed by the evacuation of children in 1939, and the 1943 report on British cities by the Women's Group on Public Welfare, initiated in response to the experience of evacuation.[1] Concern that the welfare of children left a lot to be desired was exacerbated by the murder óf Dennis O'Neill by his foster father in 1945, and the findings of the Curtis committee in 1946.[2] FSU had added to the literature of deprivation through its publication of *Problem Families* and had contributed to a discussion in which a number of welfare workers (but particularly MOHs) had engaged both during and after the war in an attempt to describe and explain the phenomenon of the problem family.[3] These processes had served to highlight uncomfortable aspects of British social life and the need for energetic action to tackle them. There were, however, too few people competent to undertake the work. Those whose personality, background or inclination had led them to undertake the care of people in difficult circumstances tended to be given the generic title 'social worker'. There was little agreement about what a social worker was, however, except that – as Eileen Younghusband pointed out – like a cat, she was traditionally feminine. Her gender also meant that she could be considered professionally inadequate. There was a tendency, which Younghusband deplored, to believe that a female social worker needed training, whereas her male colleague was assumed to have acquired all he needed to know through some all-sufficing experience of life which was seen as a substitute for, and not an enhancement of, training.[4]

The wide range of occupations in which those who might have been labelled social workers were employed in the late 1940s included recognised professions – like those of the almoner or the psychiatric social worker – as well as a number of activities, often of lesser status, ranging from casework with individuals to the running of youth clubs. Other workers performed jobs as diverse as personnel work or school attendance enforcement. At base, such disparate occupations were united by the requirement of remedying deficiencies between the individual and his or her environment.[5] In spite of her title, the almoner in the mid-twentieth century was unlikely to be found distributing charitable funds, but was more likely to have been responsible for making practical provision for the convalescent patient to cope at home, or enabling him or her to access support from the welfare services. The school attendance officer had to enforce the law in relation to children's regular presence in the classroom. Both attendance officer and almoner were frequently engaged in trying to change the individual's social setting as well as his or her attitude towards it. Many services employing social workers were narrowly specialist, or were the preserve of specific voluntary agencies. These tended to concentrate their efforts on particular areas of need – for example, residential care for children whose parents were unable to look after them – or provided services for people coping with particular disabilities, such as visual impairment or other physical handicap; but many of their employees had little or no formal training for the tasks they undertook.

With little agreement about the role and definition of the social worker, it is not surprising that there was equally little understanding of her educational and training needs. When the local authority children's and welfare services were set up in the aftermath of the Second World War, there was only limited professional education available, and much of that was inappropriate for the work that needed to be done. An investigation into the employment and training of social workers was funded by the Carnegie United Kingdom Trust and conducted by Eileen Younghusband in 1947. Her *Report on the Employment and Training of Social Workers* revealed the diverse nature of British social work and the lack of relevant and adequate training. It pinpointed much of the discontent about provision for social work education and transformed disparate ideas for improvement into recommendations and a coherent plan of action.[6] The report also demonstrated that such provision as there was fell into two main categories, neither of which could be described as adequate or comprehensive: academic courses with little practical content, and training schemes designed and implemented by social work agencies for their own staff. Social science or social administration courses were offered by a number of universities – the report listed 16 – but these varied considerably and there was no consensus on the essential elements of the curriculum. Of those courses surveyed in 1947, only 5 included the principles and methods of social work as a compulsory element; only 3 gave instruction on social structure and contemporary social problems; and only 3 believed it necessary to give students information about the statutory and voluntary social services. Traditional academic subjects predominated: 16 courses included economic or social history; 14 included economic theory; and 14 included psychology. While providing students with the opportunity to gain traditional degrees and diplomas, such courses did not equip those wishing to engage in practical social work with the necessary skills; most of them had not been designed to do so. Some courses required students to complete practical placements in social work agencies, though not, in Younghusband's opinion, to a satisfactory degree. She believed that existing courses failed to engender an understanding of the principles underlying social work or to confer practical proficiency. Those who purported to train social workers had paid too little attention to the relationship between theoretical and practical training and, in the absence of any detailed research, there was no body of principles on which such training could be based.[7] Courses organised by voluntary agencies demonstrated the opposite weakness, in that they emphasised practical experience but were weak on theoretical underpinning.[8] For example, organisations working with families – Younghusband mentioned the Family Welfare Association as an example – provided some training.[9] Specialist agencies working with children, including Dr Barnardo's and National Children's Homes, had their own training schools.[10]

The position in 1947 reflected the uneven fashion in which academic social science departments had come into being in the earlier part of the century in an attempt to give the 'breadth and educational value which only the universities could provide'. The Department of

Social Science at the University of Liverpool was the first such department to appear, in 1904,[11] closely followed by the Department of Social Science and Administration at the London School of Economics (LSE),[12] which in 1912 took over the School of Sociology that had been founded by the Charity Organisation Society in 1903.[13] The situation in 1947 also demonstrated the uncertainty of the academic departments about the tasks that their graduates might be required to perform. The long struggle to clarify the aims of university social science courses intensified after the end of the Second World War. Its central question was the purpose of university courses and whether they were intended as vocational training for social work practitioners or were purely academic, like French or biology, with no necessary vocational component. The success of the universities in retaining control over the academic content of social science courses was to contribute to the long-running confusion within social work about what constituted professional training: was it a social science degree, a diploma or certificate with or without a practical component; or was it training 'on the job', undertaken by aspiring social workers once they had completed their academic training? If the latter, was it necessary for a social worker to possess a university qualification? The confusion within the universities – where there was often pressure to increase the time for academic study at the expense of practical fieldwork[14] – was matched by that within the emerging profession, where there was understandable concern to produce competent practical workers. This confusion was to take many years to resolve.

The appearance of Younghusband's report in 1947 coincided with a period of self-criticism within professional social work bodies.[15] Indeed, as practitioner turned academic, Younghusband was an important part of this reflective process. Before beginning to teach at the LSE in 1929, she had worked for five years as a social worker in South and East London. Her sense of dissatisfaction was that of an insider, and her assessment of the inadequacies and weaknesses of the situation – the uneven pattern of training throughout the country and the consequences of unplanned and uncoordinated developments – was made as a member of an unplanned and uncoordinated occupation. As an academic, she could appreciate the pressures felt by universities whose students on practical placements had very varied experiences. The variety was largely determined by two factors: the views of the university as to what was appropriate, and the requirements of professional bodies such as the Probation Advisory and Training Board, the Central Training Council in Child Care and the Institute of Almoners, which seconded students. On the other hand, as a practitioner Younghusband understood the lack of educational opportunity for fieldworkers in more general forms of social work. She believed this to be a function of the shortage of training places rather than indifference to the value of training, but given the small number of suitable courses, the position was unavoidable and could not quickly be remedied. Moreover, graduates from university social science departments represented only a tiny minority of those who went on to become social workers, most of whom had undertaken no professional training at all.

As the 1947 report was in preparation a number of PSU workers were pondering their futures. By choosing social work as a career, they found themselves considering membership of an occupation characterised by confusion and the lack of a clear professional identity. The need for training for the tasks they had set themselves during the war had been an important issue in those units that had practised what they called family casework, and is evidence of the intention of many workers to continue in some form of welfare work when the war was over. Some attempts to arrange professional tuition had not met expectations – informal seminars in sociology conducted by a tutor resident at the university settlement in Liverpool had not been notably successful[16] – but within the unit houses workers followed a path of self-education, reading as much relevant material as they could find, taking counsel from friends and supporters in local colleges and universities and, by organising case conferences both within and between units, learning through sharing experiences with other colleagues.[17] Such ad hoc training put PSU well within the traditions of other specialised agencies, such as the Charity Organisation Society,[18] and was to provide the foundation for more formalised schemes when the war was over and FSU was established. At the end of the war, however, and in spite of their considerable practical experience – or perhaps because that experience had demonstrated the need for training – a number of unit members were anxious to gain recognised professional qualifications. Few, unlike Younghusband's traditional social worker, were female. To that extent they were not representative of those who were seeking training at universities or working in voluntary agencies in the immediate post-war period. Neither did they fit the stereotypical image of middle-class social workers. When he sought advice from academic staff at the LSE in 1945, Ken Richardson (a Liverpool PSU worker then employed by the PNCMH) made it clear that PSU members who wished to exchange their pre-war occupations for social work lacked appropriate qualifications and may not have been able to meet university entrance requirements. Many had no more than elementary school education; those who possessed university qualifications were the exceptions. As with the question of their religious affiliations,[19] the PSU workers differed in their accounts of their own social, and therefore educational, experience. Some were keen to stress their middle-class backgrounds, others to demonstrate that they came from working-class stock.[20] Richardson appears to have wondered whether the three-month course with the PNCMH that some had completed would be an adequate compensation for an otherwise limited education, and would be sufficient qualification for admission to the mental health course at the LSE.[21] He need not have worried; as Younghusband was to note in 1951, many university social work courses in the 1940s had more places than they could fill. In spite of the demand for social workers, agencies frequently chose to employ people without formal qualifications with the result that the need for workers was not reflected in the demand for university places.[22] In the immediate post-war period, a number of FSU workers successfully completed relevant courses as a prelude to a career in social work.[23]

Richardson's choice of a mental health course was not without significance; nor was the choice of the LSE surprising. The first mental health course in Europe had been set up there in 1929,[24] and it had become one of the most prestigious in the country. Furthermore, there were few other vocational courses open to would-be social workers; the sort of training offered by the Probation Service, the Institute of Almoners and some other specialised bodies would not have been suitable preparation for the work that PSU members had in mind. The mental health course, on the other hand, would have fitted their understanding of the social work task. The importance they attached to the high incidence of mental illness or incapacity in the families with whom they worked, reinforced by their experience with the PNCMH, meant that it was only natural that unit members should look to further psychiatrically oriented training when thinking of the future.

Even so prescient a commentator as Younghusband was to be

surprised both by the pace of change and by the extent of the demand for social workers in the years after the war. In her supplementary report, written in 1951 because her observations of 1947 had so quickly become out of date, she reflected on a scene which was very different in many respects from that of four years earlier. Changes in the employment of social workers went along with a growing acknowledgement of their value. In part, this was a function of the new machinery of state welfare services, in which the social worker was an essential element. These services caused a shift in the way her position was perceived. From being a 'doer of good works in voluntary organisations' the social worker had become a valued professional. As social work had become the concern of the state, social workers were increasingly employed by local authorities or other statutory bodies, in contrast to their traditional position within charities or voluntary agencies. Some had continued in their previous employment but found that their employers had changed. Almoners and psychiatric social workers had become part of the National Health Service (NHS) and were to be found working in the new state-managed hospitals, while posts for boarding-out and children's officers were created by local authority children's departments, inaugurated in 1948.[25]

In spite of their increased numbers and more widely recognised functions, the degree of professionalism exhibited by social workers continued to be extremely variable. In the years immediately after the war there were too few trained personnel to meet demand, and social work agencies, whether voluntary or statutory, either chose or were forced to employ untrained workers.[26] The 1959 *Report of the Working Party on Social Workers in the Local Authority Health and Welfare Services* noted that 89 per cent of those working in welfare or social work still had no generally recognised social work qualification.[27] This was borne out by a study of a town in the north of England where 72 social workers were employed in the mid-1950s, of whom only 5 had had a professional social work training while 42 had undertaken no training of any kind.[28]

Although commentators in the late 1940s and early 1950s were urging a broad approach to the solution of family problems – an approach which took account of the structural and social components of individual distress – and arguing that there could be no sound practice of casework without an understanding of the principles and function of social reform, community organisation and social group work,[29] it was psychodynamic work which became the dominant mode of intervention.[30] This was influenced to a great extent by work done at the Family Discussion Bureaux established in London in 1948 and taken over by the Tavistock Institute in 1956.[31] In 1951, the Tavistock had also extended the influence of psychodynamic methods by diverting resources for social work education from the training of psychiatric social workers to the provision of full-time courses for small groups from any recognised branch of casework.[32] Fred Philp, then fieldwork organiser in Liverpool, took advantage of this and was seconded to follow an advanced social work course at the Tavistock in 1954.[33]

The emphasis on the importance of mental health which had characterised the PSU/FSU's early work continued over the ensuing decades and appeared to be reinforced by experience. The Liverpool FSU's annual report for 1955–56 noted that of the 105 families on their books during the previous years, 22 parents had spent time in mental hospitals or were ascertained mental defectives (sic); 17 children had been treated at child guidance clinics; and 29 children were attending or had attended special schools. Even these figures, the report concluded, underestimated the amount of emotional disturbance in families.[34] The following year, the Kensington and Paddington unit reported that of the 20 families with whom the unit had been working for more than two years, 15 were characterised by the poor mental health of both parents.[35] In 1960 the unit noted that about a quarter of FSU families had at least one parent who had been diagnosed mentally ill.[36] A description of its clients in a document associated with the setting up of a Combined Casework Unit in Hackney in 1962 noted that:

> Most of the families are 'problem families', having difficulties in many areas of their lives but particularly in financial management and child care. In all cases parents have deep-seated personality problems which make it difficult for them to establish satisfactory relationships with others or to profit from the social services available in the community.[37]

So clear an idea of their client group encouraged a number of senior FSU workers either to request secondment to relevant courses or to make the decision to leave the organisation in order to study for a professional qualification. Two Liverpool workers enrolled on the mental health course at the LSE between 1956 and 1958,[38] as did one of their colleagues from the South London unit.[39] The 1960s saw several more workers becoming students at the LSE and at the universities of Manchester, Leeds and Liverpool[40] (which offered similar opportunities) in spite of the Ministry of Health's refusal to recognise FSU employment as equivalent to mental health service experience for the purpose of qualifying for the grant aid by which many such students were supported.[41] In a number of cases, FSU financially supported those who enrolled on university courses.[42]

Although professionally qualified staff remained in short supply throughout the 1950s and beyond,[43] FSU appears to have been able to attract a much higher proportion of qualified social workers than most local authority welfare or children's departments. According to a paper compiled by its national secretary in 1959, FSU could claim that 16 per cent of the successful applicants to the agency had a social science degree, and 64 per cent had a social science diploma. It is difficult to be certain from such a breakdown whether this constituted an 80 per cent qualified intake; many courses would not have contained a vocational training element although some, for example the BA in Sociology at the University of Liverpool, included a substantial practical component. Student reports suggest that in some terms students might have spent as much as 25 days on placement.[44] Although the figures present some problems of interpretation, the high proportion of applicants to FSU who had undertaken courses with some relevance to social work was unlikely to be mirrored elsewhere and suggests that the organisation held a particular appeal for qualified workers. The possession of relevant academic experience did not guarantee a post in the organisation, however. In the 1950s, as many applicants were rejected as were accepted, however impressive their academic qualifications. Jones also claimed that 92 of the workers accepted by FSU had completed university courses of one sort or another; this, again, must have been a unusually high figure.[45] It is borne out by the records of the national personnel committee which, in the early 1960s, notes that recruits to FSU were, in many cases, graduates with some sort of social work qualification.[46] In 1976, an FSU national policy report noted that 70 per cent of FSU workers were professionally qualified;[47] in 1981 the figure was 90 per cent.[48]

David Jones's study of the intake in 1959 also threw up other interesting characteristics of FSU recruits. Of those appointed, 96 per cent were single; 20 per cent were under 23; 72 per cent were aged between 33 and 39; 8 per cent were aged between 30 and 39.[49] In many of its aspects, the FSU's staff profile was the same as that of its wartime predecessor. Workers were young and unattached, and their average length of service was less than three years. In part this was a result of the conditions under which they worked. Most units still required their personnel to be resident and to be on call for long hours at a time, including at weekends. It was the sort of work which enticed the young and idealistic, but held less attraction for people with family responsibilities.

The weaknesses, as they perceived them, of some university courses led FSU, which attached great importance to intensely personal social work, to adopt a cautious attitude towards the qualifications of prospective workers and, on occasion, to prefer an unqualified applicant with the 'right' personality to a graduate who did not appear to fit the FSU mould. It was never assumed that an applicant for a social work post was necessarily suited to work in a unit simply because she or he held a recognised university or college qualification. In spite of any training they may have had, all candidates had to undergo a period of instruction and assessment before their suitability was agreed. To that extent, FSU did not differ markedly in its practice from other agencies, whether local authorities or voluntary societies who, in Younghusband's words, 'shaped the semi-finished product of an academic course to the particular pattern of a specialised agency'.[50] However, other organisations may not have formalised the training in the same way that FSU did.

One of the motives behind the centralised organisation of training and the design of a formal FSU scheme in the early 1950s was a desire to safeguard the agency's methods of work. The fear that local authorities might set up rival units, which purported to be FSUs but which did not benefit from the organisation's training and organisation, had first been aired in Manchester in 1951 when a pilot scheme was drawn up.[51] It was hoped that a recognised FSU training course might help to separate the genuine article from its imitators. The Manchester scheme provided different training for different types of trainee, implicitly acknowledging the range of candidates who were accepted by the organisation. Those without a relevant academic qualification were to undertake the longest training, which lasted 12 months and included practical work under the supervision of the fieldwork organiser and some theoretical instruction arranged either by the unit or by a committee of the national organisation. This theory element was to occupy up to one-quarter of the course time, and would include economic history, the history and development of social services, the functions of the main welfare services, and psychology.[52] This may have represented a unrealisable dream. There is little evidence from the records kept on trainees that a scheme with so substantial an academic component was ever put into effect; the training offered to those applicants without formal academic qualifications appears to have been exactly the same as that received by those who had them. The position of the national organisation was reinforced by the requirement that all candidates were to be subject to scrutiny by the national training committee which would take ultimate responsibility for trainees.

It may be that the implementation of the ambitious Manchester scheme, as well as a more simple one in Sheffield,[53] were overtaken by events. In the year that the scheme was drawn up, FSU's contribution to the development of professional social work was recognised by the award of a grant of £15,000 over five years from the Carnegie United Kingdom Trust Fund.[54] The money was earmarked for training, and this prompted the appointment of a national training working party under the chairmanship of Tom Stephens. The brief was to consider the selection of workers, the types of instruction they should receive, and the content, organisation and duration of any training.[55] The scheme that resulted had much in common with the one designed in Manchester. A six- to nine-month period of instruction was envisaged on the assumption that the course was neither a substitute for academic social science training nor a new social work qualification, but was designed to meet the particular needs of workers with problem families – families whose care played a central part in the organising principles of the syllabus. Students were to be required to understand the nature of the statutory and voluntary social services with particular reference to the problem family and to social casework. They would be made aware of methods of dealing with such families and acquire some knowledge of the experimental work that had already been done. Mental health and ill-health, epilepsy, child development and maladjustment, and family relationships were to constitute another section. Social casework, recording and reporting were included, as was a practical section on homemaking, budgeting, parentcraft, health and hygiene, and household repairs. In 1953 Manchester, Liverpool, and Kensington and Paddington were recognised as the principal training units.[56]

Although the national office had controlled the appointment of staff from the earliest days of the organisation, the handling of the

Carnegie grant further demonstrated the centralising ambition of the national staff. The mechanisms for managing the grant were reserved to London, specifically, the national personnel and training committee, chaired by Tom Stephens, which reserved the right to select candidates, oversee their training and receive regular reports on their progress.[57] This highlighted a confusion about the location of control that was to increase during the 1960s and 1970s.[58] While such a large grant clearly required central direction, that fact that the detailed control of appointments was retained in London – where interviews took place, sometimes with scant reference to the unit in which an applicant was eventually to be placed – sat uneasily in an organisation which stressed the importance of local links and the relative autonomy of local units. Some aspiring caseworkers were required to remain trainees for a longer than usual period in order to prove that they had reached the desired standard, and the decision about any necessary extension was taken in London by the personnel committee.

Trainees were placed in units as vacancies occurred. Occasionally an applicant's personal circumstances were taken into account and a placement found near her or his home. Residence in the unit house was compulsory throughout the 1940s and 1950s, and for longer in some units; for some trainees this was a less than comfortable experience. In Liverpool in 1956, two trainees who were forced to share a room because of the shortage of space expressed some resentment, although it made little difference.[59] Trainees were required to spend a number of weeks working alongside more experienced staff before they were allowed to take on small caseloads. In most cases the fieldwork organiser would take responsibility for monitoring their progress, although all members of the unit would be available to offer support and advice. In some units, the extra work incurred by the presence of trainees gave rise to complaint. In 1952 the Liverpool unit, which had repeatedly been asked to take on trainees who would leave the unit on completion of their training, argued that this placed an unacceptable burden on the local workers who were expected to invest a lot of effort but saw little benefit accruing either to their unit or their clients.[60] From the national organisation's point of view, there was little option but to use the established units as training grounds. FSU was under pressure to expand and to open branches in cities throughout Britain. There was no shortage of aspiring workers, but there were few experienced staff competent to undertake the task of training. In 1956 the Liverpool unit actively tried to address this and to recruit a psychiatric social worker so that she or he could take responsibility for the training of prospective FSU workers and university students on placement at the unit.[61]

The lessons learned during training were reinforced by conferences organised for trainees and, later, for all staff. Some of these covered a wide variety of topics; one held in Liverpool in April 1952, for example, covered narrowly specific subjects such as the 1948 Children Act; historical issues such as 'Poor law and unemployment assistance prior to the National Assistance Act 1948'; and more practical topics including 'Meeting the material needs of families', 'Meeting the needs of children' and, significantly, 'How valuable is a social science diploma in FSU work?'[62]

FSU may have questioned the value of some university courses, but within academic social work there were some attempts to encourage a correspondence between the demands of the courses and the needs of the agencies. Some universities had devised methods for keeping closely in touch with practice which antedated the post-war developments in social work training. As Younghusband had noted in 1947, members of academic staff sometimes held posts as practitioners within social work agencies; for example, in both Birmingham and Bristol during the immediate post-war period, the wardens of the university settlements were also university tutors in practical social work. In Liverpool, the training secretary of the Liverpool Personal Service Society was also a part-time member of the university Department of Social Science, and the senior psychiatric social worker at the Maudsley Hospital taught in the Department of Social Science and Social Administration at the LSE.[63]

The acclaim which FSU's family casework had received made the agency a popular choice with students and teachers for practical placements. This meant that FSU's responsibilities towards its own trainees had to be considered alongside responsibilities to colleges and other training institutions for which FSU provided opportunities for practical experience. The earliest references to student placements come from the Manchester unit which accepted students from the local university in 1944.[64] Within a year or so, the Liverpool unit followed suit and offered placements to students from the University of Liverpool and Josephine Butler House (which trained Anglican Moral Welfare workers), as well as from other university courses.[65] These students were rapidly followed between 1945 and 1950 by others from the LSE, the Manchester School of Domestic Science,

Leeds University, University College Cardiff, Bedford College, University College Leicester, Southampton University, Selly Oak College Birmingham and Hull University.[66] Soon after its establishment, the Kensington and Paddington unit agreed to receive students on placement from a number of universities and colleges. The practice helped to cement relationships with training institutions, and the fees received by the units were a valuable source of funds.

In the ensuing years student placements with FSU continued to be in great demand, and by the early 1960s practical experience in specific units had become very desirable; the Kensington and Paddington unit was particularly highly regarded. In addition to its own trainees and those students on undergraduate and postgraduate courses at universities, FSU was asked to provide training opportunities for local authority employees. A child-care officer from Lancashire County Council did a period of training at the Liverpool unit in 1957,[67] as did a child-care officer from Warrington children's department.[68] An area children's officer from Denbighshire did a spell with the Liverpool unit in 1963,[69] and the following year the children's officer from Glamorgan requested that FSU provide three-month training placements for some of her staff.[70] Members of other professions also used FSU as a training placement. Health visitors spent time at the Liverpool unit in 1959, as did a Home Office trainee probation officer and students from the Institute of Almoners.[71] Medical students spent some time observing the work of the Islington unit in 1964,[72] and prison officers in training at Wakefield jail spent periods on placement with Sheffield FSU in the late 1960s.[73] Interest was also shown by workers from other countries: in 1944, a Malay student spent some time working in the Manchester unit,[74] and in 1957 an employee of the Hong Kong Welfare Department following a course at the LSE chose to do a placement in the Liverpool unit.[75] In 1963, a worker from the Pestalozzi Frobel-Haus in Berlin also spent time training at the Liverpool unit.[76] Although this was gratifying – the level of demand for placements indicated the esteem in which the organisation was held – the constant stream of students continued to put strain on the staff. In 1960, the Liverpool unit reported that it had received more applications for training placements than it could accept,[77] and this was not unique. At a meeting in March 1964, fieldwork organisers from all units voiced concern about the increasing demands for training places and supervision that were being made on units.[78]

Personal links go a long way towards explaining the relationships which so rapidly developed between individual units and universities. In most university departments a tutor was given special responsibility for arranging the students' practical work. To perform the task effectively the tutor would need to be in close touch with agencies in his or her area. In Manchester in the 1940s Penelope Hall and Barbara Rodgers, both of whom worked at the Department of Social Administration at Manchester University, used their personal contacts to strengthen relationships between their department and the local unit. In Liverpool also there were strong links between the unit and its local university, fostered by T. S. Simey from the Department of Social Science and reinforced when Penelope Hall moved to the university. It is less clear how the Department of Social Science at University College Cardiff came to hear about the vacancies, but two Cardiff lecturers, Maisie Jukes and Walter Birmingham, spent time as residents in the Liverpool unit in the 1940s before sending some of their students there for practical experience.[79]

FSU was not alone in fielding requests for placements. Its experience was shared by other agencies, statutory and voluntary, and increased as the number of social work students rose from the early 1960s onwards. The number of agencies involved in the practical training of social workers prompted concerns about the maintenance of standards. The lecturers who ran training courses began to question the quality of student experience, and attempts were made to achieve some standardisation in order that students should receive roughly equal treatment regardless of the agency in which they were placed, and also that they should acquire the right degree of professional competence. In Liverpool, a well-developed scheme was in place. A practical advisory committee composed of representatives of the Liverpool University Department of Social Science and the training agencies had to be consulted before a new agency could be accepted for training purposes. If accepted, organisations were automatically given a seat on the committee, which was responsible for developing policy and monitoring standards. It received reports on every student, and approved the marks awarded for practical work.[80] Another example of an attempt to coordinate practical training and safeguard standards was provided by the Association of Family Case Workers, which had 17 recognised agencies on its books in the late 1940s.[81]

From the 1950s onwards, 'generic' casework courses – designed to provide the necessary basic skills for social workers, regardless of the branch of the profession in which they had chosen to work – were slowly introduced. Younghusband's central recommendation in her 1947 and 1951 reports had been the establishment of a postgraduate school for social workers, to be staffed with experienced practitioners and dedicated to teaching and research. This was rejected as too costly by the Carnegie trustees, to whom an application for funding was made, although the LSE was keen to offer a home to such a school and the Joint University Council for Social and Public Administration gave the idea qualified approval.[82] The Carnegie Trust did award a grant of £20,000 over four years to support a modified scheme which resulted in the creation of an applied social studies course at the LSE in 1954.[83] Younghusband directed this experiment from 1954–58.[84]

Younghusband's experience of the LSE course informed the recommendations for desirable norms in social work training set out in her 1959 report. Established in 1955 to inquire into the 'proper field of work, and the recruitment and training of social workers at all levels... in the local authority health and welfare services... and in particular whether there is a place for a general social worker with an in-service training as a basic grade',[85] the Younghusband committee reviewed a profession lacking coherence and comprising a complex series of services that had evolved independently of each other and had reached different stages of development.[86] Steered by a group of people who had a long-standing interest in the quality of social work training[87] it addressed the lack of training, particularly for welfare officers and mental welfare officers, and argued that if no nationally agreed training were developed, welfare departments would be the only local authority departments staffed by officers who were without a recognised qualification.[88] The report covered almost every aspect of professional practice and outlined the need for systematic enquiry into the relation between theory and practice.[89] It also recommended instruction in the supervision of practical work and the teaching of interviewing and reporting techniques, together with an assessment of the ways such skills should appear in a training programme. The report also noted the desirability of providing guidance for tutors on the levels of attainment which should be expected from students. It assumed a basic minimal content to any course and assumed that the skills peculiar to any form of social work could be added to that base.

Younghusband's report on social work training[90] also encouraged the introduction of vocational courses in colleges of further education and the extramural departments of universities. These were largely designed for non-graduates who wished to become social workers, and for social work agencies who were increasingly keen to employ trained staff at a time when they were in very short supply. Incidentally, the 'Younghusband courses' (as they became known) encouraged fresh thinking in services which, according to Barker, were in danger of deterioration. The provision of training courses for child-care, health and welfare officers in the 1960s gave educational opportunities both to established local authority employees and to new recruits.[91] Although the introduction of such courses initially resulted in a two-tier profession, those who successfully completed them were eventually given an equal footing with their graduate colleagues.

As the 1959 Younghusband report was published, some FSU workers were beginning to reflect on the training that their own organisation offered and suggest ways of updating it. Sheila Kay, fieldwork organiser in the Liverpool unit, claimed that FSU training had not changed in the previous decade – although methods in social work had – and that, as a result, FSU was losing good recruits to other agencies, particularly to statutory ones. She argued that one way forward might be to alter, or even abandon, the period of specialist FSU training to bring it more into line with other professional organisations, which generally accepted graduates of generic social work courses without giving them further instruction. Kay believed that FSU should avoid any suggestion that it had a monopoly on intensive casework which required particular education for its workers.[92] She was mounting a challenge to the notion that there was something different about FSU's methods; while there may have been a difference in the 1940s and the early 1950s, this was much less true in the late 1950s and early 1960s. The increasing confidence of the profession as a whole – exemplified by the growth in specialist literature and the increasing number of courses designed to produce competent practitioners – together with a greater public understanding of the social work task put FSU at the forefront of many developments, but the agency was no longer so distinctive as to require special training.

Later that same year, as if to give official recognition to FSU's place in the mainstream of social work practice – but also emphasising the degree of common ground between its practice and that of other agencies – a course of theoretical training for experienced workers was jointly planned by FSU, the Family Welfare Association, the Invalid Children's Aid Association and the Moral Welfare Association, and was accepted by the University of London as an extramural course.[93] A similar development took place in Liverpool when FSU, together with the Council for Social Service, the Liverpool Personal Service Society and the University of Liverpool, set up a course for voluntary social workers to be run by the university's extramural department.[94]

1959 also saw the appointment of Fred Philp to the FSU's national office staff with special responsibility for training, research and publication. His duties included the organisation and conduct of annual caseworkers' conferences and periodic study courses; general supervision and development of training for caseworkers and field-work organisers, including the preparation of training materials; and liaison with universities and other training organisations. He became secretary to the newly formed research committee and, as the member of staff responsible for publication, was expected to oversee the preparation of technical material for internal use, including material for annual reports, appeals and general publicity.[95] It was a powerful position, with the potential to influence the organisation's shape during the next stage of its development. In addition to his responsibilities within the organisation, it was agreed that Philp should become tutor on a course for probation officers and women public health officers.[96]

After Philp's appointment as national secretary in 1962 the formalisation of training continued with the appointment of unit training officers who took administrative responsibility for student placements, and helped to plan their programmes and to support those staff who were supervising students. FSU's contribution to social work training was increasingly recognised. The Islington, South London, Manchester, Oldham, Bristol, Bradford, Leeds, Leicester and Birmingham units had all been visited by representatives of the Joint Committee on Family Casework Training by December 1961 and the remaining units received them during the next few months, eventually to be rewarded by an official recommendation of their suitability to take students in training.[97] FSU workers were also in demand as lecturers in colleges and universities and in various advisory capacities. David Jones was appointed to the Council for Training in Social Work in 1962.[98] Peter Leonard moved from the

South London unit to the post of lecturer at the University of Liverpool in 1963,[99] and Eric Brown went from the Liverpool unit to teach at Chiswick Polytechnic later the same year.[100] Sheila Kay, the Liverpool fieldwork organiser, was appointed lecturer at the University of Liverpool in 1966.[101]

Given the increasing emphasis on training, and FSU's willingness to offer placements to students on the non-graduate training courses set up in technical colleges and colleges of further education after the recommendations of the 1959 Younghusband report, it comes as a surprise to read Philp's report to the FSU personnel committee in the summer of 1967. Having reviewed the difference between salaries paid by FSU and those paid by local authorities – a comparison which demonstrated FSU's failure to keep pace with current levels of pay – Philp suggested that young social science graduates were not necessarily the best people to help those families referred to FSU. While recognising the difficulties attendant in such a question at a time when the need for social workers to receive appropriate training was generally accepted, he stated his conviction that there was little reason to believe that workers with professional training were substantially more helpful to families than untrained people in the past. He compared young social science graduates with other 'lively, concerned young people without social work training, and older people without academic training but with a natural sympathy for families and children', and suggested that the former might have less to offer.[102] In the climate of the 1960s, it must have taken some courage to enunciate what amounted to heresy and flew in the face of opinions being voiced throughout the profession. It also ran counter to the climate in FSU where professionally trained workers were increasingly in demand. However, his attitude chimed with earlier PSU/FSU criteria for the selection of workers, which had stressed the importance of the 'right' personality above academic qualifications. To some extent Philp was giving expression to an attitude against which the social work profession had fought for more than half a century. As Chris Jones argued in the late 1970s, a major part of social work's struggle to achieve professional status had involved attempts to exorcise the perception that it was an activity which could be undertaken by anyone with a sympathetic manner.[103] In 1981, Butrym, Stevenson and Harris agreed, echoing the sentiments of the Charity Organisation Society's C. H. Loch when they argued that clients had the right to be protected from incompetence and abuse and that there was no better way of ensuring this protection than to train social workers properly.[104]

The unification of professional courses on broadly generic syllabuses during the 1960s completed a process which had begun in some universities in the 1950s. The LSE applied social studies course had contributed to the breaking down of barriers between the different branches of social work, a development which had been anticipated some years earlier by another notable social work educator, Roger Wilson. In a paper to the British Conference on Social Work in 1950, Wilson had noted that the fast-emerging specialities in social work had the potential to enrich each other and to be fed by a broad experience of family casework.[105] The LSE course had been approved as suitable for students wishing to undertake family casework, medical social work and probation work, but not all professional social workers agreed about its value; in spite of the inclusion of psychodynamic methods in the syllabus, it was not recognised by the body representing the most specialised group, the Association of Psychiatric Social Workers.[106] It was, though, part of the process of making social work an intellectually respectable subject which could and should be taught in a university department. In 1956, Younghusband had compared social work to subjects such as social medicine, social research, social anthropology, psychiatry and psychology, and she pilloried the universities for failing to recognise what was involved in the different methods of applying the social sciences.[107] Although the applied social studies course amalgamated with the LSE child-care course in 1958, it was not until 1970 that applied social studies and mental health courses were integrated into the Diploma in Social Work Studies.[108] This process, albeit extended over more than a decade, eventually helped to demonstrate that a social worker qualified in one branch did not need to retrain to become competent to work in another, and that the common ground of casework was more fundamental than the differences between specialities. In addition, it gave social work students the same standard of professional education as that enjoyed by those on mental health courses, who had historically been thought to be better trained than other social workers;[109] and it was based on a clear partnership between the university and fieldwork agencies.[110] It demonstrated that to run a series of separate courses was to deny students the enrichment which resulted from associating with each other, to waste precious resources, and to perpetuate an emphasis on administrative structure and difference at the expense of similarity and educational content.[111] This coincided with the creation of local authority social services departments in 1968 (in Scotland) and 1971 (in England and Wales), which rendered anachronistic the earlier divisions between social work specialisms and required social workers to handle problems posed by a variety of clients, regardless of their difficulty or their age.

The increasing number of generic courses and the merging of courses for graduates and non-graduates, together with the introduction of higher degrees for social workers from the mid-1960s, marked the beginning of the realisation of Younghusband's ambition that social work training should provide students with skills which would equip them to tackle a variety of human needs, and of her dream that social work should gain academic respectability, taking its place among other recognised professions with its own literature, specialist training and research programmes. The first academic chairs in social work were established by the mid-1970s.[112] Younghusband's wider ambitions for the profession were also eventually realised. In 1972, the Certificate of Qualification in Social Work replaced a number of specialist qualifications awarded by the previous training bodies. The Certificate in Social Service was introduced by the Central Council for Education and Training in Social Work in 1975. It was designed for staff already in a range of posts other than designated social work positions, most of which were to be found in residential institutions. An ambition necessary to the professional ambitions of any profession – that it should have recognised training procedures – had eventually been achieved.

These developments did not meet with general approval. In addition to the widely voiced concern that specialised work such as child-care and mental health required particular training, the considerable expansion in the number of social work courses led one commentator to remark ruefully in 1976 that there had been 'a serious degree of dilution and depression of standards on many courses', compounded by two major reorganisations of the social services.[113] Younghusband would not have agreed. In the following decades, however, the criticisms levelled at social workers and the uncertainty that attended any consideration of their role and their training became part of a widespread national discussion. The competence of many practitioners and their supervisors was questioned, as were the administrative procedures which resulted in dangers to some children being overlooked, or cases getting lost in the gaps between the responsibilities of medicine, social work, education and police work.[114] In the aftermath of tragedies such as the death of Maria Colwell in 1973, some within the profession argued that the professional skills and specialised expertise of social workers in the pre-reorganisation children's departments had been lost within the more varied and less specialist working environments of the new social services departments.[115]

Further developments in the organisation of social work training during the 1970s resulted in the creation of student training units (STUs). These were largely experimental and were established in a variety of social work settings, both statutory and voluntary, financed by grants from the Department of Health and Social Security.[116] They were intended to provide practical placements for students under the supervision of experienced social workers. One was set up at Newcastle FSU in October 1973, and by 1978 the organisation was responsible for five more such units,[117] each employing the services of a full-time training officer and funded by the DHSS on condition that at least 800 student training days were provided by each STU. By 1978, FSU as a whole was providing approximately 10,000 training days a year for professional students in England and another 1,000 days a year for pre-professional students – that is, those who were on courses which did not lead directly to a professional qualification. Edinburgh FSU had a half-time teaching unit funded by the Scottish Office which was required to provide 300 student placement days a year.[118]

The Newcastle FSU student training unit deliberately fostered relationships with three local social work courses, two at the University of Newcastle and one at Newcastle Polytechnic. This was an attempt both to ease the pressure for placements and to build up relationships with academic staff in nearby colleges.[119] Newcastle was not the only unit to see the potential of close links with local colleges. For example, the director of the first applied social studies course at Goldsmiths College (part of the University of London) worked with the unit organiser of the East London FSU in the early 1970s to devise a model of group work practice and teaching. Under this scheme, a small number of students went to the unit for half a day per week and they were responsible for one of the unit's group projects. Their work was supervised by two unit staff members.[120]

FSU's student training units were not always an unqualified

success. The Newcastle unit's increasing emphasis on an integrated approach to work with families in the late 1970s had an adverse effect on its appeal to lecturers on social work courses. The mismatch between what students were taught in their colleges – inevitably determined by the content of the university-designed curriculum – and what they experienced in the field resulted in a drop in the number of student placements, in this case because it was feared that the students would gain too little casework experience.[121] Moreover, it proved difficult to find suitably experienced staff to act as supervisors within the unit. There was some indication that the job of training officer was not one which was held in particularly high esteem within the profession. In 1974, the Oldham unit had found it difficult to recruit a student training officer, noting that social workers saw it as an unattractive, dead end job.[122] Later that year it was argued that to become a student training officer was a sideways or even a downwards move – in that it was not one of the main routes up the social work hierarchy[123] – and therefore held few prospects for promotion. The criticism was directed at the demands of an already defined hierarchy and its failure to integrate tutorial responsibilities rather than at any particular agency or scheme of training, but it suggested that professional education was not being given a high priority.

Placements for college and university students did not constitute the only contribution made by FSU to social work education; some units, Camden for example, organised post-qualification courses for social workers. By the late 1970s, FSU's active involvement in in-service training for its own workers included an induction programme for new staff and specialist courses on social work method (especially group and community work), work with the under-fives, and work with families whose children had suffered non-accidental injury. In addition, the organisation offered management courses for senior workers and courses in administration for its secretaries.[124]

In spite of what it believed to be its formative influence on students, and the close links it had enjoyed with colleges and universities for more than 30 years, by the late 1970s FSU considered that its impact on educational institutions was less than it might be. Possible remedies were suggested by the 1978 working party on development. A two-way traffic of personnel was mooted, with FSU staff contributing to academic courses and practising academics joining local management committees, though no practical suggestions for the implementation of such schemes were made. The section on training in the working party's report is perhaps the least confident part of the whole document, and suggests that in this area FSU had found itself at something of a crossroads. The organisation's past contribution was acknowledged, and its present activities listed, but the general tone suggests that although future opportunities could be glimpsed there was no certainty that the organisation would be able to grasp them. To a great extent, this mirrored the position of the agency within social work provision. Its values and practice had become mainstream and in some areas it was thought to be lagging behind current thought. On the basis of its history, FSU attempted to position itself within social work educational provision as the agency best equipped to contribute knowledge about the most under-privileged client groups. Working party members must have realised that this view could be challenged, not least by local authority social services departments whose staff dealt with many more families in acute distress than FSU; but the working party was also realistic about its present state and faced up to some of the internal difficulties created by the inadequacies of FSU training. It acknowledged the continued tensions produced within the agency as a result of its long-standing reputation for providing valuable experience for students, as well as the need to achieve a balance between the unit's core activities with families and its role as a training agency. This was a major concern which had exercised workers in some units since the early 1950s, but had clearly not been resolved satisfactorily by 1978. Moreover, FSU's reputation was not as good as it had once been. Indifferent evaluation reports on the work of FSU's student training units had been made by the Central Council for the Education and Training of Social Workers (CCETSW) and the DHSS. No further detail is given, but it appears that the agency's methods of work and standards were being questioned. Recognition that the organisation's reputation might suffer as a result led to mild criticism of the evaluation process by the working party, coupled with an attempt to limit further damage. It was recommended that a framework for future evaluations should be agreed with the DHSS and the CCETSW,[125] and that there should be closer liaison with FSU's national office. Implicit in this is the notion that the national committees might have been able to present a better picture than the local units, perhaps by providing a more comprehensive overview; but this cannot disguise FSU's recognition that it had lost its place at the forefront of practical social work training.

If FSU was aware of its deficiencies, it was also aware of its inability to remedy them without recourse to public funds. The working party argued that CCETSW's proposals for expanding the provision of post-qualification courses offered FSU the opportunity to provide practical placements for students on such courses. At the same time FSU recognised its inability to meet CCETSW's standards. It would need a training officer and extra funds, for which application would have to be made to the DHSS.[126] In order to make certain that all staff had the opportunity of professional training, the working party also urged the national office to apply to the DHSS secondment scheme for funds to allow staff to be seconded to appropriate courses.[127] Although its more ambitious plans appear not to have been realised, FSU's training programme for the following year reflected advances in techniques and broader patterns of intervention which were increasingly elements in its practice, as they were in social work generally. One of the assistant directors reported to the national management committee in May 1979 that induction courses, courses for supervisors and courses on management skills for senior workers were planned. Sessions on running groups, using video, family therapy, research projects, and running drop-in centres were also envisaged.[128]

As was to be expected in an organisation which gave a considerable degree of autonomy to individual units, student experiences varied from place to place. Complaints from universities and colleges about the inconsistency of approaches to the resolution of family problems were reflected in anxieties expressed by the caseworkers. In 1966, their committee had complained that training varied too much from unit to unit and suggested that there should be greater systematisation and a national plan of training,[129] but the importance attached to local determination and traditions continued throughout the 1970s and beyond. Placement reports reveal the variety of emphasis and practice within FSU. A student of the University of Liverpool in 1975 had a very different experience on placement in the local unit from a student at Westhill College, whose practical experience was at the South Birmingham unit. In the case of the former, the report contains considerable detail about the psychology both of the student and of the families with whom she worked, says little about structural factors and gives a clear indication that families' problems were believed to be internal to them, in that they were the consequence of inadequate relationships.[130] In South Birmingham, on the other hand, a different atmosphere prevailed, with emphasis being placed on environmental factors which contributed to families' distress and the search for remedies in practical or campaigning activities, like the local housing action group and the youth club.[131] A later report on a student at the South Birmingham unit contains comments which reveal a significant shift away from many of the attitudes which characterised the organisation's earlier history:

> Broadly the gains of this placement have been exposure to community action, in particular some experiences of taking on the local state. This has meant embracing some aspects of conflict theory in practice... there has been a significant shift in [his] perception of the benevolence of welfare agencies in this respect (I believe he now sees the DHSS and the Housing Department as organisations who do not necessarily act in the interests of the working class... he has had his eyes opened regarding the conditions of a poor housing estate).[132]

The supervisor exemplified a school of thought which argued that, too often, social workers were trained to act in the interest of ruling elites and against the interests of their clients.[133]

No such socialist-inspired theory met a student on placement in the more therapeutically ordered atmosphere of Merton FSU. He was commended for initiating psychosocial diagnoses and formulating joint treatment plans with the families in his care;[134] and a student from Brunel University, also on placement at Merton FSU in 1975, appears to have had to confront his own problems rather than those of the families on his caseload. His university tutor wrote to the unit to say, 'It looks as though you have helped him really to come to grips with the problems that face him inside him... '[135] The style of work of the Merton unit might have been exactly what tutors at Brunel were looking for. In 1982, an article by a member of staff on the social work course argued against the inclusion of a large theoretical element in social work training, on the grounds that thought is based on emotional experience and that immersion in experience has to come before theorising.[136]

There was, however, a plurality of belief in social work education.[137] It must be assumed that those colleges and universities which sent students to the South Birmingham unit were influenced by radical social work theory. Reports throughout the late 1970s and 1980s demonstrate South Birmingham's continued interest in community and group work which aimed not to reconcile the family to its plight and its circumstances, or even to change the patterns of its internal functioning, but to put pressure on various authorities for changes in the type or provision of services.[138] One student's 'contract' with the unit in its role as a training agency required her to work with the local claimants' union, to help with tribunals for supplementary benefit claimants, and to support the housing action group and the women and health group.[139] The unit also held seminars on topics like behaviour modification, running public meetings and organising pressure groups. The short-term casework offered to a small number of families was not conducted on psychodynamic lines but concentrated on practical issues and their resolution.

External events prompted a more public consideration of the work and training of social workers. In 1987, in part as a result of anxiety created by the publication of a report into the killing of the child Kimberley Carlile by her mother's partner which criticised social workers and other agencies responsible for the child's supervision for failing to recognise danger signals, a recommendation was made that training for social workers should be increased to three years and that all candidates should have a proper grounding in law, child-care and child abuse.[140] Changing perceptions of need and changing patterns of service delivery prompted reconsideration of social work training courses, and it was suggested that the original distinction between the mainly in-service Certificate in Social Service and the college- and university-based Certificate of Qualification in Social Work was no longer appropriate.[141] Discussions about the length and nature of training for social workers continued throughout the rest of the twentieth century, as did public criticism of what were perceived to be their failings.

By the late 1980s, FSU's contribution to social work training, although still significant, no longer allowed students to experience pioneering and unusual approaches to family problems. Senior FSU workers were products of conventional social work courses and brought with them the current values and standards of the profession. Students may still have seen high-quality work done by dedicated social workers, but they also worked alongside others whose professional training might have been in teaching or counselling, as well as ancillary workers who specialised in providing the sort of practical support that FSU social workers might have given a generation earlier. Moreover, as will be seen, its increasing dependence on financial support from statutory bodies limited the freedom to experiment and innovate which had been such an exciting feature of the organisation for students of an earlier generation.

# NOTES

**1.** Women's Group on Public Welfare, *Our Towns, A Close-Up: A study made during 1939–42 with certain recommendations by the Hygiene Committee of the Women's Group on Public Welfare* (Oxford, 1943).

**2.** Ministry of Health and Ministry of Education, *Report of the Care of Children Committee* (Curtis report) Cmnd 6922 (HMSO, 1946).

**3.** See above, ch.2.

**4.** E. Younghusband, *Report on the Employment and Training of Social Workers* (Edinburgh, 1947), pp4–5.

**5.** The confusion about the exact nature of the social work task persisted until at least the mid-1980s. R. Pinker, 'The threat to professional standards in social work education: A response to some recent proposals', *Issues in Social Work Education*, 4 (1984), p6.

**6.** M. Barker, 'Eileen Younghusband 1902–1981: A personal appreciation', *Issues in Social Work Education*, 1 (1981), p80.

**7.** Younghusband, *Employment and Training of Social Workers*, pp30ff.

**8.** Younghusband, *Employment and Training of Social Workers*, pp30ff.

**9.** Younghusband, *Employment and Training of Social Workers*, p8.

**10.** Younghusband, *Employment and Training of Social Workers*, p41.

**11.** Younghusband, *Employment and Training of Social Workers*, p30.

**12.** K. Russell, S. Benson, C. Farrell and H. Glennerster, *Changing Course* (London, 1981), p10.

**13.** J. Lewis, *The Voluntary Sector, the State and Social Work in Britain* (Aldershot, 1995), p81.

**14.** E. Younghusband, *Social Work in Britain: 1950–1975*, 2 vols (London, 1978) vol 2, p30.

**15.** E. Younghusband, *Social Work in Britain: A supplementary report on the employment and training of social workers* (Edinburgh, 1951), p51.

**16.** See above, p30. Cf A. Cohen, *The Revolution in Post-War Family Casework: The Story of Pacifist Service Units and Family Service Units, 1940–1959* (Lancaster, 1998), p51.

**17.** T. Stephens, *Problem Families: An experiment in social rehabilitation* (London, 1945), pp71–2.

**18.** Russell et al, *Changing Course*, p10.

**19.** See above, p16.

**20.** Cohen, *The Revolution in Post-War Family Casework*, p39.

**21.** Letter from Ken Richardson to Sybil Clement-Brown. ULSCA D495(HQ) PSU5-8.

**22.** Younghusband, *Social Work in Britain: A supplementary report*, p3; Younghusband, *Social Work in Britain, 1950–1975*, vol 2, p27.

**23.** Minutes of the Liverpool FSU committee, July 7 1954. ULSCA D495(LI) M2/1. Minutes of the FSU national executive committee, June 6 1956. ULSCA D495(HQ)M2/4. See also minutes of the FSU national executive committee, October 26 1962. ULSCA D495(HQ)M2/5.

**24.** Russell et al, *Changing Course*, p12; Younghusband, *Social Work in Britain, 1950–1975*, vol 2, p190.

**25.** Younghusband, *Social Work in Britain: A supplementary report*, p3.

**26.** Younghusband, *Social Work in Britain: A supplementary report*, p3.

**27.** Ministry of Health, Department of Health for Scotland, *Report of the Working Party on Social Workers in the Local Authority Health and Welfare Services* (Younghusband report) (HMSO, 1959).

**28.** B. Rodgers and J. Dixon, *Portrait of Social Work: A study of social services in a northern town* (Oxford, 1960), p158.

**29.** V. Cormack, , 'Principles of casework', *Social Work*, 4 (1947), p69.

**30.** See the discussion on the relationship between social work and psycho-analysis in W. Boehm, 'The contribution of psychoanalysis to social work education', in E. Younghusband (ed.) *Education for Social Work* (London 1964), pp86ff.

**31.** E. Irvine, 'Renaissance in British casework', *Social Work*, 13 (1956), p189; R. Chambers, 'Professionalism in social work', in B. Wootton (ed.), *Social Science and Social Pathology* (London, 1959), p359.

**32.** Irvine, 'Renaissance in British casework', p192; Younghusband, *Social Work in Britain: 1950–1975*, vol 2, p23.

**33.** Minutes of the Liverpool FSU committee, July 7 1954, October 12 1954. ULSCA D495(LI)M2/1.

**34.** Liverpool FSU annual report for 1955–56. ULSCA D495(LI)M11/9.

**35.** Kensington and Paddington FSU annual report for 1956–57. ULSCA D495 (WL)M5/4.

**36.** Kensington and Paddington FSU annual report for 1960–61. ULSCA D495 (WL)M5/8.

**37.** Basis of the operation of the Combined Casework Unit, February 23 1962. ULSCA D495(HQ)B3/1.

**38.** Liverpool FSU executive committee reports, July 1 to September 30 1956 and April 1 to June 30 1958. ULSCA D495(LI)M3/1.

**39.** Minutes of the Liverpool FSU executive committee, June 4 1956. ULSCA D495(LI)M3/1.

**40.** For example, secondments are reported in the minutes of the FSU national executive committee, October 26 1962, May 22 1963, March 17 1965, July 20 1966, March 12 1968. ULSCA D495(HQ)M2/5.

**41.** FSU national secretary's report, July 21 1960 to October 5 1960. ULSCA D495(HQ)M3/13.

**42.** Minutes of the FSU national executive committee, 6 June 1956. ULSCA D495(HQ)M2/4. 17 March 1965; 6 October 1965; 20 July 1966. ULSCA D495 (HQ)M2/5.

**43.** In 1950, 300 students qualified as social workers, compared with 3,123 in 1975. Younghusband, *Social Work in Britain: 1950–1975*, vol 2, p33.

**44.** Reports on student placements 1947–1950, held in the Department of Sociology, Social Policy and Social Work Studies, University of Liverpool.

**45.** David Jones, papers dated April 16 1959 and April 17 1959. ULSCA D495(HQ)M3/3-12.

**46.** Minutes of the FSU national personnel committee, ULSCA D495(HQ)M3/13–15 passim. Minutes of the Liverpool FSU committee record the qualifications of caseworkers appointed to the unit from as early as 1948. These included social science diplomas and certificates in youth work. ULSCA D495(LI)M2.

**47.** Minutes of the Islington FSU committee, October 4 1976. ULSCA unlisted.

**48.** FSU evidence to the National Institute of Social Work Committee of Enquiry into Social Work, April 1981. ULSCA unlisted.

**49.** David Jones, paper dated April 17 1959 comparing some of the formal characteristics of both successful and unsuccessful applicants to FSU. ULSCA D495(LI)M17.

**50.** Younghusband, *Employment and Training of Social Workers*, p33.

**51.** Minutes of Manchester FSU unit meeting, January 10 1951. ULSCA D495 (MA)M2/1.

**52.** Minutes of the Manchester FSU casework sub-committee, January 18 1951. ULSCA D495(MA)M3/1.

**53.** Minutes of the Sheffield FSU committee, September 11 1951. ULSCA D495(SH)M1/1.

**54.** Report of the Liverpool FSU executive committee to April 30 1952. ULSCA D495(LI)M2/2.

**55.** Minutes of the FSU national personnel and training committee, April 19 1951. ULSCA D495(HQ)M3/13.

**56.** Minutes of the FSU national executive committee, December 9 1953. ULSCA D495(HQ)M2/3.

**57.** Report of the working party on training (1951). ULSCA D495(HQ)M3/13.

**58.** See below, ch.7.

**59.** Report of the Liverpool FSU executive committee, September 1 1955 to March 23 1956. ULSCA D495(LI)M3/2.

**60.** Minutes of the Liverpool FSU executive committee, August 18 1952. ULSCA D495(LI)M3/2.

**61.** Minutes of Liverpool FSU committee, June 30 1956. ULSCA D4945(LI) M2/1.

**62.** Papers of a conference for FSU trainees in Liverpool, April 1952. ULSCA D495(HQ)M3/5.

**63.** Younghusband, *Employment and Training of Social Workers*, p52.

**64.** Manchester PSU report for November 1944. ULSCA D495(MA)M1/1.

**65.** See, for example, minutes of the Liverpool PSU committee, January 13 1943. ULSCA D495(LI)M1/3. Minutes of the Liverpool PSU committee, August 7 1946. ULSCA D495(LI)M1/6. June 18 1947. ULSCA D495(LI)M3/1.

**66.** Liverpool FSU, casework reports, 1945–1950. ULSCA D495(LI)M4.

**67.** Report of the Liverpool FSU executive committee, April to June 1957. ULSCA D495(LI)M3/2.

**68.** Report of the Liverpool FSU executive committee, October to March 1957. ULSCA D495(LI)M3/2.

**69.** Report of the Liverpool FSU executive committee, January to April 1963. ULSCA D495(LI)M3/2.

**70.** Minutes of the FSU fieldwork organisers' meeting, March 6 1964. ULSCA D495(HQ)M3/1.

**71.** Report of the Liverpool FSU executive committee, April 1 to June 30 1959; January 1 to March 31 1960. ULSCA D495(LI)M3/2.

**72.** Minutes of the FSU national executive committee, May 13 1964. ULSCA D495(HQ)M2/5.

73. P. Goldring, *Friend of the Family: The Work of Family Service Units* (Newton Abbot, 1973), p172.

74. Minutes of the Manchester PSU committee, November 1944. ULSCA D495(MA)M1/1.

75. Report of the Liverpool FSU executive committee, January to March 1957. ULSCA D495(LI)M3/2.

76. Report of the Liverpool FSU executive committee, January to April 1963. ULSCA D495(LI)M3/2. The Pestalozzi system of education stressed the importance of taking into account the mental, physical and spiritual capabilities of individual children.

77. Report of the Liverpool FSU executive committee, August 1960. ULSCA D495(LI)M3/2.

78. Minutes of the FSU fieldwork organisers' meeting, March 6 1964. ULSCA D495(HQ)M3/1.

79. Minutes of the Liverpool PSU committee, April 3 1946; Liverpool PSU report for the month ending August 31 1946. ULSCA D495(LI)M1/5.

80. Younghusband, *Employment and Training of Social Workers*, p45.

81. Younghusband, *Employment and Training of Social Workers*, p51.

82. Younghusband, *Social Work in Britain: 1950–1975*, vol 2, pp20–2; Younghusband, 'Trends in social work education', *Social Work*, 13 (1956), p256.

83. S. Clement Brown and E. Gloyne, *The Field Training of Social Workers* (London, 1966), pp12ff; Younghusband, *Social Work in Britain: 1950–1975*, vol 2, p24. Chambers, 'Professionalism in social work', p360.

84. Barker, 'Eileen Younghusband 1902–1981', p80.

85. Younghusband, *Social Work in Britain: 1950–1975*, vol 1, p204.

86. Younghusband report, para 16.

87. Dame Geraldine Aves's biographer claims that she, Robin Huws Jones (director of the social science course at University College, Swansea), and Younghusband were 'in a kind of private triumvirate during the four years of the working party's existence', although technically, as a civil servant and Head of the Ministry of Health's Welfare Division, Aves was an observer. P. Willmott, *A Singular Woman: The Life of Geraldine Aves, 1898–1986* (London, 1992), p122.

88. Barker, 'Eileen Younghusband 1902–1981', p81.

89. More than 20 years later, the profession was still considering the need to relate theory to practice. J. Hearn, 'The problem(s) of theory and practice in social work and social work education', *Issues in Social Work Education*, 2 (1982), pp95ff; M. Payne, 'Relationships between theory and practice in social work: Educational implications', *Issues in Social Work Education*, 10 (1990), pp3–11.

90. FSU gave evidence to the working party. Minutes of the FSU national personnel and training committee, November 2 1955. ULSCA unlisted.

91. Barker, 'Eileen Younghusband 1902–1981', p81.

92. S. Kay, 'Notes on the FSU training scheme' (1959). ULSCA D495(HQ) M14/3.

93. FSU national secretary's report, May 12 1960 to July 12 1960. ULSCA D495(HQ)M2.

94. Report of the Liverpool FSU executive committee, August 1960. ULSCA D495(LI)M3/2.

95. 'Function of the training officer', no date. ULSCA D495(HQ)M13/3.

96. Minutes of FSU national executive committee, March 16 1960. ULSCA D495(HQ)M2/4.

97. Minutes of the FSU national personnel committee, March 14 1962. ULSCA D495(HQ)M5/10.

98. Minutes of the FSU national executive committee, October 26 1962. ULSCA D495(HQ)M2/5.

99. Minutes of the South London FSU committee, May 14 1963. ULSCA D495(SL)M1/2. Minutes of the FSU national executive committee, May 22 1963. ULSCA D495(HQ)M2.

100. Minutes of the FSU national executive committee, July 24 1963. ULSCA D495(HQ)M2.

101. Minutes of the Liverpool FSU committee, July 31 1966. ULSCA D495 (LI)M2/1.

102. A. F. Philp, report to FSU personnel committee, June 29 1967. ULSCA D495(HQ)M3/14.

103. C. Jones, 'Social work education, 1900–1970', in N. Parry, M. Ruston and C. Satyamurti (eds), Social Work, Welfare and the State (London, 1979), p78.

104. 'Social work should not be entrusted to novices, dilettanti or to quacks...', quoted in Jones, 'Social work education', p77; Z. Butrym, O. Stevenson and R. Harris, 'The role and tasks of social workers', Issues in Social Work Education, 1 (1981), p16.

105. Cited in E. Howarth, 'The present dilemma of social casework', Social Work, 8 (1951), p530.

106. Chambers, 'Professionalism in social work', p360.

107. Younghusband, 'Trends in social work education', p242.

108. Russell et al, Changing Course, pp19ff.

109. Younghusband, 'Trends in social work education', p253; Younghusband, Social Work and Social Change (London, 1964), p20.

110. Younghusband, Social Work in Britain: 1950–1975, vol 2, pp24–5.

111. Younghusband, 'Trends in social work education', pp252ff.

112. York University was the first to introduce a two-year master's course in social work in 1966. Younghusband, Social Work in Britain: 1950–1975, vol 2, pp31 and 32. See also Jones, 'Social work education, 1900–1970', p78.

113. E. Irvine, 'The right to intervene', in E. Irvine (ed.), Social Work and Human Problems (Oxford, 1979), p54. Reprinted from Social Work, 21 (1964); see also Pinker, 'Threat to professional standards', passim.

114. See, for example, R. Bourne, 'What are we training social workers for?', New Society, 54 (1980), pp223–4.

115. J. Packman, The Child's Generation (Oxford, 1981), pp172ff.

116. Younghusband, Social Work in Britain: 1950–1975, vol 2, p67.

117. These were at Birmingham, Bradford, Leicester, Oldham and Sheffield. FSU working party on development, The Development of Family Service Units (London, 1978), p51.

118. FSU working party on development, The Development of Family Service Units, p51.

119. Notes on student training unit, October 1973 to August 1974. ULSCA unlisted.

**120.** D. M. Smith (ed.), *Families and Groups: A unit at work* (London, 1974), preface.

**121.** Minutes of Newcastle FSU committee, January 20 1977. ULSCA D495 (NE)M1; R. Baker, 'Is there a future for integrated practice? Obstacles to its development in practice and education', *Issues in Social Work Education*, 3 (1983), p10.

**122.** Minutes of Oldham FSU committee, April 29 1974. ULSCA D495(OL) M1/1.

**123.** Minutes of the Oldham FSU executive committee, November 25 1976. ULSCA D495(OL)M1/2.

**124.** FSU working party on development, *The Development of FSU*, pp51–2.

**125.** FSU working party on development, *The Development of FSU*, p52.

**126.** FSU working party on development, *The Development of FSU*, pp51 and 53.

**127.** FSU working party on development, *The Development of FSU*, p53.

**128.** Minutes of the FSU national management committee, May 22 1979. ULSCA D495(HQ)M2/6.

**129.** Minutes of the FSU national executive committee, July 20 1966. ULSCA D495(HQ)M2/5.

**130.** Report on student from University of Liverpool on placement with Liverpool FSU in summer 1975. ULSCA D495(HQ)M5/3.

**131.** Reports on students from Lanchester Polytechnic, ULSCA D495(SB)C2/5; Selly Oak Colleges ULSCA D495(SB)C2/1; and Birmingham University on placement at South Birmingham FSU, 1981. ULSCA D495(SB)C2/3.

**132.** Report on student from Westhill College on placement at South Birmingham FSU, October 1981 to June 1982. ULSCA D495(SB)C2/1.

**133.** Payne, 'Relationships between theory and practice', p8.

**134.** Report on student from Croydon College of Design and Technology on placement at Merton FSU, for nine months from summer 1975. ULSCA D495 (ME)C1.

**135.** Report on student from Brunel University on placement at Merton FSU, for nine months from autumn 1975. ULSCA D495(ME)C1.

**136.** M. Barker, 'Through experience towards theory: A psychodynamic contribution to social work education', *Issues in Social Work Education*, 2 (1982), p4.

**137.** Butrym, Stevenson and Harris, 'The role and tasks of social workers', p5; Payne, 'Relationships between theory and practice', pp3ff.

**138.** Reports on students placed at South Birmingham FSU. ULSCA D495 (SB)C2/1-13.

**139.** Report on postgraduate student from Birmingham University on placement at South Birmingham FSU, July to December 1982. ULSCA D495(SB)M4/3.

**140.** Press release from Central Council for Education and Training in Social Work, December 1987.

**141.** Press release from Central Council for Education and Training in Social Work, December 1987.

# 6

# Changing Relationships
# with the State

Even before the Second World War, the increasing part played by the state in the provision of welfare services since the beginning of the twentieth century had led some commentators to foresee the demise of voluntary agencies. For example, in 1937 T. S. Simey claimed that the role of the voluntary sector in social welfare would decrease in importance as the statutory sector assumed a greater prominence. He believed that the voluntary sector had a supplementary function and that it was an unsatisfactory substitute for properly organised public services.[1] His assertion was based on the belief that voluntary societies were unable to provide services on the scale necessary to relieve the social distress that was increasingly evident in the 1930s, in part because they were incapable of securing sufficient funds to pay for the staff and equipment necessary to meet future levels of need. In addition, he believed them to be lacking in professionalism.[2]

Simey's prophecy was only partly accurate. The structural re–organisation which resulted from the introduction of the machinery of the welfare state after 1945 increased the rate at which overall state responsibility for some forms of social welfare was assumed and had some effect on the mix of provision.[3] It did not, however, confirm the suspicions of those who, like Simey and Lady Allen of Hurtwood,[4] believed that British society had outgrown the need for philanthropic activity.[5] In Nicholas Deakin's words, it changed 'the size and shape of the space within which the voluntary sector had to operate',[6] but the picture was not clear-cut. Many modifications to areas of responsibility did not result directly from the formal introduction of the post-1945 measures, nor were some changes as dramatic as has sometimes been assumed.[7] Government intervention in welfare issues, particularly if measured by public expenditure, had grown rapidly during the inter-war years while all sections of the voluntary sector experienced financial difficulty,[8] but in spite of their financial problems and the possibility of a changing relationship with the state, voluntary agencies retained their autonomy. To some extent they were, even if some failed to realise it, in a strong position in relation to the statutory provision of social services and had the explicit support of the new Labour administration. Clement Attlee, whose experience of work within the sector must have given him a particular perspective, argued for the humanising effect of voluntary activity on national life.[9] Herbert Morrison believed that the voluntary spirit was essential to democracy.[10] In his introduction to the *Nuffield Social Reconstruction Survey*, published at the end of the Second World War, G. D. H. Cole dismissed the notion that all social service activities should be taken over by the state.[11] The practical consequences of these attitudes were noted in a 1950 survey of Merseyside which highlighted the reliance of the state on charitable organisations and noted that much of the new welfare legislation was dependent for its implementation on the activities of voluntary societies.[12]

This was not immediately evident, however, and agencies did not shrink from expressing their concern. The Church of England Waifs and Strays Society (later to be renamed the Church of England Children's Society) responded to the report of the Curtis committee published in September 1946[13] by drawing attention to its own long-standing reputation as a provider of assistance to children and families, and seeking to distance itself from those examples of poor-quality child-care uncovered during the committee's investigations. Nevertheless, the fear that the criticisms directed at some children's organisations might come to be associated with all of them and have an adverse effect on the reputation of its own institutional care prompted an anxiety that popular financial support for running its children's homes would dwindle.[14] This concern was compounded by the passing of the 1948 Children Act which resulted in the setting up of local authority children's departments and the appointment of children's officers. The following year, the society commented ruefully that the public was beginning to think that everything to do with children was being absorbed by the state.[15] Other child-care agencies expressed similar anxieties. Dr Barnardo's, one of the giants of residential child-care, believed that the new children's departments posed a real threat to the continuation of its work and expressed the fear that the newly appointed children's officers might interpret their role as one which permitted them to interfere in the running of the society's homes. As a commentator in the late 1950s noted, having been dislodged from its position as a major player in the field of child-care, Dr Barnardo's was forced to recognise that local authorities 'hitherto hardly deserving of the status of colleagues' had suddenly acquired supervisory responsibilities for children in voluntary care[16] – even those in the care of Dr Barnardo's. Other charities found themselves in a similar position, sharing with some medical practitioners with interests in family welfare a 'deep and powerful dislike of the change which has taken place'.[17]

The perception that the state was taking over responsibility for most forms of welfare appears to have been widespread. A survey in 1948 suggested that 99 per cent of those interviewed believed that philanthropy had been made superfluous by the welfare state.[18] In addition, some believed that the potential donor to charitable causes was being deprived of the pleasure of giving by the encroachment of the activities generated by a proactive state and the level of taxation necessary to finance them. An erstwhile supporter of Toynbee Hall, a settlement house in East London, complained to the warden in 1946 that '... a totalitarian government is robbing the individual so that he can no longer enjoy the immense pleasure of supporting beneficent activities of this kind'.[19]

Work with families in difficulty that was frequently undertaken by charitable organisations was symptomatic of the mixed provision of services characteristic of the immediate post-war period. It has been argued that the voluntary sector was believed to be the appropriate vehicle for intervention in family life and for the delivery of services to families.[20] Although reasons of sensibility might have dictated the continued use of the voluntary sector for family work, it was – as the Merseyside survey demonstrated[21] – reasons of finance which helped to ensure that the state was nearly as distant from such a sensitive area of intervention after the post-war developments as it had been in the 1930s. However, the view that the voluntary sector was invariably a more appropriate vehicle than the state to offer support to families was challenged in the 1950s. The National Council of Family Casework Agencies assured members of the Younghusband working party in 1956 that there was no reason why a family caseworking service should not be offered by the local authority,[22] something that Barbara Kahan, as children's officer in Dudley from 1948 to 1951, and later in Oxfordshire, had already begun to demonstrate.[23] The London County Council (LCC), which appointed six caseworkers to work with families using FSU-style methods in 1957, continued the trend.[24] In its 1959 report, the Younghusband committee went further. It highlighted the expansion of local authority services and the improvements in the standard of service they offered; those high standards, Younghusband suggested, which had hitherto been associated with the work of some of the voluntary agencies, were now also to be found among statutory bodies,[25] permitting them to expand their range of provision. As Packman has noted, some local authorities appeared to function very much as voluntary agencies had traditionally done. For example, in the 1950s Oxfordshire children's department:

> ... built up its own store, and persuaded churches, local traders and even its own foster parents to hand on discarded cots and prams, clothing, toys and household goods and even food... to be given to families known to be needy.[26]

Whether it was improvements in local authority standards or the realisation that some statutory authorities were adopting their methods that prompted their anxiety, voluntary organisations continued to fear that the growing range of state services posed a threat to their traditional role.

But those who believed that they were witnessing the demise of voluntary action were mistaken, and instead of commenting on their decline, Eileen Younghusband was to assert confidently in 1951 that voluntary societies were working in an active and healthy partnership in the newly extended social services and that their major troubles sprang from lack of funds rather than from redundancy or from rivalry with the statutory authorities.[27] Her views were supported by those engaged in the work of the voluntary sector. On Merseyside, the Liverpool Council of Social Service argued against what it saw as the mistaken assumption that the need for voluntary agencies would die as public social services grew. It noted that the voluntary sector had traditionally worked within the field of emotional and domestic difficulties, had experimented with a variety of approaches to human problems and that its projects had been characterised by a flexibility of method. Using Liverpool as an example of such varied charitable work it listed child welfare (particularly the prevention of cruelty to children), youth work, family casework and the provision of leisure activities for the aged.[28] It argued that the voluntary sector had an important part to play in protecting the moral fibre of the people from the 'sapping activity of the welfare state'. However, it pointed out that the growing financial difficulties experienced by voluntary organisations posed a serious threat to the delivery of their services.[29] While confirming the voluntary societies in their roles, Younghusband also noted the limitation imposed on their services by the burden of increased taxation, which had the effect of cutting off some of the old sources of charitable giving.[30] A few years later she was to comment on the 'dizzying success and devastating failure' faced by voluntary family casework agencies: success in their methods and vindication for their sometimes controversial techniques, but failure to raise the necessary funds to continue and expand.[31]

These observations would have come as no surprise to FSU. Unlike some other agencies, FSU had not viewed the advent of the welfare state with foreboding. Without the long history of almost autonomous charitable service that characterised other organisations concerned with the family – such as the Charity Organisation Society/Family Welfare Association – or organisations concerned with the care of children in foster homes and residential institutions – such as the Church of England Waifs and Strays Society or National Children's Homes – FSU had no sense that its particular role was to be compromised or its contribution made redundant. On the contrary, its certainty that the sort of intensive family casework it practised was outside the immediate scope of the statutory bodies enabled it confidently to carve out its own space and to anticipate working alongside them. Underlying that confidence was the conviction that the statutory agencies would not, at least in the short term, wish to involve themselves directly with problem families, and that FSU's work in this area would be enhanced, not restricted, by the development of local authority services. This confidence was well judged. Long before it was in a position to set up a national network of units, requests for caseworkers to work with problem families had begun to arrive on the newly appointed national secretary's desk, so that the dilemma facing the organisation was not how to carve out a niche for itself within the welfare state, but how to meet the demand for its services from local authority departments. As the National Assistance Board had noted in 1949, the statutory services were forced to acknowledge their need of the voluntary organisations, particularly so far as work with poor and dysfunctional families was concerned, because the board's officers had neither the time to provide the almost continuous supervision such families were thought to need nor the special skills to effect the education or re-education of parents.[32]

The inability of the statutory services to provide appropriate care and the consequent need for the intervention of voluntary agencies gave FSU considerable freedom of action in its work with seriously disadvantaged families. A measure of autonomy and independence helped to safeguard the commitment to innovation and experiment to which the organisation attached high importance. As it argued in 1954, perhaps unconsciously echoing Lord Beveridge's observation a few years earlier, 'pioneer work can best be done under voluntary auspices. It is the proper function of voluntary organisations.'[33]

If Younghusband's observations about the fear of redundancy resulting from state activity did not apply to FSU, then her comment about the limitations on expansion as a result of inadequate funding certainly did. Like many (perhaps most) other voluntary organisations, its ambitions were perennially hampered by a shortage of money. Lord Balfour's energetic attempts to raise sufficient funds to enable the post-war agency finally to shed its amateur clothes and become a professional organisation took time to come to fruition and failed to meet the expectations that had been raised when plans for the new agency had first been laid. Its new status as a formally constituted organisation meant, among other things, that it had to pay reasonable salaries to the workers. Levels of pay within the voluntary sector generally were known to be less than generous,[34] but FSU's were particularly low and still calculated on the 'pocket money' basis that had governed their payment during the war. The weekly sum paid to workers was only 10s 0d a week in 1945 and the extra funding the organisation needed in order to increase that to a proper level was considerable. Hopes of raising £5,000 in order to put the Manchester and Liverpool units on to a more permanent footing, and to enable the new London unit to open, had not been realised by June 1947, six months after an appeal had been launched. An already difficult situation was compounded by the Chancellor of the Exchequer's decision to limit the tax recoverable from covenants to the standard rate of income tax. An earlier expectation that the money recovered from the covenanted gifts of a small number of wealthy supporters who paid tax at the highest level would benefit FSU to the tune of 19s 6d for every £1 donated was not realised,[35] and this steep drop in anticipated income dealt a severe blow to hopes of a rapid move towards the establishment of a peacetime agency. It was not until the late spring of 1948 that there was sufficient money in the bank to enable the two northern units to take on the mantle of the new organisation and for the new unit to be opened in London.[36]

For a short time small sums from the central funds were given to the branches in order to help them get off the ground; the Manchester and Liverpool units were given £750 each in October 1947, for example,[37] and further monies were passed to all three units in February 1949;[38] but to allow that situation to continue for too long would have run counter to the underlying philosophy of the agency, which was committed to a local base with each unit forming an integral part of its local social services, and being financed by local interests. Moreover, prolonged support from London would have been impossible; the national organisation had very little in its own bank account which, by November 1949, stood at just £320 9s 1d.[39]

The acknowledgement by some local authorities that the agency could make a valuable contribution to post-war reconstruction led some of them to agree to fund FSU's activities in their areas. Oldham Corporation, for example, found the money to pay for a problem family worker, seconded from the Manchester unit, in July 1949.[40] Over the next decade, in cities such as Manchester and Sheffield where units had already been established, children's officers facilitated the award of grants to FSU to encourage intensive work with families or to enable the organisation to expand into new districts.[41] However, there were mixed feelings within the organisation about the wisdom and the practicality of relying too heavily on funds from statutory authorities, and a strong sense that such funds would never be adequate. By the mid-1950s, the recognition that the service would need financial support from a variety of sources in order to survive led the Liverpool unit to aver that a voluntary society could not rely wholly on grants from the state or trust funds, and that individual subscribers were badly needed.[42]

While the importance of individual generosity was acknowledged, FSU also recognised that many potential individual subscribers were unlikely to be able – or even to wish – to finance the sort of expansion which seemed necessary. The plight of neglected or ill-treated children could be relied upon to excite sympathy and encourage donations, as the child rescue charities had demonstrated for more than a hundred years, but poorly organised families were unlikely to have the same appeal. As Lord Beveridge had pointed out, 'The general public are apt to regard family misfortunes as the fault of the people who suffer them, and not a case for charitable giving'.[43] Local authorities, therefore, were among the most obvious targets for appeals for funds, because they had already shown themselves to be in need of the services that FSU could provide. Furthermore, the organisation's confidence in the value of what it could offer to local authorities was underlined by the sense that preventive work with families would save money for the state. Unlike the NSPCC, which in the 1940s believed that neglectful parents should be prosecuted, or many children's departments that dealt with families at crisis point,[44] FSU's approach of trying to work with the family, and enabling parents and children to remain together by raising standards of housewifery and child-care, was cheaper than institutional care; but it could not be provided free. If workers such as those employed by FSU helped families to function, even if at a fairly low level, and to keep parents and children together, considerable sums of public money which might have been expended on caring for those children in foster homes or institutions would be saved. The argument that some of that money should be diverted to FSU seemed incontrovertible.[45]

On the other hand, there was a degree of ambivalence about FSU's position within social service provision. In 1958, Arthur Collis, one of FSU's supporters and himself an ex-PSU worker, highlighted the dangers of too great a dependence on grants from local authorities. He foresaw demands for results and 'startling improvements' on the part of funders which might be impossible to achieve, even after a long period of casework with some families.[46] Although such demands appear not to have been made in the early days of FSU, the expectation that local authorities should be rewarded for their generosity by visible improvements in the lifestyles of those families for whom they were funding services was not too far ahead. In the 1950s, however, units such as those in Manchester and Oldham benefited considerably from the generosity of their local authorities and appeared unaware of the dangers that increasing dependence on a single source of income might bring. Other units experienced chronic financial difficulty. For example, in spite of energetic fund-raising and some local authority grants, the Liverpool unit found itself in a poor financial state in October 1953 with just enough money in the bank to last until the end of the year;[47] things were little better the following year.[48] In 1957, the city council requested government permission to increase its grant to FSU.[49] In February 1960, the unit had enough money to keep going until June,[50] but the possibility of running out of funds was always just around the corner.[51]

Liverpool was not alone. Founded in 1953 with a grant from the City Parochial Foundation,[52] the Islington unit moved quickly into debt and lived a precarious hand-to-mouth existence at least for its first three years. In November 1954 and February 1955 it appealed to the national committee for financial aid, noting that not only did it have insufficient funds for its day-to-day expenses and its salary bill, but that lack of money also meant that its resident workers did not have enough meat and fresh fruit in their diet to keep them healthy.[53] By the mid-sixties the anxiety that the unit might not survive had subsided, but by then it had become heavily dependent on grants from Islington Borough Council and the LCC children's committee, and seemed nervously aware of the need to enlarge its sources of income.[54]

Islington's experience reflected the general situation. The proportion of FSU income which came from local authority grants, while covering the entire costs of only a few units, increased steadily. The LCC grant to the Kensington and Paddington unit in 1952 was £200, just under 10 per cent of its total annual expenditure of £2,090. In 1962, local authority monies accounted for more than 60 per cent of the unit's income; out of a total of £10,163, the LCC gave £4,540 and the combined grants from the Middlesex County Council and the London boroughs of Kensington, Paddington and Willesden added a further £1,650. Although the unit differentiated between regular subscriptions and occasional donations and noted that subscriptions accounted for only 10 per cent of the total income, in the 1950s and 1960s there seemed to be no sense that too great a dependence on one source of finance might hold dangers for the organisation. Changes began to take place during the next ten years. By 1978 the unit (now renamed the West London unit) claimed that it received the smallest state support in the organisation, with 55 per cent of its annual income coming from a variety of local authority and government grants, including the Urban Aid Fund and money from the Job Creation Programme.[55] The situation in the Kensington and Paddington unit was not unusual. Camden unit, whose annual budget in 1974 was £23,351, received £19,374 from the local council, earned £1,641 in training fees and received only £4,228 in subscriptions and donations.[56] By 1978 its income pattern had altered so that it received only 57 per cent of its annual funds of £38,111 from state sources, had increased its private income to 13 per cent and had secured a European Economic Community grant equivalent to 18 per cent of its income.[57]

Some local authorities considered grants paid to FSU to be money well spent. In 1965, Manchester children's department reviewed and expanded its grants to voluntary bodies and approved the decision to allocate the largest amounts to FSU and the NSPCC, seeing them as agencies closely involved with families whose children were in danger of going into care.[58] However, not all local authorities saw FSU's activities in this light. In 1969, a report from the Islington children's department suggested that FSU's attempts to raise funds to support a traditional family casework service were misdirected, because local authorities were increasingly providing such a service themselves. Instead, it argued, FSU should justify its existence by devoting more of its resources to experimentation and to pioneering new ways of working with poor families.[59]

Units' levels of financial support varied considerably. In a review of FSU's first decade the Liverpool unit had noted that in 1958 all units received some assistance from their local authorities and two had all their costs met by the cities in which they worked.[60] Bristol FSU was one of those units which enjoyed total local authority funding. From its inception, it had been organised differently from the others. The deputy MOH, Dr R. C. Wofinden, had maintained a long-held interest in problem families and had contributed colourful correspondence to medical and public health literature on the subject since his time in the department of public health at Rotherham.[61] Under the Bristol Corporation Act 1950, the local authority was granted power to establish a rehabilitation service for what were euphemistically termed 'special families' and, if necessary, to delegate this work to a voluntary agency.[62] It was under the provisions of this regulation that the health committee approached FSU in 1952 with the suggestion that a unit might be established in the Southmead area of the city. By the end of the year, an agreement had been reached with the national organisation, even though it ran counter to FSU's normal practice which insisted that a local committee, carrying considerable responsibility, was essential. The Bristol health committee wanted to bypass any such local management and to liaise directly with FSU national office. Instead of working through its own local management committee, the Bristol unit was to be responsible to a sub-committee of the Bristol department of public health.[63] Bristol FSU thereby became an agent of the department in 1953, reporting to the MOH alongside such unambiguously statutory officials as the Port Health Services Officer and the Public Analyst.

On the face of it, the unit had found itself an almost invulnerable position, firmly ensconced within the Bristol department of public health. The security, as it was perceived, of total local authority funding was short-lived, however, and the Bristol unit's financial dependency was an important factor in its closure in 1967.[64]

The reasons for the withdrawal of funds from Bristol FSU are complex. By the early 1960s, the local authority children's department was already beginning to lay claim to some of the work which had previously been done by the department of public health, and the two had begun to cooperate on some projects. For example, in 1959 they combined in the provision of home helps to look after children 'temporarily deprived of maternal care or that of a female guardian'.[65] In 1963, the passage of the Children and Young Persons Act provided the Bristol children's department with an opportunity to expand its work with problem families, hitherto the responsibility of the department of public health. The Act gave local authorities power to practise preventive social work primarily in order to reduce the numbers of children being taken into care or brought before juvenile courts.[66] The alacrity with which the children's department acted may indicate that it had just been waiting for the starting pistol. It had already anticipated the provisions of the Act by setting up a number of family advice centres around the city,[67] and within one month of the Act's implementation the children's committee reported the creation of four additional child-care officer posts and the decision that the numbers of family caseworkers would be reviewed after 12 months.[68]

In March the following year, representatives of the public health, children's, housing and welfare services committees met to discuss the implications of the new Act. Their joint recommendations resulted in the transfer of all family casework to the children's department, with the children's officer replacing the MOH as the coordinating officer. Adjustments reflecting the new arrangements were also to be made in the functioning of the area case committees, hitherto the forum for inter-departmental discussion. FSU was to continue as agent of the Bristol department of public health.[69]

Quite what was meant by that final recommendation is hard to know. The public health department had agreed to hand the problem families on its books to the Bristol children's department, so what was to be the role of FSU as an agent of the former, responsible for problem families in Southmead? A letter from FSU's national secretary in 1966 demonstrates the effect of that recommendation on FSU and the extent to which the local interpretation of the 1963 Act restricted the organisation's area of activity. Under the new arrangements, any families known to have had contact with either the children's department or the 'special families' health visitors – and many, if not most, families had originally been referred to FSU through such statutory channels – had to be referred back to those services and were not to be added to FSU's caseload,[70] which was considerably reduced as a consequence. In his day book for 1963, the fieldwork organiser Alf Strange noted the increase in the number of children's department social workers in the Southmead area, and the corresponding decrease in referrals to FSU.[71] The department had elected to employ its own staff to do preventive work with families, even though the Act empowered it to use the services of voluntary organisations. This raises questions about why – given that FSU had been established in the area for ten years and believed that it enjoyed substantial local support – the children's officer chose to use her own social workers to operate in Southmead rather than leaving FSU to work there while she built up operations in other parts of Bristol.

One reason may be found in FSU's style of working. Caseloads were deliberately kept very low in order to work intensively with particularly needy families, but the health visitors who were doing similar work and had always been Bristol's key practitioners in this area carried much larger caseloads. In 1957 FSU, which had three workers, was actively involved with a total of 52 families (in some years it was fewer); by contrast, the three health visitors doing problem family work had caseloads of approximately 50 families each.[72] The unequal loads must have caused reflection if not resentment. Even if it was argued that FSU took responsibility for the more difficult families, its concentration on one small geographical area makes that unlikely. Later criticisms of some FSU social workers by their local authority counterparts were to focus on the relative sizes of caseloads,[73] and the fear that a few families referred to FSU received preferential treatment at the expense of many others with similar problems; Bristol may well have been experiencing an early version of this unease.

There is also evidence that the unit had its own internal difficulties. The workers lived together in one small house and were on call for long periods of time. They ate together; the fieldwork organiser's wife even cooked for them all in the early days, although she gave this up in 1958. Such close association between work and home resulted in tensions which were exacerbated by problems concerning gender, with the fieldwork organiser experiencing difficulty in managing his female caseworkers. Early in the unit's life Alf Strange had written to the national secretary attributing responsibility for the strains in the unit to his 'inadequacy with the opposite sex', which he believed was 'something to do with the folly of the emancipation of women and the correlation of the latter with duodenal ulcers'.[74] Subsequent correspondence suggests a continued state of tension between Strange, his wife and the caseworkers. The local authority records give no clue, but the FSU archive, much richer in everyday information, paints a picture of a depressed and dysfunctional community.

Internal management was not the only problem. The local authority must have been conscious that the unit's style of work made it vulnerable to criticism. Bristol FSU had locked itself into a 1940s model of practice. Other units had begun to abandon the requirement that all workers should be resident and constantly available. Some other units were actively challenging tradition and changing their practice in the light of new theories and a rapidly evolving sense of professional identity among social workers. The Bristol unit retained a style of life and functioning which had worked well in wartime but was becoming increasingly inappropriate in the late 1950s and 1960s. In some aspects of its work tensions had developed between the unit and the department of public health. For example, in cases of child neglect, especially where the NSPCC had become involved, there were clearly differences of opinion about where responsibility should lie, and anxieties about the dangers posed to the unit's relationships with families should they become involved in any prosecution and be expected to appear in court against their clients.[75] Other units must have faced similar problems, but the Bristol unit appeared unable to resolve the tensions inherent in its position as both an agent of a statutory authority and a friend of the family. Incidentally, it also demonstrated an almost unavoidable danger in the FSU approach. A stress on the importance of keeping parents and children together and on the need to support parents in their role could lead to a failure to appreciate adequately the needs of children in difficult or potentially dangerous situations.

The local authority had also questioned the narrow geographical boundaries of the unit's work. Earlier in its history Canon Mervyn

Stockwood, chair of the health committee, had tried to persuade the unit to accept referrals from other parts of the city; and in 1960 Dr Sarah Walker, the Medical Officer of the maternity and children's sub-committee to which the unit was directly responsible, had questioned the future of FSU's work in Southmead, even suggesting that there might be other areas of the city where the need was greater.[76] However, such suggestions were successfully resisted and the narrowly local emphasis of the work was retained.

Faced with an organisation which appeared to be inflexible, the children's department's decision to use its own child-care officers to visit families who would formerly have been referred to FSU is understandable. So is that of the Bristol department of public health which, a year or so later, declined to provide £5,000 a year any longer for a style of work which had appeared to be limited and outdated.[77] Both the children's and the public health departments drew attention to the increased powers made available to the local authority as a result of the 1963 Act – although, given the terms of the Bristol Corporation Act under which FSU had been invited in the first place, it is questionable whether the increase was as large as all that. The 1950 Act had empowered the city to establish a rehabilitation service for families, and if necessary to delegate this work to a voluntary agency;[78] the relevant provisions of the 1963 Act were not so different. The new legislation may simply have provided a convenient excuse for a difficult course of action. Officers of the departments concerned, like one of the MOHs seven years earlier, also commented on the illogicality of continuing a service like that offered by FSU in just one district of a large city.[79]

In 1965, the Bristol department of public health began to use other – presumably cheaper – welfare assistants to do much of the work previously done by FSU, such as visiting families and helping women with domestic tasks and budgeting.[80] As the unit had lost its role and had neither a local management committee to support it nor any machinery for fund-raising, it was forced to close when the Bristol department of public health finally withdrew its funding at the end of 1966. Whatever its short-term advantages, then, the relationship with the Bristol MOH and his department resulted in unwelcome consequences.

Within FSU, the Bristol unit's experience was unusual. The factor which precipitated its closure – the Children and Young Persons Act of 1963 – was given a mixed reception in the organisation as a whole.

Some observations had been anticipated by witness statements to the Younghusband committee which reported in 1959, and are indicative of the tensions between the statutory and voluntary sectors, especially when practice once seen as innovative and the prerogative of voluntary agencies became mainstream and was taken over by the state. In such a situation, the committee believed that it detected a reluctance on the part of voluntary agencies to relinquish responsibility.[81] No such reluctance coloured the Kensington and Paddington unit's response to the new legislation. It welcomed the prospect of more preventive work with families.[82] Other units believed that the Act held a threat to the organisation, in spite of its emphasis on prevention which, it might be argued, vindicated the agency's approach. On one hand, by giving local children's departments responsibility for performing the sort of work hitherto done by organisations like FSU it called into question the possible viability of units in some areas. On the other, it carried the possibility of overload. Were children's departments to avail themselves of the provision in the Act for close cooperation between statutory and voluntary organisations, and to refer preventive work with families to bodies like FSU, the latter might be required to review its policy of small caseloads and intensive care. Should that be the case, there might be a reduction in the distinctive contribution that FSU could make.[83] In addition, an increased demand for its services could have a serious effect on FSU's finance and personnel. As the Act came into operation, however, discussion at the fieldwork organisers' committee in September 1965 revealed varied patterns of referrals from children's departments, some of them of long standing and all reflecting the range of attitudes and approaches to be found in local authority departments. For example the Bradford unit, which like Bristol enjoyed a close relationship with the local department of public health, had little contact with the local children's department. While its funding arrangements continued, it expected little contact with the children's department. The Leeds unit, which worked closely with the local welfare department, similarly expected few referrals from the children's officer. The Birmingham unit, on the other hand, was in receipt of an increased local authority grant to enable it to provide a family casework service to some parts of the city because the enlarged children's department was still unable to cope with the demands being made on it. The London units all accepted significant numbers of referrals from their local children's departments,[84] and some noted an increase.[85] Other local situations revealed good relations with children's departments and locally determined arrangements for referral.[86] Liverpool City Council appointed four social workers to undertake preventive work with families thought to be at risk of eviction, and seconded them to FSU for training.[87] By 1967, the whole of Islington FSU's local authority grant came from the children's department.[88] In spite of the anxiety generated by the passing of the 1963 Act, FSU continued to be able to make its own distinctive contribution and fears of its demise proved to be unfounded.

Nevertheless, some consequences of the Act did not disappear. Uncertainty about their role was just one problem faced by units during the 1960s. Shortage of suitable personnel was another crucial factor in FSU's inability to expand or even maintain its current strength. Although a surprisingly large number of wartime members of the PSUs had opted to stay in the new organisation after 1948, many had gone back to their peacetime occupations. Those who remained had been spread rather thinly around the Liverpool, Manchester, and Kensington and Paddington units, and new units as they came along. Recruits came forward in considerable numbers, but they needed to be trained. The training, which was done under the supervision of more experienced caseworkers, was short – generally no more than six months – but even so it was impossible to match supply with demand. An already difficult situation was made worse as a result of the 1963 Act. The national secretary Fred Philp drew attention to the hunger for staff of the newly enlarged children's departments in his report to the personnel committee in June 1967.[89] To Philp's mind, the threat to FSU's traditional way of working posed by this expansion involved more than the competition for good workers; it also reflected the development of a profession of which FSU had believed itself to be a leading practitioner. An increase in the preventive work done by local authorities threatened to displace FSU. As he explained in a letter to Sir Donald Allen, Clerk to the Trustees of the City Parochial Foundation, creative original development might in the future be more difficult.[90] Moreover, Philp believed that it would not be not possible to attract better people to FSU unless salaries were competitive. It was a point that he had made before[91] and it helped to underline his fear that FSU was already beginning to fail to attract the most promising students and suggests that he foresaw considerable change ahead.

Although a particular application of the provisions of the 1963 Act and its own internal difficulties together contributed to the Bristol unit's failure, a fundamental reason for its weakness in relation to the local authority was its financial dependence. Glasgow FSU, another unit which received 100 per cent of its funding from the local authority, experienced a similarly sudden end to its activities. Founded in 1965 and situated on a large local authority housing scheme in the Castlemilk area of the city, it had a very general threefold remit: advice, assistance and work with families.[92] Within a decade its work was threatened by increased activity on the part of both the statutory authorities and another voluntary agency. When a local authority area social work team moved to Castlemilk in 1976, and was followed by a branch of the Citizens' Advice Bureaux, most of the unit's work seemed to have been taken over by other agencies. Although threatened, it believed that it could identify a number of areas of work in which it could expand local provision,[93] but in spite of public acknowledgement of the contribution that FSU had made to a deprived area by the director of social work for Strathclyde Regional Council, the unit's grant was withdrawn and its work ceased.[94] Like the Bristol unit, Glasgow had suffered its fair share of internal difficulties and uncertain leadership. At base, though, the reasons for closure in both cases appear to include a reduction in the confidence of the local authority in the work of the unit, a denial that FSU had a monopoly on any special skills or mystique, and the consequent withdrawal of financial support. As the deputy director of social services for Glasgow had commented:

> We in the social work department can do the FSU job if we can get the right type of workers. Our area teams could do it. There would have to be an element of specialisation within the team and we would have to find people with an aptitude for working with intensive casework families.[95]

Tensions between FSU and their local authority funders characterised relationships at Bishop Auckland, too. The initial approach to FSU had been made by the housing manager of the Bishop Auckland Urban District Council in the mid-1960s. At first, FSU was unable to respond. During the following five years a small group of local people – councillors, teachers and local clergy – began to meet regularly to discuss the problems of one particular estate. As a result, discussions about the possibility of a unit being opened in the area took place with both the national director and the unit organiser of the Newcastle FSU. The unit eventually opened in 1973. Funding for the venture was agreed on a block grant basis, 75 per cent being met from the local authority funds and the balance provided by FSU. No long-term funding strategy was formalised, although it was understood by FSU that the local authorities would gradually assume the total funding of the agency.[96] In the event, after a period characterised by a strained relationship with the local council, particularly about differences in methods of work with families whose children were suspected of suffering non-accidental injury, the grant was withdrawn. As it had no other substantial sources of income, the unit was forced to close in 1979.[97]

The loss of local authority approval was not the only danger to the future of those units which were almost entirely dependent on local authority funding. Reorganisation of services and the redrawing of boundaries created anxiety in those units affected. From 1962, as a consequence of the changes brought about by the implementation of the Greater London Plan, the South London unit which had hitherto been partly funded by the LCC had to begin to work with the London boroughs of Lambeth and Southwark, Bermondsey and Camberwell.[98] The prospect led to a resolve to augment its income from statutory authorities with other sources,[99] and thereby to gain a degree of independence and increased security. Concern that FSU's future might be at stake was not altogether unfounded. A Lambeth councillor on the South London FSU committee suggested in 1964 that consideration be given to the possibility of the unit coming entirely under the control of the local authority.[100] Four months later discussion centred round the difficulties local authorities were facing in the task of finding the most effective ways of organising welfare services and noted that, while some would like to provide the services themselves, others found it expedient to make use of the expertise of organisations such as FSU. The FSU committee bolstered its confidence in the future by clinging to the conviction that it was almost impossible for local authorities to carry out the amount of work that was required, and suggested that for at least the following year they were likely to continue to use local voluntary organisations; but questions were raised about the possible effects on FSU's independence. One Lambeth councillor had made it clear that his authority would expect substantial representation on the management committee if it allocated financial resources to the unit,[101] thus signalling a wish for increased accountability from FSU and greater statutory control of voluntary activity in general. That the local council allocated £15,000 to support a range of voluntary organisations in the borough just a few weeks later suggests that the councillor may have had ambitions which his authority was unable to realise and that its own resources were unequal to the demands being made on its services.[102]

With the exception of Bristol all units were managed locally. The appointment of local committees charged with the overall responsibility for their units and with raising the necessary funds for the work to continue was intended to reinforce the ties between each unit and its locality. In some cases the committee was dominated by local authority representatives, both elected members and officers. The Bradford unit, founded in 1953, was a case in point. It originated as a result of the initiative of the Bradford public health department,[103] was later transferred to the supervision of the Bradford children's department and, like the unit in Bristol, received 100 per cent of its funding from the local authority. Unlike Bristol, though, it was managed by a local committee to which, after 1963, the City of Bradford children's officer acted as secretary.[104] Although the Bradford FSU committee was characterised by a weighty local authority representation, it was still officially independent of it. In other units the membership was more varied, and included representatives of religious groups, local colleges and universities, and other agencies – both voluntary and statutory – with an interest in the welfare of the family.

Local units also became involved in cooperating with projects and initiatives organised by local authorities. During the 1960s officers of the Manchester children's department were keen to coordinate the work of voluntary bodies in Manchester. The children's officer took the initiative in forming a coordinating committee made up of representatives of his own department as well as those from the welfare, education, health and housing departments; the Catholic Rescue Society, the NSPCC, and FSU were also invited to join the committee. With mechanisms for improved communication, such as area case conferences about 'at risk' families, it was believed that the organisation of more effective delivery of services would be achieved.[105]

Such experiments in cooperation resulted from one of the concerns of the 1960s, which was that of discovering the most effective way to deliver a range of services to meet the needs of families and their individual members while avoiding duplication of effort and organisation. Consideration of how best to manage the personal social services resulted in the setting up of the Committee on Local Authority and Allied Personal Social Services in England and Wales under the chairmanship of Sir Frederick Seebohm. The committee reported in July 1968, and recommended the creation of unified social service departments.[106] As a result, the Local Authority Social Services Bill began an eventful journey through Parliament – interrupted by a General Election – in February 1970. The incoming Conservative government adopted the central recommendations of the Seebohm committee, and by October 1971 the DHSS had taken over responsibility for children's departments from the Home Office, thus unifying central government responsibility for the personal social services.[107] It also assumed responsibility for encouraging the provision of services which would be family-centred, community-based and contain a preventive element. Indirectly, it assumed support for the voluntary sector and, as Jeremy Kendall and Martin Knapp have pointed out, many local authorities did increase their financial contributions. The position was uneven though; some traditional metropolitan Labour-controlled authorities remained suspicious of the voluntary sector while some Conservative authorities expected it to pay for itself.[108]

The publication of the Seebohm report and the implementation of the 1971 Local Authority (Social Services) reorganisation exposed both the insecurity of FSU's position in many areas, and the fragility of its relationships with some local authorities. The FSU fieldwork organisers, when discussing relationships with local authorities in anticipation of the publication of the Seebohm report, noted that Tower Hamlets authority planned to take over all voluntary agencies.[109] Their fears may not have been unfounded. Tower Hamlets council had long entertained reservations about the value of voluntary agencies and at the annual general meeting of the East London Family Service Unit in 1970 it was clear that these were shared by some of its employees. A local authority social worker challenged the unit staff either to resign and to earn more in local authority employment, or to delineate a plan for sub-contracting work from the local authority. The only justification for the unit's existence, he argued, lay in its ability to supply services not already provided by the local authority; it could no longer rely on a 'benevolent statutory service to continue to hand over money to keep it going'.[110] As in the case of the fears expressed about some of the implications of the 1963 Act, things turned out differently. In 1978, the annual report of the East London unit recorded the fact that most of its referrals came from social service departments – a considerable change from 1969, when it had been noted that the borough had a policy of not referring any cases to voluntary organisations and when the grant to the unit had been cut by £3,000.[111] In spite of the resources of the local social services department – a large local authority social work team, family advice centre, and youth facilities – which had encouraged a social worker to warn FSU of its impending demise eight years earlier, the unit was still thriving and providing a local service. What is more, local and central government grants accounted for most of the unit's income: £39,489 of a total of £49,785.[112] The situation in East London is illustrative of the more general position noted by the Wolfenden committee in the late 1970s; tight controls on their expenditure had led to an alteration in attitude among some local authority social services departments and a disdainful view of the role of the voluntary sector had faded, to be replaced by a more welcoming attitude.[113]

In Oldham, the basis on which the local authority grant had been calculated had long been a cause of anxiety; the unit firmly believed that the grant should be tied to the wages bill – as was the case in East London from 1973 for example[114] – in order to keep FSU salaries in line with local authority ones. FSU workers' pay had consistently lagged behind because it had proved impossible to attract money from voluntary sources sufficient to fill the gap between the unit's local authority grant and the proceeds from independent fund-raising.[115] The reorganisation of local authority social services in Oldham gave rise to some alarm. The director of social services recognised the role currently being played by FSU and made it clear that he saw the unit operating in two main ways in the future, as a demonstration unit in casework skills and as an agency which devoted its energies to solving difficult and often intractable family problems;[116] but he declined to increase its funding. While the designation of the task suited the local unit's rather conservative approach, the director's comments did nothing to alleviate the long-term problem of what the unit perceived to be inadequate financial support. By 1975, the FSU committee was trying to think of other ways of making the agency more attractive to the local authority.[117] Oldham social services department was not tempted by any of its suggestions. Its own financial position was so precarious that it gave the unit only £10,000 of its £15,000-plus costs, and the unit was forced to make one worker redundant.[118] From the local authority's point of view the rationale must have been clear; with 27 of its own posts frozen because of acute difficulties in local authority funding, it could hardly have been expected to give priority to a voluntary organisation. The unit, however, thought otherwise and compared its position unfavourably with units in other towns; by that measure, it argued, the grant from Oldham Metropolitan Borough Council to its local unit was much lower than that given to other units by their local authorities.[119]

Had it been looking towards the north east, Oldham FSU would have found confirmation of its argument. In 1973, the Newcastle unit, too, was short of funds and believed its future to be in jeopardy.[120] The local authority came to the rescue and awarded a grant of £16,500 for its activities the following year: one of the largest grants hitherto given by a local authority to any unit.[121] However, there was price to pay; the social services department in Newcastle believed that the unit should increase its workload, while the unit believed that it was vital for the number of families on the books to be kept low.[122] Two years later, local authority representatives argued that the money given to FSU could be better spent on the council's own services. Although FSU believed this to be the view of only a minority of councillors, it recognised that greater care needed to be taken in relationships with the local authority and that the unit had to demonstrate that its approach was cost-effective.[123]

Newcastle was not alone in having to reconsider the extent to which it was accountable for the way in which local authority grants were spent. Units had increasingly to justify their expenditure as local authorities found themselves short of money and became aware of savings which could be made were they to divert money hitherto given to the voluntary sector, and to make increased use of the resources of their own social services departments. Clearer guidance was sometimes given to units about the work that was to be done in return for a grant from the local authority, and in some areas units anticipated greater control over their activities. The West London unit, for example, feared considerable change once the Seebohm recommendations had been implemented and questions were raised about the future role of the organisation, but its anxieties were without foundation in the short term. Although the unit argued that 'FSU does not wish to continue beyond the point of useful service',[124] the new social services department clearly did not believe that point to have been reached, although it did set out to manage FSU's contribution by requesting that it maintain its concentration on families who needed long-term help. It stressed the needs of young, unmarried mothers, young couples with acute housing problems, those who were homeless and those whose relationships were threatened by the pressures they were experiencing, and it suggested that these groups were candidates for FSU's help.[125] The department also appears to have expected that the unit would concentrate its work and resources on a smaller geographical area than had hitherto been the case.[126] In Rochdale, where the local authority provided 100 per cent of the unit's funds, the director of social services claimed to appreciate the versatility of FSU's ways of working. Although he argued that it was difficult to quantify the value of its work, he believed that as many as 28 children from 23 families had been kept out of local authority care as a result of FSU's activities.[127]

Local authorities, strapped for cash in the 1970s following the oil price shock of 1973 and the acute national financial problems which resulted from the International Monetary Fund's imposition of cuts in public expenditure in 1976, could be forgiven for resisting any attempt to draw them into the internal competition about levels of funding which increasingly characterised aspects of inter-unit discussion within FSU. A crucial part of the relationship between the local authorities and local units was, of course, the question of whether the local authority got value for money. Perhaps especially after the 1971 local government reorganisation, and the later reductions in local government expenditure, comparisons were made between the statutory and voluntary sectors, particularly in relation to the relative sizes of their social work caseloads. This was no new problem. FSU's caseloads, while considerably smaller than local authority ones, were also smaller than those of comparable agencies, a situation which has led at least one commentator to refer to FSU as a 'luxury service'.[128] When they were making plans for the Combined Casework Unit in Hackney in the early 1960s, it became clear that the Family Welfare Association, although providing similar services, expected its social workers to carry loads of about 25 to 30 cases, while FSU's workers had caseloads of between 12 and 18.[129] In 1977, acknowledging with gratitude FSU's ability to regulate the size of its caseloads, Ruth Popplestone (an assistant director of FSU) argued the organisation's case and claimed that, particularly in cases of non-accidental injury to children, limited loads and minimal administration were essential to allow the worker to get on with the essential work without distraction.[130] However, Popplestone did not address the frequently voiced complaint that intensive care for a small number of families was being bought by some local authorities from FSU at the expense of less care for a large number of equally needy ones. In 1978 the national organisation recognised the possibility that low caseloads could bring unwanted critical attention to a unit's activities and urged that funding authorities should be made aware of the wide range of services frequently offered by units in addition to face-to-face casework.[131] Although units ran clubs, used the unit house as a meeting place for an assortment of groups, and involved themselves in a wide variety of group work projects and community activities, the time-consuming casework methods which were still its trademark resulted in FSU coming under scrutiny even from its own workers. At least one unit felt itself under pressure to demonstrate value for money, especially when its local authority produced a prioritised list of agencies to which financial help was to be given, and FSU found itself towards the bottom. As a result, methods of work were changed and the throughput of clients increased.[132]

Disquiet was also expressed about what was perceived to be FSU's practice of reserving the right to choose the clients with whom it worked. Although it appears that in the 1940s and 1950s many local government departments had referred to FSU those families for whom they felt unable to do any more, in later years the position may have been reversed and some local authority social workers began to resent what they saw as FSU's practice of leaving the most difficult cases on the books of the local authority. The FSU working party on development, however, noted in 1978 that the timing of and rationale for referrals seemed to depend as much 'on expediency for the referring agency as on the family's needs or the appropriateness of the units' services', thus suggesting that FSU had much less agency in the process than was popularly believed.[133]

After the mid-1970s there was agreement across the political spectrum on the desirability of the expansion of the voluntary sector in the personal social services and some alleviation in their financial plight. Evidence to the members of the Wolfenden Committee on Voluntary Organisations suggested that many local authority departments were unable to provide either long-term support or short-term intensive care to families with multiple problems and that many were prepared to finance FSU to meet the need.[134] The traditional strengths of the voluntary sector had been its flexibility and its ability to innovate and experiment. In the early 1960s commentators had begun to note the increasing importance attached to the statutory social services and to comment that

> Social imagination is the true function of voluntary organisations. In time, responsibility for that which they have pioneered may be taken over by the public authorities and become universal. If the voluntary organisation goes on being able to see new needs and to devise effective remedies it lives: if not, it dies.[135]

The Seebohm report of 1968 had urged that social service departments should play:

> ... an important part in giving support, both financial and professional to vigorous, outward-looking voluntary organisations which can demonstrate good standards of service, provide opportunities for appropriate training for their workers, both professional and voluntary, and show a flair for innovation.[136]

But innovative activity is difficult to sustain. As the Wolfenden report of 1978 pointed out, most voluntary organisations begin their lives as the pioneers of some service or other and subsequently become providers of that service in a more routine way. 'It is an interesting question how far voluntary organisations continue to act in a pioneering way, once their opening phase is over.'[137] The director of social services in Sheffield at the beginning of the 1970s certainly believed that he could see the process of moving from innovation to routine in the local unit. He noted that FSU had originally justified its existence by its experimental, pioneering work, but that the local unit had not changed during the pervious decade and needed to find a new role:

> It's time for them to re-think their role... FSU was the pioneer of intensive casework, but now they have succeeded. Intensive casework is accepted. Local authorities are going to say: 'If we're to pay for another caseworker, we're going to employ him ourselves.' And they will be right. FSU must find something else to pioneer and experiment with. It's the function of voluntary bodies to try new things, not to go on doing what they've always done for years past.[138]

For its part, FSU feared that some local authorities understood neither the nature of the innovative process[139] nor its potential to threaten relationships between units and local authorities, many of whom placed a very high priority on conformity with their procedures, particularly in areas in which unit activities overlapped with local authority responsibility.[140] As value for money became an increasing concern of the major funders (in FSU's cases the local authorities), evidence of money well spent was frequently sought and had the potential to limit genuine experiment by its expectation that success was guaranteed.[141] By the late 1970s some local authorities were steering FSU into more routine work and entering into contracts with local units which required that certain work be done in particular places if the unit wished to qualify for financial assistance. In those cases where the unit was heavily dependent on the local authority, freedom for manoeuvre was seriously curtailed; but this position reflected the reality of the relationship. As Nicholas Hinton of the National Council for Social Service pointed out in 1978, the Voluntary Service Unit at the Home Office had stated that the primary determinant in terms of criteria for funding must be that the organisation is working to a policy which is in accordance with the department's own policy.[142] Too close a correspondence between local authority expectations and voluntary willingness to accede to them could result in the erosion of the voluntary sector's ability to question or criticise the status quo,[143] especially if it were thought that the next year's grant might be at risk. In an ideal world, Hinton argued, the combination of constructive criticism in the development of policy, discussion of differing ways of tackling problems, and a considered approach to the question of which services would be best provided by statutory organisations and which by voluntary, could benefit service provision.[144]

The FSU working party on development noted the difficulties attendant upon expecting local authorities to fund innovative work. The nature of innovation necessarily involved the risk that a good new idea might turn out to be impracticable. Local authorities, themselves operating within tight budgets, were understandably keen to steer clear of funding projects which appeared to carry a high risk of failure. The FSU working party's suggestion that central government funding might usefully be sought, although illustrated with some suggestions, did not seem much more realistic. Nevertheless there was a belief in FSU circles that, as in the earliest days of its history, FSU practice should be one step ahead of the statutory authorities.[145] Moreover, its central management believed that in small and large ways, individual units had been responsible for much creative and innovative work, some of which had become a permanent feature of the unit's workload.[146] The organisation was also aware that it had long since moved away from the situation of the 1940s and 1950s, when its work was unusual and its values and practice were those which local authorities had wished to employ or emulate but lacked the resources to do so. It had not lost its missionary zeal, however, and the sense of its own competence which had provided the driving force for its work in the 1940s also informed the convictions that led the working party to claim a didactic role for its work in the 1970s. Writing about FSU experiments, it argued that every effort should be made to feed the lessons back into local authority departments, not as anecdotes but as tried and tested pieces of work.[147]

In addition, the organisation recognised that experimental work might appear to constitute criticism. FSU's national officers recognised the difficulties attendant upon directing or appearing to direct policy arguments against FSU's funding authorities, and sought to protect local relationships and avoid unnecessary conflict by recommending that issues be taken up nationally rather than locally.[148] The argument was based on the recognition that day-to-day problems in any one unit would raise general principles, and the belief that national action was the best way to take the matter forward.[149] It also recognised the need for the national body to be well informed and able to act when public policy was under review by central government.

By the late 1970s, 23 FSUs were spread throughout the country, and more expansion was thought unlikely and undesirable. Instead, the organisation planned to increase its influence and believed that it might do this more effectively if it allied itself formally with other organisations such as the National Council of Social Service, and pressure groups including the Child Poverty Action Group, the Finer Joint Action Committee, the Right to Fuel and the Disability Alliance. A explicit interest in social policy was demonstrated by the establishment by the national office in 1977 of a social policy group, part of whose brief was to ensure that FSU should seek every opportunity to make representations to government departments and relevant committees on matters concerning the family. In addition, it was thought desirable to create a network for discussion, with each unit setting up its own social policy group and establishing a link with the national group responsible for social policy matters. It was also recommended that there should be an annual review of priorities for social action by FSU as a whole.[150]

FSU was working in a new climate, characterised by a greater degree of accountability and a greater degree of dependence. Evidence of the tune being called by the body which paid the piper was discussed in the FSU's director's report of 1983, where attention was drawn to two separate projects which had been terminated because they had fallen foul of their local authorities; in both cases the units had adopted the position of energetic defenders of the rights of their clients. In Salford, the unit's actions in raising publicly issues associated with local housing conditions led to accusations that they were stirring up anger among the tenants, and the project was terminated at a month's notice. A health project in Oldham received similar treatment. The publication of a report on service delivery, based on work with 40 mothers, produced by the unit in the early 1980s met with outrage from the local health authority which believed that the unit was stabbing them in the back. As a result, the project was brought to an abrupt end.[151] The South Birmingham unit, too, encountered tensions in its relations with its local authority. Unit workers believed that a variety of techniques were being used in the early 1980s to try to thwart their attempts to empower service users and to influence the standard of service delivery they received from the local authority in the form of improved housing or better refuse collection.[152] Their approach in the 1980s was informed by the radical social work principles of devolving power to local people that most South Birmingham FSU workers espoused. The move from a social to a community work methodology had not always been smoothly executed and had led to stresses within the unit team and a reconsideration of their philosophy in relation to those who used their services. The sometimes painful examination of the role of the worker vis-à-vis the service user led them to consider the nature of power and its occasionally hidden effects. It eventually drove them to try to encourage local people to become more involved in decisions concerning the work of the unit, and to enable them to gain the experience and courage necessary to mount campaigns against the local authority.

Lessons to be learned from the withdrawal of local authority support were not readily grasped. The West London unit (formerly the Kensington and Paddington unit) had noted in the mid-1960s the dangers of too great a dependence on local authority generosity. Although the LCC, Middlesex County Council, and the borough councils of Willesden, Kensington and Paddington were together providing the unit with sufficient funds to cover all its staffing costs, the desirability of maintaining some independent income was noted.[153] However, the organisation's dependence on public funds increased steadily. In 1978, the average amount of unit income derived from public funds had risen to 86 per cent. Competition for local authority funds based on comparison with other units led the treasurer of the Thamesmead unit, in his report for 1985–86, to note that other units throughout the country were receiving a higher proportion of their income from central and local government than Thamesmead and to argue that it ought not to be the exception. Five years earlier, a similar comparison had been made by the Manchester unit, when it argued that it was at 'the bottom of the league' for local authority support, and that while many units received between 60 and 90 per cent of their income from local authorities, Manchester raised more of its own funds than any other unit.[154] In 1982, the Liverpool unit, which was receiving about 50 per cent of its budget from the city council, noted that this was the smallest percentage received by any unit in the country and agreed that it should press for an increase to 75 per cent over the next four years.[155] By 1984, it had achieved 60 per cent, though the temptation to compare itself unfavourably with other units was still strong and it noted that the national average was now 90 per cent.[156]

Crucial to the discussion about the relationship between the state and voluntary organisations is the question of values. Voluntary organisations claim to exist because they are different from the state, because their motivations are fuelled by values essentially different from those of the state;[157] but values are not static and can change or be adopted by other agencies. To some extent FSU exemplified that process, something that Fred Philp had observed in the wake of the closure of the Combined Casework Unit at Hackney in 1967. He argued that a voluntary organisation must show itself to be better than or different from its statutory counterpart and that FSU was not providing anything distinctive, except in its more generous use of time and reduced pressure of work.[158] He believed that the unit in Hackney may have been doing work of high quality, but that it had not been able to appeal to the local authority on the grounds that it had provided a better service or one which was clearly different.[159] Although local units accepted grants from local authorities with gratitude, some found it difficult to understand why councillors and officials failed to show interest in the detail of the work they funded.

An aggrieved note in the records of the Liverpool unit in 1984 expresses the management committee's disappointment and disapproval when, having issued invitations to an open day to every one of the city's 90 councillors, not one turned up.[160]

FSU, like other voluntary organisations, became part of the emerging contract culture in the 1980s. The greater control which this gave to the funding body, together with the changes in practice which were frequently built into the description of any service agreements made between local authorities and FSU, contributed to the process whereby criticism of the organisation began to evaporate. At the end of 1989 a new service agreement was drawn up between Birmingham social services department and South Birmingham FSU for the latter to focus particularly on under-fives, the group targeted as a top priority for voluntary sector funding by the local social services committee.[161] As a condition of its local authority grant, FSU undertook to provide short-term help for families, operating as a team and on a multi-skill basis, and some day care provision for under-fives. The staff level required to implement this was reflected in a change in the balance of staff common to many units, which now employed fewer social workers and more workers from other disciplines. Education workers had already become an important feature of work in some units. In others, nursery teachers or nursery nurses began to take on crucial aspects of the unit's work with families, and family support workers who gave help to families in their own homes came to take their place within the unit teams. In addition, volunteers offered their services for a variety of tasks – from helping to run a unit's second-hand clothes store to taking an active part in self-help programmes, from casework to membership of committees – and took on an important role in many units. The Sheffield unit, for example, had made extensive use of voluntary helpers since the 1960s, using them at first to help with children's groups or addressing envelopes, and later allowing them to work with selected clients.[162] Some were themselves past or present service users, exemplifying the erosion of the sharp boundary between the client and the worker that had been in progress for several years.

FSU was no more certain of its local authority funding in the 1980s than it had been in the 1940s. Neither was it any more clear about whether such funding was an advantage or a disadvantage, even though it had become essential. At one level little had changed – in 1980 as in 1940, units were taking on tasks put their way by the local authorities – but at another the relationship had undergone considerable change. Freedom to carry out those tasks in novel ways was often restricted by local authority requirements, a situation which had been foreseen in 1958 by one of FSU's earliest members[163] but had been largely ignored in the interests of growth and of establishing new units. (It is an argument rehearsed more recently by writers like Robert Whelan, who bemoan the voluntary sector's dependence on statutory funds.[164]) By 1980, FSU's distinctiveness no longer lay in its new approach to old problems. Its clothes were now worn by other organisations, including the traditional child rescue agencies and local authority departments. It could no longer command almost unqualified support and admiration. To a great extent, it had become just another voluntary social work agency, dependent for its survival on its ability to play the tunes requested by its major funders, the local authorities.

# NOTES

**1.** T. Simey, *Principles of Social Administration* (Oxford, 1937), cited in J. Wolfenden, *The Future of Voluntary Organisations: Report of the Wolfenden Committee* (London, 1978), p18.

**2.** Simey, *Principles of Social Administration*, p143. G. Finlayson, 'A moving frontier: Voluntarism and the state in British social welfare 1911–1949', *Twentieth Century British History*, 1 (1990), pp183ff.

**3.** Finlayson, 'A moving frontier', p204.

**4.** Lady Allen was an energetic critic of poor standards of residential child welfare and the absence of a properly coordinated administration. H. Hendrick, *Child Welfare: England 1872–1989* (London, 1994), p212.

**5.** J. Grier, 'A spirit of friendly rivalry? Voluntary societies and the formation of post-war welfare legislation', in J. Lawrence and P. Starkey (eds), *Child Welfare and Social Action* (Liverpool, forthcoming).

**6.** N. Deakin, 'The perils of partnership: The voluntary sector and the state, 1945–1992', in J. Davis Smith, C. Rochester and R. Hedley (eds), *An Introduction to the Voluntary Sector* (London, 1995), p43.

**7.** For further discussion on the relationship between the state and voluntary agencies, see M. Brenton, *The Voluntary Sector in British Social Services* (London, 1985); A. Digby, *British Welfare Policy: Workhouse to Workfare* (London, 1989); G. Finlayson, *Citizen, State and Social Welfare in Britain, 1830–1990* (Oxford, 1994); R. Lowe, *The Welfare State in Britain Since 1945* (London, 1993).

**8.** J. Lewis, *The Voluntary Sector, the State and Social Work in Britain* (London, 1995), pp14–15.

9. Finlayson, *Citizen, State and Social Welfare*, p281.

10. Council minutes of Dr Barnardo's Homes, April 1946. ULSCA D239/B1/2. I am grateful to Julie Grier for this reference.

11. Deakin, 'The perils of partnership', p41.

12. Liverpool Council for Social Service, *The Outlook for Voluntary Social Service on Merseyside* (Liverpool, 1950), pp5–6.

13. Ministry of Health and Ministry of Education, *Report of the Care of Children Committee* (Curtis committee), Cmnd 6922 (HMSO, 1946).

14. Church of England Waifs and Strays Society annual report for 1948. See also S. Mencher, 'Factors affecting the relationship of the voluntary and statutory child-care services in England', *Social Service Review*, 32 (1958), p27, n7.

15. Church of England Waifs and Strays Society annual report for 1949. However, this claim of independence was based on a shaky interpretation of the past; a fifth of children accommodated by the Waifs and Strays Society were 'poor law children being paid for by local boards of guardians'. R. Parker, *Away From Home: A history of child care* (Ilford, 1990), pp21–3, 27–30. Quoted in B. Holman, 'The voluntaries: Another perspective', in R. Whelan (ed.), *Involuntary Action: How voluntary is the voluntary sector?* (London, 1999), pp36–7.

16. Mencher, 'Factors affecting the relationship of the voluntary and statutory child-care services', p27.

17. An address by Professor D. R. MacCalman at the Conference of the National Council of Family Casework Agencies, October 1953, from *Social Work*, 10 (1953), p746.

18. M Chesterman, *Charities, Trusts and Social Welfare* (London, 1979), p84.

19. Sir R. Waley-Cohen to J. J. Mallon quoted in Deakin, 'The perils of partnership', p40.

20. See J. Maxwell, 'Children and state intervention', in A. M. Rafferty, J. Robinson and R. Elkan (eds), *Nursing History and the Politics of Welfare* (London, 1997), pp232–3.

21. Liverpool Council for Social Service, *The Outlook for Voluntary Social Service*, pp5–6.

22. Oral evidence of the National Council of Family Casework Agencies, Association of General and Family Caseworkers and Liverpool Personal Service Society, November 23 1956, quoted in Lewis, *The Voluntary Sector, the State and Social Work*, p120.

23. Personal communication from Barbara Kahan, May 1990. J. Packman, *The Child's Generation* (Oxford, 1981), pp55ff.

24. Packman, *The Child's Generation*, pp55ff. See above, p101. Minutes of the Kensington and Paddington FSU committee, October 15 1957. ULSCA D495 (WL)M1/2.

25. Ministry of Health and Department of Health for Scotland, *Report of the Working Party on Social Workers in the Local Authority Health and Welfare Services* (Younghusband report) (HMSO, 1959), para1035ff. Report to Liverpool FSU executive committee, June 1959. ULSCA D495(LI)M3/2.

26. Packman, *The Child's Generation*, p61.

27. E. Younghusband, *Social Work in Britain: A supplementary report on the employment and training of social workers* (Edinburgh, 1951), p2.

**28.** Liverpool Council of Social Service, *The Outlook for Voluntary Social Service*, p9.

**29.** Liverpool Council of Social Service, *The Outlook for Voluntary Social Service*, p9.

**30.** Younghusband, *Social Work in Britain: A supplementary report*, p2. See above, pp176, 179.

**31.** Younghusband, 'Social work in public and voluntary agencies', *Social Work*, 17 (1960), p3.

**32.** National Assistance Board annual report for 1949, quoted in E. Howarth, 'The present dilemma of social casework', *Social Work*, 8 (1951), p528.

**33.** Liverpool FSU annual report for 1954–55. ULSCA D495(L1)M11/8. In 1948, Lord Beveridge had argued 'British people are apt to dislike new things till they have tried them... Experiment has come in the past through Voluntary Action and is most certain to come that way'. Lord Beveridge, *Voluntary Action* (London, 1948), p224.

**34.** Liverpool Council for Social Service, *The Outlook for Voluntary Social Service*, p10.

**35.** A. Cohen, *The Revolution in Post-War Family Casework: The Story of Pacifist Service Units and Family Service Units 1940–1959* (Lancaster, 1998), p50.

**36.** Minutes of the FSU national executive committee May 2 1948. ULSCA D495(HQ)M2/2 .

**37.** Minutes of the FSU national committee November 28 1947. ULSCA D495(HQ)M2/1.

**38.** £350 each was given to the Manchester and Kensington and Paddington units, and £250 to Liverpool. Minutes of the FSU national executive committee, February 18 1949. ULSCA D495(HQ)M2/2.

**39.** Minutes of the FSU national committee, November 18 1949. ULSCA D495(HQ)M2/2.

**40.** Minutes of the Manchester FSU casework committee, September 26 1949. ULSCA D495(MA)M3/1.

**41.** Sheffield City Council gave £500 to the local unit in February 1950. Minutes of the Sheffield FSU committee, February 13 1950. ULSCA D495(SH)M1/1. Manchester children's department gave £200 to FSU in 1956. B. Holman, *The Corporate Parent: Manchester Children's Department 1948–71* (London, 1996), pp46 and 121.

**42.** Liverpool FSU annual report for 1956–57. ULSCA D495(LI)M11/10.

**43.** Beveridge, *Voluntary Action*, p302.

**44.** A. Collis, 'Casework in a statutory and voluntary setting', *Social Work*, 15 (1958), p453.

**45.** Kensington and Paddington FSU annual report for 1954–55. ULSCA D495(WL)M5/2.

**46.** Collis, 'Casework in a statutory and voluntary setting', pp456ff.

**47.** Minutes of the Liverpool FSU committee, October 6 1953. ULSCA D495 (LI)M2/1. The Liverpool children's committee made annual grants to FSU of approximately £700 during the 1950s. The department of public health also made annual grants to the organisation. See minutes of the children's committee, June 18 1952. Liverpool Record Office (LRO) 352MIN/CH1/1/1. Minutes of the children's committee, December 14 1960. LRO 352/MIN/CHI/1/4. I am indebted to Julie Grier for these references.

**48.** Minutes of the Liverpool FSU committee, December 7 1954. ULSCA D495(LI)M2/1.

**49.** Minutes of the Liverpool FSU committee, April 16 1957. ULSCA D495 (LI)M2/1.

**50.** Minutes of the Liverpool FSU committee, February 11 1960. ULSCA D495(LI)M2/1.

**51.** See, for example, minutes of the Liverpool FSU committee, October 6 1960, January 19 1961, January 11 1963, March 2 1965, October 13 1965, January 26 1966. ULSCA D495(LI)M2/1. November 3 1975, January 26 1976, March 23 1977. ULSCA D495(LI)M2/2.

**52.** Minutes of the Islington FSU committee, October 20 1953. ULSCA unlisted. V. Belcher, *The City Parochial Foundation 1891–1991: A trust for the poor of London* (Aldershot, 1991), p284.

**53.** Minutes of the Islington FSU committee, November 9 1954, February 8 1955, May 3 1955, August 16 1955, September 6 1955, October 11 1955, December 6 1955, February 14 1956, April 17 1956. ULSCA unlisted.

**54.** Minutes of the Islington FSU committee, August 19 1965, January 9 1967. ULSCA unlisted. Collis, 'Casework in a statutory and voluntary setting', pp456ff.

**55.** FSU working party on development, *The Development of Family Service Units* (London, 1978), p86.

**56.** Camden FSU annual report for 1974–75. ULSCA D495(CA)M4/2.

**57.** FSU working party, *The Development of FSU*, p86.

**58.** Holman, *Corporate Parent*, p129.

**59.** Report from Islington children's department. ULSCA unlisted.

**60.** *Liverpool FSU 1948–58*, ULSCA D495(LI)M2/1.

**61.** See above, pp50ff.

**62.** Bristol Corporation Act 1950. 14 Geo 6, Part VI, p52. Bristol Record Office (hereafter BRO).

**63.** Bristol FSU annual report for 1955. ULSCA D495(BL)M4.

**64.** For a fuller account of Bristol FSU, see P. Starkey, 'The Medical Officer of Health, the social worker and the problem family, 1943–1968', *Social History of Medicine*, 11 (1998), pp421ff.

**65.** Letter from R. C. Wofinden about a family help scheme he had observed in Kent. Minutes of the children's committee and sub-committees, 1958–1961, minutes of the children's committee, June 9 1959, BRO. At the meeting of the children's committee, October 30 1959, it was agreed that such a service should be started in Bristol, under the auspices of the public health department and the children's department. Minutes of the children's committee and sub-committee, October 30 1959. BRO.

**66.** Hendrick, *Child Welfare*, p227.

**67.** Letter from T. Johnstone (Bristol children's officer) to Alf Strange (Bristol FSU fieldwork organiser), November 23 1964. ULSCA D495(BL)M2.

**68.** Minutes of the children's committee, October 30 1963. BRO. See also report of the MOH for 1963, 57. BRO 33416(30)c.

**69.** Minutes of the meeting of the representatives of health, children's, housing and welfare service committees, March 10 1964. BRO.

**70.** Letter from A. F. Philp to R. C. Wofinden, September 21 1966. ULSCA D495(BL)M2.

**71.** Note in day book by Alf Strange, June 12 1963. ULSCA D495(BL)M5.

**72.** Report of the MOH for 1957, B14. BRO 33416(28)c.

**73.** P. Goldring, *Friend of the Family: The Work of Family Service Units* (Newton Abbott, 1973) p180. Clients also noticed the difference in size between local authority and FSU caseloads, and believed that as a result FSU was able to make more time to deal with individual problems. P. Phillimore, *Families Speaking: A study of fifty-one families' views of social work* (London, 1981), p77.

**74.** Letter from Alf Strange to David Jones, May 7 1956. ULSCA D495(BL) M2.

**75.** A series of letters from Alf Strange to David Jones, between July and November 1956, details an incident in which the NSPCC publicly criticised the actions of the local authority over the case of a neglected child. Although the letters do not make it explicit, it would appear that FSU had been visiting the family concerned and that its method of working was being criticised by the NSPCC. ULSCA D495(BL)M2. Cf. minutes of the Bristol FSU staff meeting, July 3 1959. ULSCA D495(BL)M1. See also undated document, *Co-operation with the NSPCC*. ULSCA D495(BL)M2.

**76.** Note in day book by Alf Strange, 7 December 1960. ULSCA D495(BL)M5.

**77.** Letter to Philp (national secretary of FSU) from the Town Clerk of Bristol, January 26 1967. ULSCA D495(BL)M2.

**78.** Bristol Corporation Act 1950, 14 Geo 6, Part VI, p52. BRO.

**79.** Confidential memo to all members of the FSU national executive and personnel committees from the national secretary, February 6 1967. ULSCA D495 (BL)M2.

**80.** Report of the MOH for 1965, p49. BRO 33416(31)a. See also Bristol FSU report on Mothers' Group, no date but probably c1958. ULSCA, D495(BL)C1.

**81.** Younghusband report (HMSO, 1959), para 1035.

**82.** Kensington and Paddington FSU annual report for 1964–1965. ULSCA D495(WL)M5/12.

**83.** Minutes of the FSU fieldwork organisers' meeting, October 28–29 1963. ULSCA D495(HQ)M3/1.

**84.** Minutes of the FSU fieldwork organisers' meeting, September 20–21 1965. ULSCA D495(HQ)M3/1.

**85.** Kensington and Paddington FSU annual report for 1964–65. ULSCA D4945(WL)M5/12.

**86.** Minutes of the FSU fieldwork organisers' meeting, September 20–21 1965. ULSCA D495(HQ)M3/1.

**87.** Minutes of the children's committee, January 8 1963. LRO 352/MIN/CHI/1/4.

**88.** Minutes of Islington FSU committee, January 9 1967. ULSCA unlisted. By 1978, the London borough of Islington was known for its generosity to voluntary organisations and, according to the Wolfenden report, gave more in grant aid than any other local authority. Wolfenden, *The Future of Voluntary Organisations*, p91.

**89.** Children's departments, the branch of the social services with which FSU had closest dealings, had expanded from a few hundreds in 1948 to 3,500 20 years later. See B. Kahan, The child care service', in P. Townsend (ed.), *The Fifth Social Service: A critical analysis of the Seebohm proposals* (London, 1970), p61.

**90.** Letter from Philp to Sir Donald Allen, Clerk to the Trustees of the City Parochial Foundation, September 17 1964. ULSCA D495(HQ)B3/4.

**91.** Philp, *Report on the Combined Casework Unit to FSU National Committee* (1967). ULSCA D495(HQ)B3/6.

**92.** See 'Helping out the family', *New Society*, 43 (March, 1978).

**93.** Paper discussed at Glasgow FSU team meeting, February 26 1976. ULSCA D495(HQ)B2/3.

**94.** Report by the director of social work, Strathclyde Regional Council, March 1976. ULSCA D495(HQ)B2/3.

**95.** Quoted in Goldring, *Friend of the Family*, p185.

**96.** D. Holder and M. Wardle, *Teamwork and the Development of a Unitary Approach* (London, 1981), pp13–14.

**97.** Holder and Wardle, *Teamwork and the Development of a Unitary Approach*, pxiii.

**98.** Minutes of South London FSU management committee, November 20 1962. ULSCA D495(SL)M1/2.

**99.** Minutes of South London FSU management committee, January 22 1963. ULSCA D495(SL)M1/2.

**100.** Minutes of the South London FSU management committee, July 7 1964. ULSCA D495(SL)M1/2.

**101.** Minutes of the South London FSU management committee, October 20 1964. ULSCA D495(SL)M1/2.

**102.** Minutes of the South London FSU management committee, December 8 1964. ULSCA D495(SL)M1/2.

**103.** Minutes of the FSU national executive committee, February 1 1952. ULSCA D495(HQ)M2/5.

**104.** Minutes of the FSU national executive committee, October 7 1964. ULSCA D495(HQ)M2/5.

**105.** Holman, *Corporate Parent*, p128.

**106.** *Report of the Committee on Local Authority and Allied Personal Social Services* (Seebohm report) Cmnd 3703 (HMSO, 1968).

**107.** K Bilton, 'Origins, progress and future', in J. Cypher (ed.), *Seebohm Across Three Decades* (Birmingham, 1979), pp5–9.

**108.** J. Kendall and M. Knapp, *The Voluntary Sector in the UK* (Manchester, 1996), p56.

**109.** Minutes of FSU fieldwork organisers' meeting, March 20–21 1967. ULSCA D495(HQ)M3/1.

**110.** Minutes of the East London FSU annual general meeting, 1970–71. ULSCA D495(EL)M7/23; cf. Goldring, *Friend of the Family*, p191.

**111.** Minutes of the FSU personnel committee, June 6 1969. ULSCA D495 (HQ)M3/15.

**112.** East London FSU annual report for 1977–78. ULSCA D495(EL)M7/30.

**113.** Wolfenden, *The Future of Voluntary Organisations*, p84.

**114.** East London FSU annual report for 1972–73. ULSCA D495(EL)M7/26.

**115.** Minutes of the Oldham FSU committee, March 15 1975. ULSCA D495(OL)M1/3.

**116.** Minutes of the Oldham FSU committee, October 28 1974. ULSCA D495 (OL)M1/3.

**117.** Minutes of the Oldham FSU committee, April 28 1975. ULSCA D495 (OL)M1/3.

**118.** Minutes of the Oldham FSU annual general meeting, July 30 1975. ULSCA D495(OL)M1/14.

**119.** Letter from director of FSU to 'Edith' (chair of Oldham FSU committee), May 6 1975. ULSCA D495(OL)M7/1.

**120.** Minutes of Newcastle FSU committee, March 15, 1973. ULSCA D495 (NE)M1/1.

**121.** Minutes of Newcastle FSU committee, May 16 1974. ULSCA D495(NE) M1/1.

**122.** Minutes of Newcastle FSU committee, September 20 1973. ULSCA D495(NE)M1/1.

**123.** Minutes of Newcastle FSU committee, January 16 1975. ULSCA D495 (NE)M1/1.

**124.** West London FSU annual report for 1968–69. ULSCA D495(WL)M5/16.

**125.** Minutes of the West London FSU committee, February 12 1975. ULSCA D495(WL)M1/4.

**126.** Minutes of the West London FSU committee, February 12 1975. ULSCA D495(WL)M1/4.

**127.** L. M. Price, quoted in Goldring, *Friend of the Family*, p190.

**128.** Goldring, *Friend of the Family*, p167.

**129.** Basis of operation of Combined Casework Unit, February 23 1962. ULSCA D495(HQ)B3/4. In some cases it appears that FWA workers carried even larger loads. Mayer and Timms, for example, note that the norm was between 30 and 35 cases to each worker. J. J. Mayer and N. Timms, *The Client Speaks: Working class impressions of casework* (London, 1970), p19.

**130.** R. Popplestone, 'Moving the balance from administration to practice', *Social Work Today*, 8 (1977), p14.

**131.** FSU working party, *The Development of FSU*, p25.

**132.** G. Smith and J. Corden, 'The introduction of contracts in a family service unit', *British Journal of Social Work*, 11 (1981) p291.

**133.** FSU working party, *The Development of FSU*, p26.

**134.** Wolfenden, *The Future of Voluntary Organisations*, p46.

**135.** Younghusband, *Social Work and Social Change* (London, 1964), p48.

**136.** Seebohm report, paras 495–6.

**137.** Wolfenden, *The Future of Voluntary Organisations*, p47.

**138.** A. B. Armitage, quoted in Goldring, *Friend of the Family*, p187.

**139.** FSU working party, *The Development of FSU*, p35.

**140.** Holder and Wardle, *Teamwork and the Development of a Unitary Approach*, p17.

**141.** FSU working party, *The Development of FSU*, p6.

**142.** N. Hinton, 'Which way for the personal social services?', *Social Work Service*, 18 (1978), p32.

**143.** N. Hinton, 'The relevance of the voluntary sector', *Social Work Today*, 9 (1977) p21; Hinton, 'Which way for the personal social services?', p33.

**144.** N. Hinton, 'Which way for the personal social services?', p33.

**145.** FSU working party, *The Development of FSU*, p35.

**146.** FSU working party, *The Development of FSU*, p36.

**147.** FSU working party, *The Development of FSU*, p43.

**148.** FSU working party, *The Development of FSU*, p47.

**149.** FSU working party, *The Development of FSU*, p48.

**150.** FSU working party, *The Development of FSU*, p8.

**151.** FSU director's report for 1983. ULSCA D495(LI)M2/5.

**152.** P. Dobson, 'An Exercise in Consultation: Residents decide the future of a social and community work agency' (unpublished MSocSci thesis, University of Birmingham, 1987), p4.

**153.** West London FSU, annual report for 1963–64. ULSCA D495(WL)M5/11. Annual report for 1964–65. ULSCA D495(WL)M5/12. Annual report for 1965–66. ULSCA D495(WL)M5/13.

**154.** Minutes of Manchester FSU committee, January 24 1980 and September 25 1980. ULSCA D495(MA)M1/3.

**155.** Minutes of a special meeting of Liverpool FSU committee, November 30 1982. ULSCA D495(LI)M2/3.

**156.** Minutes of the Liverpool FSU committee, October 3 1984. ULSCA D495 (LI)M2/5.

**157.** Hinton, 'Which way for the personal social services?', p32.

**158.** Philp, *Report on Hackney Combined Casework Unit* (1967). ULSCA D495 (HQ)B3/4.

**159.** Philp, *Report on Hackney Combined Casework Unit* (1967). ULSCA D495 (HQ)B3/4.

**160.** Minutes of the Liverpool FSU committee, January 18 1984. ULSCA D495 (LI)M2/4.

**161.** South Birmingham Family Service Unit Service Agreement, December 21 1989. ULSCA D495(SB)M1.

**162.** Minutes of the Sheffield FSU committee, May 26 1966 and May 16 1968. ULSCA D495(SH)M1/1.

**163.** Collis, 'Social work in a statutory and voluntary setting', p457.

**164.** R. Whelan, *The Corrosion of Charity* (London, 1996); Whelan (ed.), *Involuntary Action*.

# 7

# Almost Not An Organisation

In 1948, FSU enjoyed a number of advantages. It had acquired an enviable reputation as an organisation that had developed particular and useful skills; it had no history to shed; its birth coincided with that of the children's departments and its approach seemed to complement their responsibilities; and it quickly established friendships with people in high places. But the administrative framework it set up, informed in part by an uncertainty about its long-term role, left a legacy of confusion to later generations of workers and committee members.

Discussions about the shape of the organisation had started in 1946 and the 'shadow' agency which then began to function consisted of a national committee and a national executive committee. Two local committees undertook responsibility for the Liverpool and Manchester units, which eventually came under the umbrella of the new organisation in 1948. The constitution assumed a permanent two-tier management, with one tier in London and the other in those areas in which units were established. The national committee, with a membership of not less than 7 and no more than 30, was elected at an annual general meeting. National committee powers were delegated to the national executive committee which consisted of the honorary officers (chairman, deputy chairman, honorary treasurer), other members chosen by the national committee, and a representative coopted from each local committee. The national executive committee made decisions about when and where new units should be opened. It recruited and appointed staff, organised the training and deployment of potential caseworkers, and raised funds for use in training and national projects. By the late 1950s, when serious signs of strain first began to appear, the structure had expanded in an attempt to meet the demands of a growing organisation. Provision was made for two fieldwork organisers[1] to attend national executive committee meetings.[2] Two additional national sub-committees were created – personnel, and finance and publicity – appointed annually by the national executive committee. Over the years a number of other committees, for example a research committee and a development and advisory committee, were also appointed. Membership of these committees frequently overlapped. As the organisation became more complex, senior workers in the units began to suspect that they were not properly represented, and that the management structure tended to exclude those responsible for the day-to-day work. In spite of the constitutional right of two fieldwork organisers to attend the meetings of the national executive committee, events in the late 1960s suggest that the mechanism for such representation was not in their hands nor in those of their colleagues. In January 1968, the fieldwork organisers asked that they should be able to nominate those of their number who sat on the national executive committee. Permission was granted to them to nominate candidates for three vacancies, but the committee reserved to itself the right to accept or reject their nominees, arguing that committee members served as individuals not as representatives of any one group.[3] In spite of FSU's commitment to democracy, it would appear that this did not extend to the central organ of power and that the ex officio contribution of fieldwork organisers to the most important committee in the organisation was being carefully controlled. The potential consequences of their exclusion, and that of any representative of the caseworkers, was noted by Derek Newman, a management consultant invited to examine and report on the organisation by FSU in the late 1960s. As fieldwork organisers were the main operational element in FSU and an important resource, he believed that no decision made by the national executive committee could be effective unless it had at least their toleration, if not their active support.[4]

Uncertainty about the appropriate mechanisms for selecting representatives to serve on the national executive committee reflected a confusion about where final authority should lie – with the national committees in London or with the units. Although major policy decisions were taken in London and the national executive committee had a wide view of the organisation as a whole, it was always intended that units should be based on strong local interest, be an integral part of the social services of the area and be responsive to particular local circumstances.[5] Units were set up as a result of local initiative, and local committees undertook responsibility for fund-raising and for the overall management of the work in their areas.[6] Local committees were formally appointed by resolution of the national association at its annual general meeting, but this merely gave official approval to arrangements previously agreed locally.[7] Emphasis on the importance of the local dimension created tension between the two tiers and forced the national organisation to allow such autonomy to the units that the integrity of the whole could be, and was, very easily threatened. By the late 1950s, local committees enjoyed considerable independence so long as they did not incur expenditure beyond their own resources. Although this was one limit to local freedom, it did not address the difficulty of distinguishing between matters of local concern and those of national import.

A frequent source of irritation and frustration sprang from the fact that money was raised locally but that the national organisation had a say in the way in which it was spent.[8] Energetic attempts by Lord Balfour to raise sufficient funds to get the new national agency off the ground from 1946 onwards had not altered the fundamental principle of local responsibility for local projects, which had been a characteristic of PSU. Moreover, he and Sir Donald Allen, Clerk to the Trustees of the City Parochial Foundation, a major funder of FSU in its early days, worked from the premise that the care of problem families was properly the responsibility of the statutory authorities, and that once the experiment funded by the CPF at the Kensington and Paddington unit from 1947–49 was completed, the 'authorities should take over the work, which should not be dependent on charitable funds'.[9]

It is not clear that the first national committee of FSU or the caseworkers shared such optimism about the resources and capabilities of the post-war welfare state or, if they did, that they planned the management structure of the new organisation accordingly. The financial arrangements that were employed reflected the importance attached to the local branches rather than the expectation that the organisation was a temporary expedient and that the state would take up the work once the need for it had been established. For example, grants of £750 were given to the Manchester and Liverpool units in October 1947, in order that they should be able to begin to pay salaries instead of pocket money to the workers from the beginning of 1948,[10] and in February 1949 grants of £350 each were made to the Manchester and Kensington and Paddington units, and £250 to

Liverpool.[11] At the end of 1949, after two further grants of £300 each to the Liverpool and Manchester units,[12] it was decided that no more financial aid could be given and that local committees should not commit the national committee financially.[13] No provision was made for long-term support from the centre, nor did units make any commitment to contribute towards the cost of the national administration. The underlying principle of local autonomy was articulated at various times when relationships became strained, generally by – and to the advantage of – the units. In 1959, for example, the Liverpool FSU committee used the principle of local financial responsibility to support its argument that it need contribute to the national organisation's training budget only in so far as the money was used for training caseworkers for its own unit; monies raised locally were to be used locally.[14]

As well as those tensions which resulted from the separation of fund-raising from the control of activity, others developed as a consequence of poor communication between national and local committees and the failure to devise an effective system for the relaying of concerns from local units to the centre and decisions from the centre to the units. The framework which had been designed when the original group of wartime colleagues was working together, albeit at some geographical distance, was not workable a decade and more later, when the original three units had expanded to become thirteen.[15] An undated document entitled 'The organisation of Family Service Units' – probably written during 1958 – described the complexity of the decision-making process. In an attempt to encourage consultation at all levels, items for discussion and decision might first be referred to the national executive committee by a particular local committee; referred by the national executive committee to all local committees; reconsidered by the national executive committee in the light of local committee recommendations; and referred to a sub-committee or individual for the preparation of detailed proposals; again considered by the national executive committee, then circulated to local committees and finally ratified by the national executive committee, taking into account local committee observations.[16] So cumbersome a mechanism – even if employed only infrequently – had the potential to undermine the agency's ability to act quickly and effectively. It also provided the temptation for the more powerful committees to bypass the procedure.

National and local interests frequently overlapped. The difficulties that this could engender may be illustrated by the Liverpool unit's decision in 1962 to publish an account of its 21 years of work with families in the city. The initiative for the book had come from the local committee who had encouraged Eric McKie, its long-time chairman, to write an account of the work. The national executive committee was caught by surprise. Its permission for such a publication had not been sought; when presented with the text, it did not like what it saw. An attempt was made to halt publication on the grounds that the book contained material of more than local interest and that the way in which it was presented might reflect badly on the national organisation.[17] The Liverpool committee, however, thought otherwise. It confirmed its intention to publish and argued that both the local committee and the caseworkers were satisfied that the book presented a fair account of the work of the unit. Were it to fail to gain the consent of the national organisation, the Liverpool committee expressed its intention to ignore the strictures of the officials in London and to approach the University of Liverpool, the city council and the Liverpool Council for Social Service for help with publication.[18] Faced with attempts by the national organisation to block its efforts, the local committee dug its heels in and requested that representatives from Liverpool should be present at any discussion of the book at national level.[19] As McKie was a member of the national executive committee, and should therefore have been party to any deliberations, this suggests that the question of publication was being debated elsewhere, as indeed it was. Robin Huws Jones, then Principal of the National Institute of Social Work, had been asked for his assessment. He cautioned against publication, suggesting that illustrations had been used without making clear what it was they illustrated and that 'the effect is rather to make the reader's flesh creep than to deepen and sharpen an understanding of the problem or of FSU's methods'.[20] And correspondence between Sir John Wolfenden, chairman of FSU, and Fred Philp, then national secretary, also makes it clear that the future of the book was being considered at an informal level as well as in committee.[21] Discussion focused on the use of case records, the question of whether it was appropriate that references to families should be used to illustrate the volume, and, significantly, whether casework material was the property of the national executive and could be published without its authority.[22] The issue was primarily one of the control of local activity. London may have hoped that by taking a firm line its views would win out, but the Liverpool unit managed to recruit powerful local support. Professor T. S. Simey of the University of Liverpool, who had for some time been a friend of the unit, supported McKie in his efforts and an edited version of the book, *Venture in Faith*, was eventually published in 1963. It had an introduction by Simey and a cautious, almost embarrassed, foreword by Sir John Wolfenden, national chairman of FSU.[23] Although the national committee's request that some alterations be made to McKie's original text had reluctantly been complied with, there can be no doubt that the Liverpool unit had won.[24]

The dispute over *Venture in Faith* highlights the struggle for control and the uncertainty within the organisation about where ultimate responsibility lay. The national committee had no doubt that any description of local activity was also of national concern. It did not hesitate therefore to forbid publication on the grounds that it alone could authorise anything that had more than purely local implications. In addition, the national committee announced its readiness to take legal action[25] 'and all necessary steps' to prevent the book reaching the shops.[26] The Liverpool unit, however, resisted the notion that it needed to obtain permission to publish accounts of its own work and insisted on its right to go ahead. The bitterness that was engendered persisted for many years and can have done little to improve an already uncertain relationship. Inevitably, it came to be seen in terms of personalities and long-held resentments between the national secretary and McKie. The significance of the argument was not lost on the committee of the West London unit, who commented on the important matters of principle it raised about 'the relative powers of national and local committees'.[27]

The failure to delineate clear areas of responsibility and the resultant uncertainty about authority which led to the occasional struggle for control was a legacy of the earliest days of the agency. PSU workers in Manchester and Liverpool during the Second World War had tended to sit lightly to the central organisation in London and to retain for their units a good deal of independence. Even during the war, relationships between London and the Liverpool unit had sometimes been strained. That the work in which the Liverpool unit was engaged was different from that of some other units had reinforced their sense of distance from the organisation's central office and enabled them to pursue their work with problem families with little interference. Those same pioneers formed the core of the new organisation that Lord Balfour helped to put on to a permanent peacetime footing in 1948, and many of them continued to work within or to be active on the committees of FSU well into the 1980s – providing valuable continuity with the past but, in a rapidly changing social, professional and economic climate, sometimes trapping the organisation in its history. Moreover, their pioneering work with problem families had brought them national and international recognition and reinforced their confidence in their methods and relationships, both with families and each other. Although some of the key wartime workers had moved from being provincial caseworkers to being administrators – from resisting central authority to imposing it – they continued to claim for themselves the ownership of a particular expertise and, understandably fuelled by earlier success, to endeavour to root the new organisation in the patterns of their past.[28]

In 1967 Derek Newman, a management consultant engaged by the agency, remarked that 'FSU is fascinating as an organisation because it is so nearly not one'.[29] Fascinating it may have been, but its failure to achieve organisational adulthood was to bedevil FSU's internal relationships and threaten its work for the next decade and more, as it had preoccupied its members from early in its history. Newman's inquiry highlighted structural problems built into FSU's management.[30] Such criticisms were not readily accepted by some FSU members who doubted the usefulness of the inquiry and argued that it was unlikely that 'management consultants can offer anything useful to an organisation whose work is primarily individual, creative and personal'.[31] Others, though, rejected the notion that FSU's structures were not amenable to examination from outside and found the study illuminating. In 1972, recalling Newman's comment that FSU was 'almost not an organisation' Len Hunt, the unit organiser of the Bradford unit, drew attention to FSU's continued lack of framework which, he argued, allowed it to be drawn into 'the gluepot of families with whom it works'.[32] In spite of attempts to clarify lines of responsibility and areas of management, FSU continued to suffer difficulties in ordering its affairs. In 1988, a report commissioned from Coopers and Lybrand used a similar metaphor to describe FSU's administration. It suggested that unless the 'gummed-up' management of the organisation were addressed and sorted out, it was unlikely that it would survive in its current form for a further five years.[33] Internal studies, formal and informal, solicited and unsolicited, consistently called attention to difficulties in communication and failures in management, but the organisation equally consistently found itself unable to change.

Part of the explanation for FSU's structural confusion may lie in its rapid growth. Although sometimes described as decentralised,[34] FSU's management structure was less clear than that implies. While responsibility for individual units resided in the localities, the national office retained a number of key functions including the appointment of staff, with the result that tension between the local and national arms of the organisation was always present and sometimes threatened its unity. Structural difficulties may also have been compounded by FSU's genesis as an organisation which began in two provincial branches, but which designed an administrative structure with a metropolitan centre.[35] FSU as a national movement began in north-west England. When it moved its central administration to London in 1948, it appointed as national secretary someone who was also expected to be responsible for running one of the new branches, albeit one in London. As the first national official, David Jones was also fieldwork organiser of the Kensington and Paddington unit, responsible for casework and the management of the unit as well as the affairs of the wider organisation. The national office was also the Kensington and Paddington unit office, giving a privileged status to a new local unit, but left behind in Liverpool and Manchester – particularly in Liverpool – were people who had played a major part in the wartime organisation and had been instrumental in the post-war developments. As the years went by they became increasingly marginalised. Although men such as Eric McKie – a prime mover in 1940 and an energetic if not always appreciated chairman of the Liverpool FSU committee until 1967 – sat on national committees, the distance which separated Liverpool and London was more than the geographical one of 200 miles or so.

In addition some of the original PSU members, although no longer employed by the organisation, found themselves working in London or the south of England and became involved in the work of FSU's national committees. Tom Stephens, for example, although he returned to work in the Civil Service after the war and eventually became an under-secretary in the DHSS, remained very influential in the national organisation until the late 1970s and was later involved in the Thamesmead unit.[36] David and Margaret Jones,[37] too, became actively involved in supporting new units as they came on stream.[38] Others, such as Fred Philp, who returned to work with FSU after taking part in post-war reconstruction in Europe, were appointed to senior positions within the national organisation, while yet other wartime PSU workers managed local units in West London, Bristol, Manchester and Birmingham, or joined local unit committees. At one level this provided coherence and stability, but at another it gave rise to a structure which had the potential to be dangerously dependent on friendship networks and personalities.

While the overall management structure was not robust enough to withstand the pressures exerted on it by rapid growth and confusion about the locus of authority, problems also became evident at a local level. Relationships between local committees and the units have a chequered history. Inevitably, tensions have arisen between lay committee members and professional social workers from time to time, with the former expecting to exercise a managerial function, while those whom they managed suspected that the committee had little real understanding of the task. In this FSU exhibited difficulties common to many voluntary agencies. As Jane Lewis has reminded us, the unpaid management committee is one of the key defining elements of the UK voluntary sector.[39] It is the legal entity in which the organisation exists; is assumed to represent those who wish to further its aims and objectives; and it can be held accountable for everything done in its name. However, although its legal status is clear, the practical outworking of its role has often proved to be problematic. As Margaret Harris has shown, the management committee has been an abiding source of confusion and ambiguity, and the implementation of its function has frequently been fraught with difficulties.[40]

Difficulties have clustered around a number of issues. For example, the work of the committee as the lay manager of specialist professionals, with the attendant dangers of misunderstanding and incomplete comprehension of the task being undertaken, has frequently been among the reasons for the confusion and ambiguity to which Harris alludes. In addition, particularly in those agencies working in the personal social services, the risk of misapprehension has sometimes been increased when committees have consisted of people with little real knowledge of the personal, social and economic circumstances of the clients for whom the agency is said to exist and whose needs its employees are paid to meet. At another level, the manner in which committee members are recruited may serve to perpetuate those difficulties and reinforce tensions between the committee, the staff it employs and the clients they all purport to serve. Like those of many other voluntary organisations, FSU committees have tended to be self-perpetuating. In spite of attempts to draw on a wide range of expertise, the only real qualification for membership has been acceptability to the existing committee members. Recruitment has been largely on a personal basis, with friends and colleagues recommending each other to the agency.[41]

In 1966 Sheila Kay, the Liverpool fieldwork organiser, reflected on the role of the committee and its relationship to the work of the unit. Although she acknowledged the importance of the committee as a representative of the wider local community, she questioned its understanding of the problems faced by the social workers and its grasp of issues such as the need for support and research. Kay argued that social workers in local authority departments experienced similar difficulties in their relationships with their committees, but she also drew attention to the more clearly defined structures to be found in statutory authorities.[42] Three years later Islington FSU took up the discussion. It commented on the lack of common experience and expectation between its local committee and its social workers, arguing that the unit meeting, not the committee meeting, was the proper place for decisions about changes and developments in the professional life of the unit to be taken. If that were so, then it had implications for the importance and status of the local management committee. Although the need for some outside supervision of unit expenditure and an independent audit was accepted, as was the need for some objective assessment of the work, the ability of a lay committee to manage specialised professionals was questioned. That FSU had always had local committees was not, in the view of the Islington team, a sufficient reason for continuing to support a management structure based on a fiction.[43] As one of the assistant directors was to argue in 1975, permission for a particular course of action relating to fieldwork would not normally have to be obtained from outside the unit team. In that situation, what sort of control could the committee expect, or be expected, to exercise? In fieldwork matters, unit teams were autonomous.[44] The argument exposed the weakness of the relationship. If, technically, the unit was responsible to the committee for its day-to-day operations, how could that responsibility be exercised when the committee members were, almost without exception, people without social work training or experience? Derek Newman had considered the relationships between local units and their committees during his study. He had argued that proper interaction between workers in a unit and the members of the local committee over the use of resources and style of work was vital. His experience of FSU suggested that, although ill-will was infrequent, understanding was limited. Local committees often felt too far away from the workers and the workers found the role of the committee confusing.[45]

If unit workers were uneasy about the role of the committee, the uncertainty was often reciprocated. Some committees believed themselves to be uncomfortably in the hands of the senior social workers. In Oldham in the late 1970s, for example, the call for an assessment of the roles of the committee and the unit organiser was prompted by the suspicion that the latter could deny authority to the former and manipulate the committee by selecting the material to be put to it.[46] In Liverpool, too, the lack of clarity about the roles of committee members and workers prompted a paper which sought to delineate responsibility and to reduce confusion.[47] Such efforts at tidying tended to ignore the constitution, which required that the committee bear ultimate responsibility for all aspects of unit activity. It would appear that this was not generally understood. In the mid-1970s the death of Maria Colwell resulted in severe criticism of social workers generally and prompted a predictably defensive reaction on the part of all social work agencies, whether statutory or voluntary. On being advised to tighten its procedures, the West London FSU committee expressed surprise that the national organisation expected it to take any responsibility for decisions relating to social work practice.[48] By distancing itself from professional decisions, the committee was effectively refusing to accept its constitutional position which required it to manage the central function of the agency – social work with families. Its actions may have been in recognition of the social workers' greater professional knowledge, but they allowed the committee's role to be defined as one concerned only with providing the funds and support services necessary for its employees to do their work. The following year the West London unit made a sharp distinction between the social workers and the lay committee members and did not attempt to involve the committee members in the business of professional decision making. The role of the committee was defined as involving the employment of staff; the support and encouragement of the workers; the establishment of overall unit policies; the attraction and allocation of resources; efficient administration; the care of unit buildings; and the linking of local unit policies with national policies.[49]

In 1967 Fred Philp had used what he perceived as the weaknesses in management of the Hackney Combined Casework Unit (CCU), a project of which FSU had been a part,[50] to highlight some deficiencies. He noted the failure of the Hackney committee to influence the development of the unit because it was reluctant to interfere with the work of the professional staff and the tendency on the part of both caseworkers and committee members to avoid rocking the boat. Philp appeared to attach particular significance to the Hackney CCU's assured income; because it did not have to worry about this, the committee was free of the central preoccupation of most FSU committees – the raising of funds. The Hackney CCU, with its grants from the City Parochial Foundation and Hackney Borough Council,[51] did not have constantly to worry about where the next tranche of money was to come from, an activity to which Philp appeared to attach the challenge and possibility of conflict which, he argued, was necessary in any living and developing organisation.[52] No direct reference was made to those units which also enjoyed freedom from fund-raising by virtue of their generous local authority grants, nor would such comparison have supported Philp's contention that raising money gave committees a meaningful task and helped to ensure good relations, but his observation that both committees and workers tended to want to avoid rocking the boat put the spotlight on a relationship in which outward harmony was given high priority and conflict carefully avoided.

The Hackney CCU cannot be seen as representative of the organisation as a whole. Apart from the fact that it was a partnership between three voluntary social work agencies, the reluctance to engage in potentially disruptive debate was not an attitude to be found elsewhere in FSU. If Philp was right, and conflict and challenge were essential elements in a living organisation, then FSU was beginning to show itself to have life in abundance. Symptomatic of developments was the change in its chief officer's title. In 1969 Rex Halliwell, formerly fieldwork organiser of the Bradford unit, replaced Fred Philp who had been national secretary since 1962.[53] Halliwell was the first person to become the chief executive of FSU who had not formerly been a member of a PSU; his predecessors, Fred Philp and David Jones, had been workers in the Liverpool unit during the war. His title was now 'director', a choice which for Geoffrey Rankin, fieldwork organiser in the Islington unit, signalled unreal expectations in the incumbent because it created an expectation that he should direct, which was only possible in an organisation that wanted to be directed.[54] Rankin, although sometimes seen as a maverick within the organisation, had put his finger on the problem. The structure did not allow direction even though attempts had been made to direct. FSU's attitude to Rankin, who was not afraid of saying uncomfortable things or of behaving in a way which challenged the organisation's ethos, tended to be one of half-concealed impatience, but his observations were correct. The organisation did not want to be directed, at least not by Halliwell. Rankin's comments found an echo in those of Newman, who saw the role of director as being one which stimulated initiative rather than exercised formal authority.[55] Halliwell's style of leadership tended to lean towards the authoritarian.

Events surrounding Halliwell's appointment can also be seen as symptomatic of wider changes taking place in the national personal social services. In October 1964 the national secretary had reported his anxiety that the demand for experienced social workers by local authorities would create such a scarcity as to be a brake on FSU expansion.[56] And as one fieldwork organiser at the time has since commented, Halliwell was over-promoted at a time when, in the wake of the 1963 Children and Young Persons Act and an acute shortage of qualified social workers to fill the management posts being created in local authority departments, such over-promotion was common.[57] Certainly by 1969 FSU had experienced several years of difficulty in finding suitable candidates for senior posts. For example, both the national executive committee and the fieldwork organisers' committee noted the shortage of suitable applicants for senior posts in units in Bradford and York,[58] as well as in Birmingham, South London and West London.[59] The Leicester unit found it difficult to recruit a suitable replacement for its fieldwork organiser and to fill vacancies for caseworkers,[60] and the following year it proved difficult to find a suitable candidate as fieldwork organiser in Newcastle.[61] It can have been no surprise, therefore, that advertisements for the post of director met with an unpromising response. Of the seven candidates shortlisted, two withdrew before the interviews took place and after the remaining candidates – including Halliwell – had met the selection committee, uncertainty about the suitability of any one of them led to discussions about whether to re-advertise the post. In the end it was decided to offer it to Halliwell, who knew the organisation and had been an effective fieldwork organiser at Bradford.[62] His appointment was given a guarded welcome by the other fieldwork organisers, who had doubts about the way in which the decision to appoint him had been reached and expressed regret that they had not been better informed or given more opportunity to participate in the process.[63]

The anxiety of the selection committee and the fieldwork organisers was well founded; Halliwell's appointment heralded nearly a decade of difficult relationships within FSU. He quickly lost the support of many fieldwork organisers and the confidence of national committees, but his was a difficult task. He represented a break with the past at a time when the past, in the shape of a significant number of ex-PSU workers, continued to be active and influential. He was less professionally confident than either of his distinguished predecessors, both of whom had gone on to senior social work posts outside the organisation; Jones helped to launch the National Institute of Social Work and eventually became its principal, and Philp was to become deputy director of social services for Cumbria. Halliwell was also appointed at a time when the preventive work with families which PSU/FSU had pioneered had become the new orthodoxy enshrined in the 1963 Children and Young Persons Act. Halliwell had become the leader of an organisation whose past success had led to uncertainty about its future role.

Given the structure of FSU and the tensions between the national and local arms of the organisation, Haringey was a disaster waiting to happen. During the first months of 1970 the unit at Haringey appeared to exemplify the uncertainties entertained by most units about the respective areas of national control and local autonomy and the pervasive ambivalence about direction from the national office. The difficulties were compounded by the Haringey workers' adherence to principles associated with the new radical social work which was beginning to take a hold on the profession. Problems came to light when a request from the personnel committee for a report on a new worker in Haringey was refused on the grounds that, as the four workers at the unit believed themselves to be equal colleagues, no one of them was in a position to make a report on any other. A similar response was offered when the failure of Haringey to send a representative to attend a meeting of the fieldwork organisers' committee was noted. The Haringey workers repeated their refusal to admit that any one of them was senior to the others, and argued that distinctions in status among the workers would contradict the ideas and values they had evolved in developing their unit.[64] Anxious that the methods being employed at Haringey ran counter to FSU traditions, the personnel committee requested an assessment of the unit's work. The unit workers refused to cooperate. Tom Stephens, chairman of the personnel committee, expressed the unanimous disapproval of the committee and, it could be argued, reflected the paternalistic and controlling attitudes which Haringey most wished to counter. In the interests of the families with whom the units were working, Stephens believed it vital that individual units should conform to the general pattern of organisation in so far as it was necessary for the maintenance of good standards.[65] That general pattern of organisation involved scrutiny of local activity by national officials. In the interests of those same families, the Haringey workers wanted to pursue new methods in their work and in their relationships as a unit and to reject some of FSU's traditional practices. As well as pursuing egalitarian attitudes in their relationships with each other, the Haringey workers were also attempting to break down the barrier between professional social workers and their clients by encouraging client families to take an active part in the life and management of the unit, a practice which FSU was to endorse 20 years later but which received less than enthusiastic support in the 1960s.

Haringey was a sub-unit, originally a branch of Islington and officially managed by the Islington unit, although it had little contact with the fieldwork organiser or the local committee there. It manifested in extreme form the organisational difficulties experienced by a number of units. On one hand, the Haringey workers complained of maladministration by the Islington committee.[66] On the other, its four caseworkers, free from the constraints of regular supervision, appeared to Tom Stephens and the personnel committee to see themselves as an independent democratic group, recognising no authority outside themselves.[67] To some extent Stephens's criticism was echoed by Eric Brown, who was invited to report on the work at Haringey. As a one-time fieldwork organiser in the Liverpool unit, and from 1970 lecturer in social work at Chiswick Polytechnic, he was well placed to comment. He pointed out that the four Haringey workers had usurped the functions of the local committee by incurring unsanctioned liabilities, especially in their action in appointing a fourth worker in spite of the fact that there was insufficient money to pay him – to which the three original workers responded by proposing that they fund him from their own pockets. Brown noted that they had been allowed to do this in default of some authority within the organisation 'spelling out the limits of the freedom of the workers... to decide for themselves what work to do'. It also raised questions about the responsibility for appointing staff in FSU and about the enforcement of agreements to adhere to recognised salary scales.[68]

Although critical of Haringey's cavalier attitude towards the organisational structures, Brown applauded what he believed to be exciting and original developments in the care and support of poor families. His explanation for the furore caused by Haringey drew attention to the dilemma currently facing all social workers; were they agents of social control or agents of social change? If, as the Haringey workers believed, society was discriminatory and repressive, then FSU in its traditional form could be seen as an agent of that discrimination. The underlying ideology embraced by the team at Haringey drew on the notion that casework was a confidence trick which worked best when both parties believed in the stratagem.[69] When one or other rejected it, then new approaches had to be considered.

Haringey, then, demonstrated two of the major problems facing FSU at the end of the decade. The management structure was not working, and the theoretical base on which intensive family casework had been built was being challenged. Furthermore, it represented an attempt to address difficulties which were beginning to cause concern within other local units. Most significantly, however, Haringey was illustrative of a debate which was to take place within the profession for at least the next decade. As Chris Jones was to point out in 1979, the most obvious characteristic of social work is that it is actively imposed on the working-class poor and is 'concerned to socialise its clients in what it regards as the appropriate social habits' with the aim of 'maintaining and reproducing a reliable working class'.[70] They were sentiments with which the Haringey workers might have agreed as they began to confront their reservations about being part of a profession which they perceived to be potentially oppressive. It is unlikely that the members of the personnel committee, rooted in an individualistic personalised model of practice, understood any of the points they tried to make. Brown's investigation was a final attempt to retrieve the situation, but in the event local authority funding was withdrawn, the workers resigned and the unit closed in September 1970.[71]

Problems such as those occurring in the Haringey unit have been attributed in part to the anti-authoritarian attitudes of the 1960s.[72] Difficult though that may be to substantiate, an atmosphere of distrust and discontent does appear to have developed, but it cannot be divorced from changes and tensions taking place within the social work profession as a whole. In part, the difficulties which faced FSU have also to be seen in the context of an occupation growing in confidence and becoming increasingly professionalised. FSU was not alone in experiencing such difficulties. Both Dr Barnardo's[73] and the NSPCC[74] found themselves facing critical issues of management during the 1960s.

These changes had been accelerating since the early 1960s. The introduction of the Younghusband courses into local colleges of further education and technical colleges in 1961, supplementing the long-established university courses, swelled the numbers of qualified social workers. For social work agencies, both statutory and voluntary, the introduction of these courses signalled a major alteration in traditional practice. Instead of taking unqualified would-be social workers and either giving them training or expecting them to work out their own methods for doing the job, agencies were able to advertise for and appoint workers who had benefited from nationally accredited courses and had gained recognised professional qualifications. FSU had long had its own centrally organised form of training and had insisted on an induction period for all the workers it appointed, whether or not they had received a college-based education, but the reception into its ranks of increasing numbers of professionally qualified workers inevitably altered the relationship between the workers on the ground and the committee who had hitherto organised training along traditional FSU lines. Tensions created by the growth of the social work profession were also expressed in divisions between the old and new schools of thought. Workers who had all undergone very similar academic training brought to the agencies a core set of ideas and weakened the ease with which an additional collection of values or practices could be inculcated. This was reflected in the attitudes of newly qualified workers. The FSU leadership appeared to some of them to embody old-fashioned values inherited from the original untrained PSU workers, many of whom were still in positions of authority and influence in the 1960s.

The slow adaptation to the presence of the new professionals was felt in the day-to-day life of the units. Liverpool was probably not unique in experiencing the force of the changes and in attempting to adapt to the new situation. For example, in the early days of the unit there was no money to employ cleaners, so caseworkers did the cleaning before visiting or being visited by their clients – a task tackled cheerfully, if inefficiently, by PSU workers in the 1940s, but no longer seen as appropriate in the new professional climate. Social workers argued that it was a poor use of their time and that other staff should be employed to take care of the building. They also complained that the office equipment was minimal and out of date.[75] If the local committee could be held to account for failing to ensure a proper working environment for professionally trained social workers, the workers themselves were products of a reluctance to reassess the role of the professional. Some failed properly to manage boundaries. A committee structure which did not have clearly defined areas of responsibility and generally accepted channels of communication produced uncertainty at ground level about the boundaries between professional social work and the wish to be all things to all people. In Liverpool, for example, attitudes persisted from the PSU days when all workers had been resident in the unit house and believed themselves to be on call for 24 hours a day. One man, a client from the 1940s, was allowed to continue to make excessive demands on the workers' time 20 years later. Little attempt was made to stop him treating the unit as though he had rights in it, encouraging in him a style of behaviour which tacitly gave him permission to disrupt the work – for example by interrupting interviews with clients – with impunity.[76]

Furthermore, some workers were unable easily to take on the role of the professional and to make a clear distinction between work and leisure. Some made the unit the centre of their lives, easily done at a time when some workers were still resident and when the unit building was both home and work. A senior caseworker in Liverpool during the 1960s spent most of at least one of his holidays sitting in the staff kitchen.[77] While such behaviour was probably unusual, in an organisation which had failed to acknowledge the role of the professional and expected employees to stand in the streets with collecting boxes trying to raise funds, ultimately for their own salaries, it demonstrated the uncertainty about the professional role on the part of both management and workers.

These concerns, consequent upon the failure to respond to a rapidly changing climate and exacerbated by complicated management structures and a reluctance to define clear boundaries, were being felt throughout the organisation. As the Islington fieldwork organiser argued in a discussion paper dated September 1969, another pressing problem in the organisation was the conflict between fieldwork organisers and their caseworkers.[78] At about the same time, the fieldwork organiser in Bradford diagnosed the FSU disease as being caused by FSU's acceptance of a non-hierarchical hierarchy, making fieldwork organisers (soon to be renamed unit organisers) the first among equals but ultimately responsible: the most difficult of management situations.[79] The Manchester unit experienced severe difficulties in the 1970s when its unit organiser, who had worked throughout the war with PSU and had been in post in Manchester since FSU's inception in 1948, lost the confidence of his caseworker colleagues. Resolution of a kind was achieved in 1973 when the unit organiser was persuaded to relinquish his post and to continue to work in the unit as a caseworker,[80] but the situation exemplified the difficulties that could arise when a senior member of an organisation, part of its highly creditable past, could no longer command the professional respect of his better-trained colleagues and was seen by them to represent old-fashioned amateur attitudes.

Another aspect of the relationship between fieldwork organisers and caseworkers was identified by Newman, who drew attention to the difficulties which could arise when the tensions between the fieldwork organiser's role as trainer, manager and equal colleague were not recognised by both fieldwork organiser and caseworker.[81] In an organisation which had historically emphasised mutuality between client and worker, however imperfectly this was understood, the expectation that within the units, and between the units and the national office, some sort of hierarchical relationship should on occasion come into play had the potential for confusion and failed expectations.

In Liverpool and Newcastle severe problems between caseworkers and their unit organisers arose in the late 1960s. In both units there was an attempt on the part of the caseworkers to engineer the dismissal of the unit organiser. In Newcastle, they were successful.[82] The protracted struggle between the unit organiser and two caseworkers in the unit had focused on mutual lack of confidence based to some extent on gender, with the male unit organiser claiming that 'the girls' were immature and irresponsible, and the female caseworkers accusing their male colleague of denying them the opportunity to have a say in unit policy and development, of withholding information, and of monitoring their use of time unnecessarily closely.[83] After an investigation conducted by the national organisation, the unit organiser resigned.[84]

In Liverpool, though, the move on the part of four caseworkers to resist the direction of the unit organiser, and to oust her from her post because they believed her to be lacking in certain professional skills, did not succeed. The wholehearted support of the Liverpool and District committee was thrown behind the unit organiser and those caseworkers who had opposed her leadership were forced to resign,[85] but it was a messy business. In an undated memorandum from the director to all units, a sorry list of failures of communication – between the unit organiser and the caseworkers, the caseworkers and the local committee, and the national director and the unit – were all noted. Although the confirmation of the unit organiser in her post necessitated the resignation of the caseworkers, a degree of responsibility was also acknowledged to lie with her and with the local committee. In an attempt to accept the consequences of these findings, the committee was asked to resign. In somewhat bizarre fashion, it was promptly re-appointed.[86]

The uncertainty and ambivalence about the exercise of authority within the units which the situation at Liverpool in the 1960s exemplified mirrored the relationship between the units and the national committees, where similar resistance to direction and surveillance was met. At the end of the 1960s the newly appointed unit organiser at Bradford, Len Hunt, commented on the high anxiety levels caused by ill-defined roles and constant changes; a situation which was aggravated by uncertainties and the high level of personal responsibility called for in each individual and which resulted in high staff turnover, communication difficulties and the constant threat of rumour. It could be no coincidence, he commented, that ex-FSU workers expressed feelings of relief when they moved to local authority posts where there was statutory certainty.[87] No wonder that in his report on FSU Newman detected, after two years of working with the agency, both an ambivalence towards authority and administration and a desire among fieldworkers for clearer management.[88]

Halliwell cannot be held solely responsible for the crises of the late 1960s and early 1970s, which resulted in part from the structure and relationship patterns of FSU, but his style of management exacerbated an already difficult situation.[89] His authoritarian attitudes, perhaps a function of his lack of confidence, led him to try to control access to information and influence.[90] In 1975, for example, permission for the Liverpool unit to have a representative member on the interview panel for its new unit organiser was refused,[91] thus increasing local resentment against the London officials.[92] The insecurity felt in the national office about the organisation's managerial difficulties is also apparent in the decision to appoint Tom Stephens as chairman of the national committee in 1975 'after a long search'. The committee had felt it appropriate that someone from inside should be appointed.[93] Whether that decision was made in order to prevent damage being done to FSU's reputation by exposure to the criticism of an outsider, or whether it was merely thought wise to appoint someone whose knowledge of the organisation would help in the task of resolving its difficulties, is not clear. Neither is it clear that he was the right person for the post. Stephens had enjoyed the reputation of being one of the most talented caseworkers of the original PSU in Liverpool and Manchester. The account of their wartime activities which he produced was largely responsible for bringing to public attention the plight of deprived families and provided the stimulus for the foundation of FSU in 1948. Since those days, his presence on committees had been consistently influential, but he had begun to lose the confidence of many of the staff by the late 1960s, and his judgement came to be questioned. He had become bruised as a result of his intervention in a local dispute in West London[94] and his championing of Halliwell, together with his handling of a redundancy dispute which affected the Oldham unit, suggested to many that it was time for him to break his close links with the agency.

The redundancy caused considerable concern throughout the organisation. In 1975 the reduction in the Oldham unit's local authority grant resulted in the decision to make one caseworker redundant, the choice of worker being made on a last-in, first-out basis. Supported by the national FSU staff association, the worker appealed. His appeal, heard by Stephens as national chairman and the chairs of two local committees, Jane Blom Cooper and Duncan Fearns, was upheld by two votes to one. The dissenting voice was that of Stephens, who promptly overruled the decision arguing that he was the chairman and that the other two assessors were only advisers whose advice he did not have to accept.[95] The Oldham situation demonstrated the tensions between the centre and the periphery, and the lack of trust that had built up.[96] The confirmation of the redundancy led to the resignations of two other workers in the unit because of their disagreement with management attitudes both locally and nationally.[97] The management of the case gave rise to complaints from the staff association about unconstitutional practice, both in the way that the decision to make a worker redundant had been taken and in the manner of communicating that decision.[98] It also highlighted particularly bad relations between the director and the local unit, relations which were so poor that the staff association believed that if the director were to be present at the appeal hearing the worker's case would be seriously damaged, because he had made no secret of his lack of sympathy for the situation at Oldham or for the redundant worker.[99] The conduct of the hearing also came in for criticism. The staff association challenged the large number of witnesses to the appeal brought by the management, to be met by the comment from the chairman that decisions about procedure were his prerogative.[100] The concerns which arose as a result of this case led Stephens to issue a document outlining new FSU appeal procedures and noting that the first resort to a panel consisting of a chairman and two assessors had shown up a number of weaknesses.[101] It was a further example of a style of management which was out of tune with the general mood of the organisation. Already strained relationships broke down to such an extent that Tony Hugill, in 1975 the newly appointed chairman of the national management committee,[102] commented on the amount of 'hyper-sensitivity, intolerance and intemperancy of expression in the organisation'. Things had been said and written and circulated which did no credit to their originators, and he had found in FSU less tolerance than in any other organisation in which he had worked.[103]

Those most closely involved with FSU offered a range of explanations for its difficulties. One unit organiser located the problems it faced during the late 1960s and 1970s in structure and its organic style, with a great deal hanging on the personalities involved; a less personal, more mechanistic model might have delineated clear lines of responsibility and given greater security to the workers.[104] Another pointed to FSU's tradition of using the metaphor of the family to describe the organisation. This was favoured by Halliwell, although FSU appeared to serving senior social workers to be a semi-functioning family; it tolerated a wide range of opinions but, as with any family, rivalry tended to favour the cause of the dominant sibling.[105] Len Hunt had claimed that the organisation's tendency to deny conflict in favour of uneasy and unhappy consensus resulted in a preoccupation with potentially explosive issues.[106]

In 1977 Rex Halliwell was forced to resign as director, after the humiliating experience of having to address the national conference knowing that he had lost the confidence of the staff and that his development plan for the organisation had been rejected by them.[107] His proffered resignation immediately after this event was not at first accepted by Tom Stephens, but its eventual acceptance prompted a paper on the structure of the national office, with a covering note from Stephens forbidding any statements to the press in an attempt to avoid harmful leaks. The crisis was explained in terms of the process of questioning of the management and objectives of FSU in which the organisation had been involved for some time. It pinpointed the uncertainties about authority and the blurred lines of communication. To a great extent the views expressed shared with papers of nearly a decade earlier a simplistic diagnosis of the structural weaknesses of the organisation, but little in the way of prescription for their cure. The blurring of lines of responsibility in the organisation as a whole had already been identified by Hunt,[108] Rankin[109] and Newman[110] as leading to friction and disunity, but apart from rather general strictures about the need for the new director to address publicly social policy issues and for his responsibilities and authority to be clearly defined and acknowledged, Stephens's paper offered no practical remedy.[111]

Managerial confusion was not the only cause for complaint within FSU during the troubled decades. Discontent also centred on matters of pay. Annual conferences, originally intended as opportunities for sharing experience and meeting workers from other units, gave opportunity for discontents to be aired and resulted in the formation of a caseworkers' committee in 1965; one of its aims was to redress inequalities, especially of pay. In spite of the endeavours of the national executive committee to devise a pay structure which adequately reflected the work and level of responsibility of FSU social workers, in the 1960s and 1970s it rarely achieved parity with local authority rates of pay. The Liverpool committee had reported in 1963 that local authorities and other agencies were paying annual salaries several hundreds of pounds in excess of those available to

FSU workers,[112] and the organisation was requested to review salary scales and conditions of service in an attempt to prevent senior workers from moving to better-paid posts.[113] The persistent failure to offer realistic levels of pay contributed to a rapid turnover in staff. Young, newly qualified social workers were prepared to work for a time in an organisation which was held in high esteem by the profession in order to gain valuable experience and training, but as FSU did not offer salaries sufficient to support a family such workers moved on to better-paid posts, frequently at a time in their careers when they could have offered a great deal to the organisation.[114] In 1965 the Kensington and Paddington unit complained that the organisation's proposed increased rates of pay were too low and that the local authorities were paying salaries which would need to be matched if FSU were to attract suitable applicants.[115] As late as 1977 the Liverpool unit reported that two social workers had rejected offers of posts with FSU because the pay scales were too low.[116] A national survey in 1976 had revealed that the average length of service of FSU workers was three years, and that the average age of recruits was 27.[117] Although three years' service was in line with the pattern elsewhere within the voluntary sector, and even though there was a small nucleus of long-serving senior social workers, the organisation was largely staffed by young, relatively inexperienced workers, many of whom were beginning to look for fresh challenges.

In 1978, the FSU development plan included the aim of making sure that FSU salaries compared well with local authority salary structure,[118] but it appears that this was still a forlorn hope. The following year in Newcastle, for example, concern was expressed by the committee that the salaries for all staff, not just social workers, were well below the local authorities' standards and were also below the proposed FSU national scale. Lack of parity with their local authority colleagues was making recruitment difficult and also having a bad effect on staff morale.[119]

The late 1970s were to witness a change in personnel at the most influential level of the agency. It was partly a consequence of their age that the old guard of pioneering PSU workers began to fade from positions of power, but it was also because the climate had changed and some of them had been too closely associated with those on the wrong side in serious internal difficulties. Halliwell was replaced as director by Tim Cook. Soon after Cook's appointment, Stephens resigned as chairman.[120] The new director set about his task with energy. In his report after nine months in post[121] he discussed the danger of having a management structure which could give rise to uncertainty and ambiguity, and he pointed FSU to the future by reporting progress on a comprehensive development plan which would examine every aspect of FSU's activity and offer concrete proposals for future activities and suggestions for their implementation. Although Halliwell represented the first break with the past, it was Cook who began to drag the organisation into the present.

The FSU development plan which was published in 1978 grasped a number of nettles and was emblematic of Cook's style of leadership. It represents a watershed in FSU's history. The opportunity to reformulate the organisation's aims was seized, bringing them up to date and recognising the changes in legislation and practice which had taken place in the 30 years since FSU's inauguration, and the new social and economic circumstances in which FSU had to work.[122] It openly acknowledged the difficulties faced by FSU as a result of its internal structures, and highlighted the problems of communication between the national organisation and its local branches; aspects of that difficulty included tensions between unit organisers and the assistant directors, and a failure of the proper representation of staff views to FSU's national committees. Uncertainties about the responsibilities, relationships and procedures of the constituent parts of FSU were to be clarified and regulated by the introduction of two manuals – a staff handbook and a handbook for local committees.[123] Embedded in a discussion about the role of the national office was the expectation that central direction would become stronger, with London taking initiatives on both fieldwork and social policy matters whenever possible, although a nod was made in the direction of participative management and the importance of taking the right decision in the right way.[124] After a decade of difficulty, 1978 may be seen as the moment at which FSU could hope to have a future, but it was a future which had broken many of its links with its past.

Although FSU's chronic problems, which became acute in the decade between 1968 and 1978, were largely of its own making, they were exacerbated by the wider context in which the organisation worked, and, in spite of Cook's efforts – perhaps because of the move to greater centralisation – the 1980s were also characterised by crisis. In Liverpool tension between London and Merseyside focused on the wages being paid to cleaners. Tackling head-on the long-running problem of FSU's low pay, the national office had decreed that a certain hourly wage should be paid to all cleaning staff, even though in some places this would mean paying them well above the local rate. The unit objected; London tried to insist.[125] A year later, the dispute was still rumbling on, the Liverpool unit arguing that it was unconstitutional for national office to try to enforce national rates of pay determined by London levels on units which were funded by local authorities.[126] The old problem of the central body dictating the way in which funds raised locally were spent had still not been resolved, and the argument demonstrated insensitivity to units outside the metropolis. Worse was to come. As the director who had done a great deal to drag the organisation into modern life left to become Clerk to the Trustees of the City Parochial Foundation, the West London unit, which had enjoyed a long period of stability, experienced severe difficulties in the management of staff relationships which resulted in the resignation of the unit organiser and seven other members of staff.[127] The following year, the Liverpool unit was faced with two grievance procedures and the eventual dismissal of its unit organiser in September 1986.[128]

In 1984 the Newcastle unit had sent shock waves through the organisation by attempting to shrug off its traditional methods of working and adopt a collective style of management which rejected the normal FSU hierarchies and actively encouraged the participation of service users.[129] While funding permitted the employment of adequate numbers of staff, and while the commitment to the experiment within the unit was high, it was believed locally to work quite well. However, it also illustrated the contention that while it was held to be more democratic, it ran the risk of claiming that it was morally superior to other ways of doing things and therefore could not be called into question.[130] Furthermore, it lacked the support of the national organisation,[131] and eventually suffered the complete withdrawal of local authority grant aid so that the unit was forced to close.[132] It did, however, leave a legacy in the form of Dhek Bhal, a project for Asian carers which had attracted considerable financial support and remained in the city after FSU had closed.[133] The principle at the heart of Newcastle's experiment – the empowerment of service users as embodied in Dhek Bhal – received enthusiastic endorsement from the coordinator of community care at the National Institute of Social Work, who thought it '… brilliant, an example to the rest of the country in piloting an alternative model of community development, carer and black led'.[134]

Newcastle's choice of collective management as a solution to FSU's organisational difficulties may have been unusual and ultimately unsuccessful, but the fact that it was tried is illustrative of the anxiety about leadership within the organisation. It did not, however, address the difficulties between committees and units. At this level, tensions between the managers and the managed in FSU had eased little since the 1960s, although the extent to which they caused real difficulties varied. Writing in the *FSU Quarterly* in 1986 Martin Thomas, a worker from the South Birmingham unit, commented on the membership of local management committees and used his own unit as an example of FSU's failure to recruit appropriate people. His argument reinforced the notion of a mismatch between the committee and the work of the unit and suggested that the South Birmingham committee members could appreciate neither the professional concerns of the social workers nor the situations of the clients. He identified a difficulty which affected not just his local unit, or just one social work agency, but was built into the nature of voluntary organisations. As was commonly the case, the South Birmingham unit committee was made up of professional men and women whose average income was much higher than that of the average FSU worker let alone of a unit client, and most of the committee had no connection – personal, residential or social – with the area in which the unit was set. For the committee members, their involvement provided an opportunity to offer their skills and time to a deserving cause. For the workers, the situation highlighted class differences and underlined the gap in status and power between the middle class committee members and the working class clients.

Efforts to fill vacancies on South Birmingham FSU committee with local residents – as in a similar experiment in Newcastle[135] – created almost as many problems as they solved. They may not have understood the problems facing a deprived neighbourhood, but middle class committee members did appreciate committee etiquette. Lack of confidence and unfamiliarity with the functions and procedures of committees hampered the smooth introduction of local people as members. By failing to offer them training, the unit also failed properly to equip its new recruits, with the result that discussion became dominated by a few determined or vocal residents. The use of jargon and the failure to explain the significance of issues under discussion made some new members feel uncomfortable, limited their effective contribution, and resulted in long and undisciplined meetings.

FSU's problems in developing effective management were common to much of the voluntary sector. Social workers who had made their way up the hierarchical structures had rarely had any training in management and, as Nicholas Deakin has noted, it was not until the 1980s that management teaching was incorporated into the courses offered by the social science faculties of polytechnics and universities.[136] As the Coopers and Lybrand report noted, proportionate to its size FSU's processes represented a very substantial superstructure that was 'costly in time, energy, commitment and money'. As a result its decision making tended to be slow, cumbersome and often ineffectual.[137] The report attracted adverse criticism from Jane Lewis.[138] Nevertheless, Coopers and Lybrand highlighted the failure to collate information and to make it available to all units, thus leaving the organisation as a whole repeatedly encountering and devising strategies for dealing with problems which were common to a large number of units and failing to enable a carefully thought-out response which could be fed into wider debates.

Although energetic attempts had been made to redesign FSU's management structures and to try to preserve the organisation's ethos while introducing greater clarity, it would not be until the mid-1990s that an examination of its structures could result in greater definition. The intensely personal style of its work, reflected in its style of management from the 1940s through the 1960s, whatever its advantages, had left FSU with a legacy of managerial relationships which trapped the organisation in introspection and a constant rearrangement of furniture without thoroughly re-ordering the house.

# NOTES

1. In 1969 the title of the senior social worker/manager in each unit was changed from fieldwork organiser to unit organiser.

2. *The Organisation of Family Service Units*, p1, no date but probably c 1958. ULSCA D495(HQ)M3/19.

3. Minutes of the FSU national executive committee, January 10 1968. ULSCA D495(HQ)M2/5.

4. Derek Newman, *Report on Two Years' Work with FSU* (1969), p11.

5. *The Organisation of Family Service Units*, p1.

6. The unit in Bristol was the one exception to this rule. It was opened as the result of an initiative taken by the local health committee and the MOH in March

1953. They did not want a local committee of any kind and wished to deal directly with the FSU national executive committee. Although this ran counter to its preferred practice, FSU agreed to the arrangement. The unit was funded by the local public health committee. It closed in 1966, when the committee withdrew its financial support and no other local committee was prepared to take it on. See above, pp183ff; P. Starkey, 'The Medical Officer of Health, the social worker and the problem family', *Social History of Medicine*, 11 (1998), pp421–44.

7. *The Organisation of Family Service Units*, p2.

8. See, for example, minutes of the Liverpool PSU committee, December 9 1942; minutes of the Liverpool PSU committee, January 27 1943; minutes of the Liverpool PSU committee, February 3 1943. ULSCA D495(LI)M1/3.

9. Letter to David Jones from Sir Donald Allen, Clerk to the Trustees, City Parochial Foundation, March 31 1949. ULSCA D495(HQ)M3/16.

10. Minutes of the FSU national executive committee, October 24 1947. ULSCA D495(HQ)M2/1.

11. Minutes of the FSU national executive committee, February 18 1949. ULSCA D495(HQ)M2/2.

12. Minutes of the FSU national executive committee, October 28 1949. ULSCA D495(HQ)M2/2.

13. Minutes of the FSU national management committee, November 18 1949. ULSCA D495(HQ)M2/6.

14. Minutes of the Liverpool FSU committee, February 3 1959. ULSCA D495 (LI)M2/1.

15. By the late 1950s there were units in Liverpool, Manchester, Sheffield, Bristol, Leicester, Stepney, South London, West London, Islington, Birmingham, Oldham, York and Bradford, and FSU was considering requests for units to be established in a number of other urban centres.

16. *The Organisation of Family Service Units*. ULSCA D495(HQ)M/3/19.

17. Minutes of the FSU national executive committee, October 261962. ULSCA D495(HQ)M2/5. Minutes of the Liverpool FSU committee, February 8 1963. ULSCA D495(LI)M2/1.

18. Minutes of the Liverpool FSU committee, January 11 1963. ULSCA D495 (LI)M2/1.

19. Minutes of the Liverpool FSU committee, January 11 1963. ULSCA D495(LI)M2/1.

20. Report to the FSU national executive committee to end December, 1962. ULSCA D495(LI)M12.

21. Correspondence between Sir John Wolfenden, Fred Philp and Irene Barclay, 1962–63. ULSCA D495(HQ)M3/18.

22. Letter from Sir John Wolfenden to Eric McKie, quoted at meeting of the Liverpool FSU committee, February 8 1963. ULSCA D495(LI)M2/1.

23. E. McKie, *Venture in Faith* (Liverpool, 1963).

24. Minutes of the FSU national executive committee, January 23 1963. ULSCA D495(HQ)M2/5.

25. Letter from Sir John Wolfenden to Eric McKie quoted at meeting of the Liverpool FSU committee, February 8 1963. ULSCA D495(LI)M2/1.

26. Minutes of the FSU national executive committee, October 26 1963. ULSCA D495(HQ)M2/5

**27.** Minutes of the West London FSU committee, February 13 1963. ULSCA D495(WL)M1/3.

**28.** A. Cohen, *The Revolution in Post-War Family Casework: The Story of Pacifist Service Units and Family Service Units* (Lancaster, 1998), p52.

**29.** Notes of senior workers refresher course, November 6–9 1972. D495(HQ) M3/21.

**30.** Newman, *Report on Two Years' Work with FSU*, passim.

**31.** A. F. Philp, report to personnel committee, June 29 1967. ULSCA D495 (HQ)M3/14.

**32.** Notes of a senior workers' refresher course, November 1972. ULSCA D495(HQ)M3/21.

**33.** Coopers and Lybrand, *Organising for a Purpose* (London, 1988), p7. But see J. Lewis, 'Management consultants and voluntary organisations: The cases of Relate National Marriage Guidance, Family Planning Association and Family Service Units', *Non-Profit Studies*, 1 (1996).

**34.** J. Lewis, *The Voluntary Sector, the State and Social Work in Britain* (London, 1995), p132.

**35.** For a case study of an organisation with a similar history, see A. Penn, 'The Management of Voluntary Organisations in the Post-War Period' (unpublished DPhil thesis, University of Sussex, 1992).

**36.** Cohen, *Revolution in Post-War Family Casework*, p59.

**37.** As Margaret Britten she had worked as a member of the Liverpool Pacifist Service Unit.

**38.** Interview with David and Margaret Jones, January 1996.

**39.** J. Lewis, 'Developing the mixed economy of care: Emerging issues for voluntary organisations', *Journal of Social Policy*, 22 (1993).

**40.** M. Harris, 'The role of voluntary management committees', in J. Batsleer, C. Cornforth and R. Paton (eds), *Issues in Voluntary and Non-Profit Management* (Milton Keynes, 1992), pp134ff.

**41.** P. Goldring, *Friend of the Family: The Work of Family Service Units* (Newton Abbott, 1973), p77.

**42.** S. Kay, A. Davies and S. Ambrose, 'From psychiatric social worker to family caseworker', *Social Work*, 24 (1966), p17.

**43.** Islington FSU quarterly report, October 1969. ULSCA unlisted.

**44.** R. Popplestone, 'Staff assessment in Family Service Units', *Social Work Today*, 6 (1975), p199.

**45.** Newman, *Report on Two Years' Work with FSU*.

**46.** Minutes of the Oldham FSU committee, July 25 1977. ULSCA D495(OL) M1/4.

**47.** Paper on FSU committee structure, no date but probably January 1976. ULSCA D495(LI)M2.

**48.** Minutes of the West London FSU committee, April 9 1975. ULSCA D495(WL)M1/4.

**49.** Minutes of the West London FSU committee, April 28 1976. ULSCA D495 (WL)M1/4.

**50.** See above, pp103ff.

**51.** The City Parochial Foundation gave £12,000 and Hackney Borough Council £2,000 a year to cover the running costs of the unit. Report of Hackney CCU to FSU by Fred Philp, 1967. ULSCA D495(HQ)B3/4.

**52.** Report of Hackney CCU to FSU by Fred Philp, 1967. ULSCA D495(HQ) B3/4.

**53.** Minutes of the FSU national executive committee, January 2 1962. ULSCA D495(HQ)M2/4.

**54.** Undated letter from Geoffrey (Rankin) to Rex (Halliwell). From internal evidence it is clear that this was written in October or November 1969. ULSCA D495(HQ)M3/12.

**55.** Newman, *Report on Two Years' Work with FSU*, p11.

**56.** Minutes of the FSU national executive committee, October 7 1964. ULSCA D495(HQ)M2/5.

**57.** Interview with Rose Pyle, May 1995; E. Younghusband, *Social Work in Britain: 1950–1975*, 2 vols (London, 1978), vol 2, p67.

**58.** Minutes of the FSU fieldwork organisers' meeting, February 12 1965. ULSCA D495(HQ)M14/3. Minutes of the FSU national executive committee, October 6 1965. ULSCA D495(HQ)M2/5.

**59.** Minutes of the FSU fieldwork organisers' meeting, February 12 1965, December 9 1965. ULSCA D495(HQ)M14/3.

**60.** Minutes of the FSU national executive committee, March 17 1965. ULSCA D495(HQ)M2/5.

**61.** Minutes of the FSU national executive committee, October 5 1966. ULSCA D495(HQ)M2/5.

**62.** Minutes of FSU personnel and development committee, January 14 1969. ULSCA D495(HQ)M3/13.

**63.** Minutes of the FSU fieldwork organisers' meeting, January 31 1969. ULSCA D495(HQ)M14/3.

**64.** FSU fieldwork organisers' meeting, March 17 and 18 1969. ULSCA D495 (HQ)M14/3.

**65.** Undated confidential letter from Tom Stephens to the chairman of FSU. Internal evidence suggests that the letter was written in February 1970. ULSCA D495(HQ)M3/12.

**66.** Minutes of the Islington FSU committee, August 24 1970. ULSCA unlisted.

**67.** Confidential draft letter to the chairman of FSU from Tom Stephens. Internal evidence suggest that the letter was written in February 1970. ULSCA D495(HQ) M3/12.

**68.** Eric Brown, 'Some implications of the developments at Haringey'. Paper prepared at request of FSU national executive committee (1970). ULSCA unlisted.

**69.** Brown, 'Some implications of the developments at Haringey'.

**70.** C. Jones, 'Social work education, 1900–1977', in N. Parry, M. Rustin and C. Satyamurti (eds), *Social Work, Welfare and the State* (London, 1979), pp75–6.

**71.** Note from the director to all units, August 27 1970. ULSCA D495 (HQ)M3/19.

**72.** Personal communication from Rose Pyle, May 1995.

**73.** J. Rose, *For the Sake of the Children: Inside Dr Barnardo's: 120 years of caring for children* (London, 1987), ch13.

**74.** C. Sherrington, 'The NSPCC in Transition, 1884–1983: A study of organisational survival' (unpublished PhD thesis, University of London, 1984), p237.

**75.** Personal communication from Rose Pyle, May 1995.

**76.** Personal communication from Rose Pyle, May 1995.

**77.** Memo to the Liverpool FSU local committee from the fieldwork organiser Rosemary Vear, October 15 1968, p3. Private papers.

**78.** Geoffrey Rankin, *A Personal View of FSU* (September, 1969). ULSCA unlisted.

**79.** Len Hunt, 'Why do ideas and suggestions lie fallow in this organisation?' Paper to national executive committee (?), no date, but probably 1970. ULSCA D495(HQ)B17/4.

**80.** Minutes of the Manchester FSU committee, March 22 1973. ULSCA D495(MA)M1/4.

**81.** Newman, *Report on Two Years' Work with FSU*, p20.

**82.** Minutes of the FSU personnel and development committee, April 25 1969. ULSCA D495(HQ)B17/4.

**83.** Minutes of the FSU personnel and development committee, January 14 1969. ULSCA D495(HQ)B17/4.

**84.** Minutes of the FSU fieldwork organisers' meeting, March 17 1969 and April 25 1969. ULSCA D495(HQ)B17/4. Cf. letter from Mike Wardle, chairman of the caseworkers' committee to his members, March 14 1969 and letter from 'Ros' to 'Rex', March 19 1969. ULSCA D495(HQ)B11/13.

**85.** Minutes of the FSU personnel and development committee, December 15 1969. ULSCA D495(HQ)B17/4.

**86.** Undated memo from 'Rex' to all units. ULSCA D495(HQ)B17/4.

**87.** Hunt, 'Why do ideas lie fallow?'.

**88.** Newman, *Report on Two Years' Work with FSU*, p18.

**89.** Interview with David and Margaret Jones, January 1996.

**90.** Interview with Rose Pyle, May 1995.

**91.** Minutes of the Liverpool FSU committee, January 7 1975. ULSCA D495 (LI)M2/2.

**92.** Minutes of the Liverpool FSU committee, September 16 1975. ULSCA D495(LI)M2/2.

**93.** Minutes of the Oldham FSU committee, January 27 1975. ULSCA D495 (OL)M1/3.

**94.** Letter from Tom Stephens to Dave Holder, May 26 1975. ULSCA D495 (HQ)M13/3.

**95.** Transcript of appeal, August 1975. ULSCA D495(HQ)M13/3.

**96.** Correspondence between May and July 1975. ULSCA D495(HQ)M13/3.

**97.** Letter to 'Dave' from Gill Silverside, July 9 1975. ULSCA D495(HQ)M13/3. See also *Oldham Evening Chronicle*, August 6 1975.

**98.** Letter from Dave Holder (chair of the staff association) to Rex Halliwell, June 4 1975. Letter from Rex Halliwell to Derek Coleman (the worker to be made redundant), June 4 1975. ULSCA D495(HQ)M13/3.

**99.** Letter to Felicity Craven from Dave Holder, June 30 1975. ULSCA D495(HQ)M13/3.

**100.** Transcript of appeal. ULSCA D495(HQ)M13/3.

**101.** Tom Stephens, note on appeal procedures, September 1975. ULSCA D495(HQ)M13/3.

**102.** The national executive committee was renamed the national management committee in 1974.

**103.** Tony Hugill, 'In at the deep end'. Paper presented to the national management committee, November 1975. ULSCA D495(HQ)M2/6.

**104.** Letter to Mike Wardle from Dick Harding, February 16 1977. ULSCA unlisted.

**105.** Personal communication from Mike Wardle, January 1997.

**106.** Notes of an FSU senior workers' refresher course, November 1972. ULSCA D495(HQ)M3/21.

**107.** Minutes of the Manchester FSU committee, February 24 1977. ULSCA D495(MA)M1/3.

**108.** Hunt, 'Why do ideas lie fallow?'.

**109.** Rankin, *Personal View.*

**110.** Newman, *Two Years' Work with FSU*, passim.

**111.** Paper on national office structure, March 1977. ULSCA D495(HQ)M2/7.

**112.** Minutes of the Liverpool FSU committee, January 11 1963. ULSCA D495 (LI)M2/1.

**113.** Minutes of the Liverpool FSU committee, September 10 1963, 26 January 1966. ULSCA D495(LI)M2/1.

**114.** Personal communication from Rose Pyle, May 1995. See also minutes of South London FSU committee, January 25 1966, in which the difficulties of recruiting additional workers and replacing existing ones because salaries were dropping so far behind was noted. ULSCA D495(SL)M1/3. See also minutes of the Islington FSU committee, July 10 1967. ULSCA unlisted.

**115.** Minutes of the Kensington and Paddington FSU committee, October 5 1965. ULSCA D495(WL)M1/13.

**116.** Minutes of the Liverpool FSU committee, November 23 1977. ULSCA D495(LI)M2/2.

**117.** Minutes of the West London FSU committee, September 20 1976. ULSCA D495(WL)M1/4.

**118.** FSU working party on development, *The Development of Family Service Units* (London, 1978), p54.

**119.** Newcastle FSU bimonthly report, November 1979. ULSCA D495(NE)M1/1.

**120.** Cohen, *Revolution in Post-War Family Casework*, p59.

**121.** Tim Cook, *Report to the National Management Committee after Nine Months in Post* (September, 1978). ULSCA D495(HQ)M2/7.

**122.** FSU working party, *The Development of FSU*, p4.

**123.** FSU working party, *The Development of FSU*, p57.

**124.** FSU working party, *The Development of FSU*, pp59 and 62.

**125.** Minutes of the Liverpool FSU committee, October 3 1984. ULSCA D495(LI)M2/5.

**126.** Minutes of Liverpool FSU finance committee, January 23 1985. Minutes of Liverpool FSU committee, September 2 1985. ULSCA D495(LI)M2/5.

**127.** West London FSU annual report for 1984–85. ULSCA D495(WL)M5/30.

**128.** Unlisted personal papers, 1985–86.

**129.** A Stanton, *Invitation to Self-Management* (Ruislip, 1989), p10.

**130.** C. Landry, D. Morley, R. Southwood and P. Wright, 'An analysis of radical failure', in J. Batsleer, C. Cornforth, and R. Paton (eds), *Issues in Voluntary and Non-Profit Management* (Milton Keynes, 1992), p26. See Stanton, *Invitation to Self-Management*, pp305ff.

**131.** Stanton, *Invitation to Self-Management*, pp56ff.

**132.** Letter from Lillian White to UK Grants Officer, Charity Projects, January 30 1992. ULSCA D495(NE)M7/4. Minutes of Newcastle FSU committee, March 3 1992. ULSCA D495(NE)M1/3.

**133.** Confidential report from 'Gus' (assistant director, FSU) to the national management committee, March 19 1992. ULSCA D495(NE)M7/4.

**134.** Evaluation of Dhek Bhal by Beverley Prevatt Goldstein, March 27 1992. ULSCA D495(NE)M20.

**135.** Stanton, *Invitation to Self-Management*, pp300ff.

**136.** N. Deakin, 'The perils of partnership: The voluntary sector and the state, 1945–1992', in J. Davis Smith, C. Rochester and R. Hedley (eds), *An Introduction to the Voluntary Sector* (London, 1995), p60.

**137.** Coopers and Lybrand, *Organising for a Purpose*, p6.

**138.** Lewis, 'Management consultants and voluntary organisations', p12.

# Conclusion

There can be little doubt that FSU played a significant role in the development of professional social work with families after the Second World War. To quantify the extent of that role is more difficult. It assumes that PSU/FSU workers took with them to new posts the values and methods they had learned in the organisation and were determined to develop and apply them. That may not always have been the case. However, the speed with which units were established with the enthusiastic support of local authorities is testimony to the fact that the organisation was seen to be offering, if not a solution to, then a method of alleviating the problems caused by poverty and deprivation as they affected some families. From the perspective of the early twenty-first century, it is possible to argue that the numbers may have been exaggerated and the appellation 'problem families' very loosely and often inappropriately applied, in some cases to large numbers of families whose difficulties evaporated once they had decent housing. However, most urban local authorities perceived a problem that threatened to hinder the work of reconstruction and many were anxious to secure FSU's services in order to solve it. FSU was also invited to give evidence to all major inquiries into social work as it affected the family in the post-war period. It was not alone in that, of course. Evidence was always collected from a wide range of sources, both voluntary and statutory, but that a young and very small organisation should expect to have its voice heard witnesses to the impact it had made in an area which excited official concern.

If measured by its contribution to the development of social work as a subject worthy of academic study, then FSU again scores highly. It found itself at the forefront of the move towards greater professionalisation of social work after 1945. Its innovatory methods of working with poor and dysfunctional families attracted the attention of teachers in most university social science departments that trained social workers and, even before FSU was properly constituted and certainly before its own workers had received professional training, units in Manchester, Liverpool and Kensington and Paddington were to be found offering practical experience to social work trainees. At various points in its history, particular units have been considered very desirable places in which to do student placements. Workers left the organisation to take up positions in university and college social work departments. And if FSU's success is measured in terms of the numbers of PSU/FSU workers whose career paths led them to positions of influence within the profession, then it has clearly made an impact; many of those who received their early social work experience with the organisation went on to assume senior positions in local authority social work.

Some past workers have been prepared to criticise aspects of the work and management of the organisation, but it has not proved possible to find any who were anxious to argue that their time within it was useless to them as professionals or that the clients were ill-served. Understandably, FSU's work has attracted both admiration and suspicion from professional colleagues in other organisations. Some found FSU uncooperative; the Liverpool unit was not the only one with a reputation for being unwilling to work with other agencies. Some criticised its methods. FSU's emphasis on keeping families together has led social workers from other agencies to claim that children were not always best served by such an approach and that there was a risk that their well-being might be sacrificed to an ideal that tended to see the best interests of the family being represented by the best interests of the parents. Indeed, the stress laid on parental incompetence in the early days of the agency metamorphosed into a less judgemental view of the family but one, it could be argued, in which the interests of children may not always have been paramount.

In a recent chance remark a local unit administrator impugned the organisation's management as 'very amateurish' in spite of energetic attempts made since the mid-1970s to address the problems of its organisational legacy. That may be a criticism that could equally well be directed at any number of organisations within the voluntary sector. Like other agencies, FSU has had to adapt and adjust its contribution in response to developments within the statutory sector.

It started life convinced that its work was properly the responsibility of the public authorities, and declared that it did not want to continue past the point of usefulness; but when some local authorities believed that point to have been reached and wished to take it over, FSU fought to survive even if that meant that it had to reinvent itself. To that extent, it exemplifies the dilemma facing voluntary agencies within the personal social services, where many have had to address the problems which arise from increasing dependence on local authority funding and increasing demands for accountability, but where few have been prepared to consider that they may no longer have a contribution to make.

# Bibliography

## PRIMARY SOURCES

Dr Barnardo's, University of Liverpool Special Collection and Archives.
Bristol Corporation Act 1950, 14 Geo 6, Bristol Record Office
Children's Society Archive, The Children's Society Record Office
Eugenics Society Archive, Wellcome Institute for the History of Medicine
Family Service Unit Archive, University of Liverpool Special Collections and
   Archives
Minutes of the City of Liverpool Children's Committee 1948–69, Liverpool Record
   Office
NCH Action for Children, University of Liverpool Special Collections and Archives.
Records of the Inner London Education Authority, Greater London Record Office
Reports of the Medical Officer of Health for Bristol 1950–1967, Bristol Record Office

*Report of the Royal Commission on the Poor Laws and Relief of Distress*, Cmnd 4499
   (HMSO, 1909)
Poor Law Commission, *Minority Report* Cd 4499 (HMSO, 1909)
Board of Education and Board of Control, *Report of the Inter-Departmental Committee
   on Mental Deficiency, 1925–29* (Wood report), Cd 3545 (HMSO, 1929), part III
*Hansard*, House of Commons and House of Lords Debates, fifth series
Ministry of Health and Ministry of Education, *Report of the Care of Children
   Committee* (Curtis report), Cmnd 6922 (HMSO, 1946)
Home Office, Ministries of Education and Health and Scottish Home Department,
   Joint Circular (1950)
*Report of the Royal Commission on Population*, Cmnd 7695 (HMSO, 1950)
Ministry of Health, Department of Health for Scotland, Ministry of Education, *An
   Inquiry Into Health Visiting: Report of a working party on the field of work, training
   and recruitment of health visitors* (HMSO, 1956)
Ministry of Health, Department of Health for Scotland, *Report of the Working Party
   on Social Workers in the Local Authority Health and Welfare Services* (Young-
   husband report) (HMSO, 1959)
Home Office, *Report of the Committee on Children and Young Persons* (Ingleby report),
   Cmnd 1191 (HMSO, 1960)
*Report on Children and Young Persons (Scotland)* (Kilbrandon report), Cmnd 2306

(HMSO Edinburgh, 1964)

*Report of the Committee on Housing in Greater London* (Milner Holland report), Cmnd 2605 (HMSO, 1965)

*Report of the Committee on Local Authority and Allied Personal Social Services* (Seebohm report), Cmnd 3703 (HMSO, 1968)

National Council of Social Service, National Institute for Social Work Training, *The Voluntary Worker in the Social Services* (Aves report) (London, 1969)

D. Newman, *Report on Two Years Work with Family Service Units* (London, 1969)

Department of Health and Social Security, *Report of the Committee on One-Parent Families* (Finer report), Cmnd 5629 (HMSO, 1974)

Supplementary Benefits Commission, *Low Incomes* (HMSO, 1977)

Supplementary Benefits Commission, *Annual Report 1978* (HMSO, 1979)

National Institute for Social Work, *The Report of a Working Party set up by the National Institute for Social Work at the Request of the Secretary of State for Social Services, chaired by Peter Barclay* (London, 1982)

Coopers and Lybrand, *Organising for a Purpose: Roles and relationships* (London, 1988)

# SECONDARY SOURCES

J. G. Adami, *Medical Contributions to the Study of Evolution* (London, 1918)

—— *The True Aristocracy: An address to the International Eugenics Congress, New York, 1921* (London, 1922)

R. Addis, 'Some comments on the Ingleby Report', *Social Work*, 18 (1961)

S. Ambrose, 'From psychiatric social worker to family caseworker', *Social Work*, 24 (1966)

B. Andrews and J. S. Cookson, 'Problem families: A practical approach', *Medical Officer*, 88 (1952)

Anonymous article, 'Unsatisfactory tenants and applicants', *The Society of Housing Managers Quarterly Bulletin*, 3 (1955)

A. R. H. F., 'A problem family at school', *Case conference*, 4 (1957)

E. T. Ashton, 'Problem families and their household budgets', *The Eugenics Review*, 48 (1956)

Association of Psychiatric Social Workers, *The Essentials of Social Casework* (London, 1956)

—— *The Boundaries of Casework* (London, 1956)

Association of Social Workers, *Recent Developments in Casework* (London, 1956)

J. Bagot, *Juvenile Delinquency* (London, 1941)

R. Baker, 'The challenge for British casework', *Social Work Today*, 4 (1973)

—— 'Is there a future for integrated practice? Obstacles to its development in practice and education', *Issues in Social Work Education*, 3 (1983)

I. Barclay, 'Problem families', *Social Service*, 24 (1951)

M. Barker, 'Through experience towards theory: A psychodynamic contribution to social work', *Issues in Social Work Education*, 2 (1982)

—— *People Need Roots* (London, 1976)

—— 'Eileen Younghusband 1902–1981: A personal appreciation', *Issues in Social Work Education*, 1 (1981)

R. Barker, *Conscience, Government and War* (London, 1982)

J. Batsleer, C Cornforth and R Paton, *Issues in Voluntary and Non-Profit Management* (Milton Keynes, 1992)

V. Belcher, *The City Parochial Foundation 1891–1991: A trust for the poor of London* (Aldershot, 1991)

B. Berger, 'The bourgeois family and modern society', in J. Davies (ed.), *The Family: Is it just another lifestyle choice?* (London, 1993)

B. Berger and P. Berger, *The War Over the Family: Capturing the middle ground* (London, 1983)

Lord Beveridge, *Voluntary Action* (London, 1948)

F. P. Biestek, *The Casework Relationship* (London, 1957)

K. Bilton, 'Origins, progress and future', in J Cypher (ed.), *Seebohm Across Three Decades* (Birmingham, 1979)

C. P. Blacker, *Eugenics, Galton and After* (London, 1952)

—— *A Social Problem Group?* (London, 1937)

—— 'Social problem families in the limelight', *Eugenics Review*, 38 (1946–47)

—— *Neurosis and the Mental Health Services* (Oxford, 1946)

—— *Problem Families: Five enquiries* (London, 1952)

E. Blackey, 'Building the curriculum: The foundation for professional competence', in Eileen Younghusband (ed.), *Education for Social Work* (London, 1964)

O. M. Blyth, 'Housing in Kensington: An account of the Kensington Housing Trust Ltd', *Social Work*, 2 (1942)

F. Bodman, 'Personal factors in the problem family', *Case Conference*, 5 (1958)

W. Boehm, 'The contribution of psychoanalysis to social work education', in E. Younghusband (ed.), *Education for Social Work* (London, 1964)

C. Booth, *Life and Labour of the People of London* (1904)

G. Boschma, 'Ambivalence about nursing's expertise: The role of a gendered holistic ideology in nursing, 1890–1990', in A. M. Rafferty, J. Robinson and R. Elkan (eds), *Nursing History and the Politics of Welfare* (London, 1997)

M. Boselli, 'The Family Centre of Hackney, II', *The British Journal of Social Work*, 1 (1971)

A. F. C. Bourdillon, *Voluntary Social Services: Their place in the modern state* (London, 1945)

R. Bourne, 'What are we training social workers for?', *New Society*, 54 (1980)

J. Bowlby, 'Forty-four juvenile thieves: Their character and home life', *International Journal of Psycho-Analysis*, 25 (1944)

—— *Maternal Care and Mental Health* (Geneva, 1951)

—— *Child Care and the Growth of Love* (Harmondsworth, 1953)

—— *Report on Proceedings of the National Council on Social Work (Family)* (London, 1953)

British Association of Social Workers, *Clients are Fellow Citizens* (Birmingham, 1980)

A. Broadie, 'Authority and the social caseworker', in N. Timms and D. Watson (eds), *Philosophy in Social Work* (London, 1978)

M. Brenton, *The Voluntary Sector in British Social Services* (London, 1985)

K. Brill ,'Preventive work by Children's Departments: A countryman's view', *Social Work*, 18 (1961)

S. Briskin, 'Who are the problem families?' *Case Conference*, 8 (1961)

C. F. Brockington, 'Problem families', *The Medical Officer*, 15 (February 1947)

—— 'Homelessness in children', *Lancet*, 1 (1946)

R. Burge, 'Partners not contractors', in R. Whelan (ed.), *Involuntary Action: How voluntary is the voluntary sector?* (London, 1999)

L. Burghes, *Living from Hand to Mouth* (London, 1980)

C. Burt, *The Young Delinquent* (London, 1944)

R. Butler and D. Wilson, *Managing Voluntary and Non-Profit Organizations* (London, 1990)

Z. Butrym, 'The role of feeling', *Social Work Today*, 13 (1981)

Z. Butrym, O. Stevenson and R. Harris, 'The role and tasks of social workers', *Issues in Social Work Education*, 1 (1981)

P. Cadbury, M. MacGregor and C. Wright, 'Problem families', *Eugenics Review*, 50 (1958)

M. Caedel, 'The peace movement between the wars: Problems of definition', in R. Taylor and N. Young (eds), *Campaigns for Peace* (Manchester, 1987)

A. Calder, *The People's War* (London, 1969)

D. Caradog Jones, 'Differential class fertility', *Eugenics Review*, 24 (1932)

—— 'Mental deficiency on Merseyside: Its connection with the social problem group', *Eugenics Review*, 24 (1932)

—— *Social Survey of Merseyside* (Liverpool, 1934), 3 vols

—— 'Eugenics and the decline in population', *Eugenics Review*, 28 (1936)

—— 'The social problem group: Poverty and sub-normality of intelligence', *Canadian Bar Review*, 28 (1945)

—— 'Eugenic aspects of the Merseyside Survey', *Eugenics Review*, 28 (1936–37)

—— *The Social Problem Group* (Cambridge, 1945)

A. Carr-Saunders, E. C. Rhodes and H. Mannheim, *Young Offenders* (Cambridge, 1942)

D. Carter, A. Mullender and G. Maccabee, *Using Contracts in Social Work Practice* (Nottingham, 1984)

W. E. Cavanagh, *The Problem Family: Four lectures given at an Institute for the Scientific Study of Delinquency conference, 1957* (London, 1958)

R. Chambers, 'Professionalism in social work', in B. Wootton (ed.), *Social Science and Social Pathology* (London, 1959)

M. Chesterman, *Charities, Trusts and Social Welfare* (London, 1979)

M. Church, 'Can mothers manage on Supplementary Benefit?', *Poverty*, 33 (1975–76)

M. Clarke, 'The unemployed on supplementary benefit: Living standards and making ends meet on a low income', *Journal of Social Policy*, 7 (1978)

—— 'The limits of radical social work', *British Journal of Social Work*, 6 (1976)

S. Clement Brown and E. Gloyne, *The Field Training of Social Workers* (London, 1966)

—— 'A review of casework methods', in E. Younghusband (ed.), *New Developments in Casework* (London, 1966)

A. Cohen, 'No social work without social administration', *Social Work Today*, 8 (1977)

—— *The Revolution in Post-War Family Casework: The Story of Pacifist Service Units and Family Service Units 1940–1959* (Lancaster, 1998)

R. Cohen, J. Coxall, G. Craig, A. Sadiq-Sangster, *Hardship Britain: Being poor in the 1990s* (London, 1992)

A. Cohen and J. Stewart, 'Preparing the student', *Social Work Today*, 8 (1977)

E. G. Collins, 'Family rehabilitation at Barkingside', in D. Lambert (ed.), *Change and the Child in Care* (Harpenden, 1965)

J. Collins, 'A contractual approach to social work intervention', *Social Work Today*, 8 (1977)

S. Collins, 'Working agreements in fieldwork placements: An evaluation', *Social Work Education*, 4 (1985)

A. Collis, 'Casework in a statutory and voluntary setting', *Social Work*, 15 (1958)

A. Collis and V. Poole, *These Our Children* (London, 1950)

P. Cooke, 'A Family Service Unit's approach to working with child abuse', *Child Abuse and Neglect*, 6 (1982)

D. Cooper, *The Death of the Family* (London, 1965)

J. Corden, 'Contracts in social work practice', *British Journal of Social Work*, 10 (1980)

J. Corden and M. Preston-Shoot, 'Contract or con trick? A reply to Rojek and Collins', *British Journal of Social Work*, 17 (1987)

—— 'Contract or con trick: A postscript', *British Journal of Social Work*, 18 (1988)

V. Cormack, 'Principles of casework', *Social Work*, 4 (1947)

C. Cornforth and C. Edwards, *Good Governance: Developing effective board-management relations in public and voluntary organisations* (London, 1998)

L. Cowan, *Reflections on Forty Years of Service* (Manchester Family Service Unit, 1987)

M. Crompton, *Respecting Children: Social work with young people* (London, 1980)

M. Cunliffe, 'The use of supervision in casework practice', *Social Work*, 15 (1958)

H. Cunningham, *The Children of the Poor* (Oxford, 1991)

R. Dallos and E. McLaughlin (eds), *Social Problems and the Family* (Milton Keynes, 1993)

H. Danbury, *Teaching Practical Social Work: A guide for supervisors* (London, 1979)

T. Dartington, 'Professional management in voluntary organisations: Some cautionary notes', in J. Batsleer, C. Cornforth and R. Paton (eds), *Issues in Voluntary and Non-Profit Management* (Milton Keynes, 1992)

I. Davey, 'Radical social work: What does it mean in practice?', *Social Work Today*, 8 (1977)

A. Davies, 'From psychiatric social worker to family caseworker', *Social Work*, 24 (1966)

J. Davies (ed.), *The Family: Is it just another lifestyle choice?* (London, 1993)

M. Davies, *The Essential Social Worker*, second edition (Aldershot, 1985)

A. Davin, 'Imperialism and motherhood', *History Workshop*, 5 (1978)

J. Davis Smith, C. Rochester and R. Hedley (eds), *An Introduction to the Voluntary Sector* (London, 1995)

E. H. Davison, 'Therapy in casework', *Social Work*, 12 (1955)

N. Deakin, 'The perils of partnership: The voluntary sector and the state, 1945–1992', in J. Davis Smith, C. Rochester and R. Hedley (eds), *An Introduction to the Voluntary Sector* (London, 1995)

D. Deed, 'Family casework', in C. Morris (ed.), *Social Casework in Great Britain* (London, 1961)

A. Digby, *British Welfare Policy: Workhouse to workfare* (London, 1989)

R. Dingwall, J. Ekelaar and T. Murray, *The Protection of Children: State intervention and family life* (Oxford, 1983)

P. Dobson, 'An Exercise in Consultation: Residents decide the future of a social and community work agency' (unpublished MSocSci thesis, University of Birmingham, 1987)

E. Doll, 'A practical method for the measurement of social competence', *Eugenics Review*, 29 (1937–38)

D. Donnison, *The Neglected Child and the Social Services* (Manchester, 1954)

—— 'The problem of the problem family', *Case Conference*, 3 (1957)

—— 'Social services for the family', *Fabian Research Series*, 231 (1962)

—— *Social Policy and Administration* (London, 1965)

—— *The Politics of Poverty* (Oxford, 1982)

D. Donnison, V. Chapman et al., *Social Policy and Administration* (London, 1967)

J. Donzelot, *The Policing of Families* (New York, 1975)

G. S. Dunn, 'Helping problem families', *Social Work Service*, 1 (1973)

A. Elliott, 'Problem families in Kent', *Medical Officer*, 100 (1958)

K. T. Elsdon with J. Reynolds and S. Stewart, *Voluntary Organisations: Citizenship, learning and culture* (Nottingham, 1995)

D. Evans, 'The centrality of practice in social work education', *Issues in Social Work Education*, 7 (1987)

O. E. Evans, *Redeeming the Time* (Liverpool, 1941)

Fabian Society, *Population and the People: A national policy* (London, 1946)

Family Service Units, *The Homework Project* (Edinburgh, no date)

—— *Solving Family Problems* (Leicester, no date)

—— *Social Insecurity* (London, no date)

—— *Residents Making Decisions* (Birmingham, no date)

—— *Groupwork with the Inarticulate* (Bradford, no date)

—— *Back in Touch: Parent–child relationship building through dance* (Leeds, no date)

—— *Time to Consider* (Leicester, 1975)

—— *Family Involvement in the Social Work Process* (London, 1982)

—— *Enuresis in School Children* (London, 1982)

—— *Schools, Families and Social Workers* (London, 1982)

—— *The Human Cost of Fuel Disconnections* (London, 1982)

—— *Families, Schools and Social Workers* (London, 1982)

—— *Foxhill Reading Workshop* (London, 1983)

—— *Homes Fit for People* (London, 1983)

—— *Our Motherhood: Women's accounts of pregnancy, childbirth and health encounters* (London, 1983)

—— *Access to Records: FSU policy paper* (London, 1985)

—— *Can Family Aides Prevent Admission to Care?* (Leeds, 1987)

—— *Bridges to Learning: How schools and communities can share resources* (London, 1987)

—— *Domestic Violence* (London, 1988)

—— *Dance Therapy in Family Social work and Evaluation of the Leeds Family Service Unit Dance Project* (Leeds, 1988)

Family Service Units Working Party on Development, *The Development of Family Service Units* (London, 1978)

Family Welfare Association, *The Family: Patients or clients* (London, 1961)

G. Finlayson, *Citizen, State and Social Welfare in Britain, 1830–1990* (Oxford, 1994)

—— 'A moving frontier: Voluntarism and the state in British social welfare 1911–1949', *Twentieth Century British History*, 1 (1990)

D. Ford, 'Introduction to the [Ingleby] report', *Social Work*, 18 (1961)

P. Ford, C. Thomas and E. T. Ashton, *Problem Families: The fourth report of the Southampton survey* (Oxford, 1955)

E. Fox. 'Modern developments in mental welfare work', *Eugenics Review*, 30 (1938–39)

A. Freud, *Infants Without Families; Reports on the Hampstead War Nurseries, 1939–45* (London, 1973)

A. Freud and D. Burlingham, *Young Children in War-Time: A year's work in a residential nursery* (London, 1942)

M. Frieden, 'Eugenics and progressive thought: A study in ideological affinity', *Historical Journal*, 22 (1979)

—— 'Eugenics and ideology', *Historical Journal*, 26 (1983)

D. Garnham and E. Mills, 'Voluntary action and medical research', in R. Whelan (ed.), *Involuntary Action: How voluntary is the voluntary sector?* (London, 1999)

P. L. Garside, 'Unhealthy areas: town planning, eugenics and the slums, 1890–1945', *Planning Perspectives*, 3 (1988)

L. Geismar and M. La Sorte, *Understanding the Multi-Problem Family* (New York, 1964)

D. Gittins, *The Family in Question: Changing households and familiar ideologies* (Basingstoke, 1993)

D. Gladstone, *British Social Welfare: Past present and future* (London, 1995)

—— *The Twentieth-Century Welfare State* (London, 1999)

H. Glennerster, *British Social Policy Since 1945* (Oxford, 1995)

E. M. Goldberg, 'Function and use of relationship in psychiatric social work', in Association of Psychiatric Social Workers, *Relationship in Casework* (London, 1963)

—— 'The function and use of relationship in psychiatric social work', in E. Younghusband (ed.), *New Developments in Casework* (London, 1966)

E. M. Goldberg (ed.), *The Boundaries of Casework* (London, 1959)

P. Goldring, *Friend of the Family: The Work of Family Service Units* (Newton Abbott, 1973)

J. Grier, 'A spirit of friendly rivalry? Voluntary societies and the formation of post-war welfare legislation', in J. Lawrence and P. Starkey (eds), *Child Welfare and Social Action* (Liverpool, forthcoming)

J. Griffith, *Central Departments and Local Authorities* (London, 1966)

R. Grunsell, *Born to be Invisible* (Basingstoke, 1978)

R. Hadley and M. Goldsmith, 'Development or convergence? Change and stability in a common ownership form over three decades: 1960–1989', *Economic and Industrial Democracy*, 16 (1995)

J. Haldane, 'Eugenics and social reforms', *Nation* (31 May 1924)

P. Hall, *The Social Services of Modern England* (London, 1963)

P. K. Hall, *Reforming the Welfare* (London, 1976)

A. Halsey, 'Professionalism, social work and paper 20.1', *Issues in Social Work Education*, 4 (1984)

## 258 Bibliography

C. Handy, *Understanding Voluntary Organisations* (Harmondsworth, 1988)

—— *Understanding Organisations* (Harmondsworth, 1993)

G. Hamilton, *Theory and Practice of Social Casework* (New York, 1940)

M. Hamilton, 'Groupwork with children in a family agency', *British Journal of Psychiatric Social Work*, 5 (1959)

E. Harbridge, 'Filling a gap in the arm of care', *Community Care* (5 February, 1981)

B. Harris, *The Health of the Schoolchild: A history of the school medical service in England and Wales* (Buckingham, 1995)

M. Harris, 'The role of voluntary management committees', in J. Batsleer, C. Cornforth and R. Paton (eds), *Issues in Voluntary and Non-Profit Management* (Milton Keynes, 1992)

A. Hartup, 'Families on the mend', *Farmers Weekly* (28 September, 1951)

S. Hatch, *Mutual Aid and Social and Health Care* (London, 1980)

—— *Outside the State: Voluntary organisations in three towns* (London, 1980)

J. Hearn, 'The problem(s) of theory and practice in social work and social work education', *Issues in Social Work Education*, 2 (1982)

H. Hendrick, *Child Welfare: England 1872–1989* (London, 1994)

J. Heywood and B. Allen, *Financial Help in Social Work: A study of financial help in families under the Children and Young Persons Act 1963* (Manchester, 1971)

M. Hill, *The Welfare State in Britain: A political history since 1945* (Aldershot, 1993)

N. Hinton, 'The relevance of the voluntary sector', *Social Work Today*, 9 (1977)

—— 'Which way for the personal social services?', *Social Work Service*, 18 (1978)

D. Holder and M. Wardle, *Teamwork and the Development of a Unitary Approach* (London, 1981)

F. Hollis, *Casework: A psychosocial theory* (New York, 1964)

B. Holman, *The Corporate Parent: Manchester Children's Department 1948–71* (London, 1996)

—— 'The voluntaries: Another perspective', in R. Whelan (ed.), *Involuntary Action: How voluntary is the voluntary sector?* (London, 1999)

E. Howarth, 'The present dilemma of social casework', *Social Work*, 8 (1951)

—— 'Definition and diagnosis of the social problem family', *Social Work*, 10 (1953)

J. Howells and M. Davies, 'The intelligence of children in problem families', *Medical Officer*, 98 (1957)

J. Hutten, 'Short-term contracts: A rationale for brief focal intervention by social workers', *Social Work Today*, 4 (1974)

—— 'Short term contracts III', *Social Work Today*, 6 (1975)

—— *Short-term Contracts in Social Work* (London, 1977)

M. Ingram, 'A casework study of a disturbed child and his family', in *Time to Consider: Papers from a Family Service Unit* (London, 1975)

E. Irvine, 'Research into problem families: A discussion of research methods', *British Journal of Psychiatric Social Work*, 2 (1951–54)

—— 'Research into problem families: Theoretical questions arising from Dr Blacker's investigations', *British Journal of Psychiatric Social Work*, 2 (1951–54)

—— 'Renaissance in British casework', *Social Work*, 13 (1956)

—— 'Psychosis in parents: Mental illness as a problem for the family', *British Journal of Psychiatric Social Work*, 6 (1961)

—— 'The function and use of relationship between client and psychiatric social worker', in E. Younghusband (ed.), *New Developments in Casework* (London, 1966)

—— 'A new look at casework', in E. Younghusband (ed.), *New Developments in Casework* (London, 1966)

—— 'The hard-to-like family', *Case Conference*, 14 (1967)

—— 'Education for social work: Science or humanity', *Social Work*, 26 (1969)

—— 'The needs of client groups with special problems', in E. Irvine (ed.), *Social Work and Human Problems: Casework, consultation and other topics* (Oxford, 1979)

—— 'The right to intervene', in E. Irvine (ed.), *Social Work and Human Problems: Casework, consultation and other topics* (Oxford, 1979)

—— *Social Work and Human Problems: Casework, consultation and other topics* (Oxford, 1979)

M. James, 'Common basic concepts to casework and groupwork', *Social Work*, 14 (1957)

R. Jennens and H. Dawe, *Our Teacher's Not from School* (London, 1984)

N. Johnson, *Voluntary Social Services* (Oxford, 1981)

—— *State Social Work and the Working Class* (London, 1983)

—— 'Social work education, 1900–1977', in N. Parry, M. Rustin and C. Satyamurti (eds), *Social Work, Welfare and the State* (London, 1979)

Joint University Council, *University Courses in Social Study* (1952)

—— *University Courses in Social Administration* (1956)

—— *Field Work in Social Administration Courses* (1966)

C. Jones, 'Social work education, 1900–1970', in N. Parry, M. Rustin and C. Satyamurti (eds), *Social Work, Welfare and the State* (London, 1979)

D. Jones, 'Family Service Units for problem families', *Eugenics Review*, 42 (1950)

—— 'The development of Family Service Units', *Social Welfare*, 9 (1956)

—— 'Some notes on measuring the results of family casework with problem families', *Social Work*, 21 (1964)

G. Jones, *Social Hygiene in Twentieth-Century Britain* (London, 1986)

—— 'Eugenics and social policy between the wars', *Historical Journal*, 25 (1982)

K. Jones, *Eileen Younghusband: A biography* (London, 1984)

—— *The Making of Social Policy in Britain 1830–1990* (London, 1991)

B. Jordan, *The Social Worker in Family Situations* (London, 1972)

—— *Paupers: The making of the new claiming class* (London, 1973)

—— *Poor Parents: Social policy and the cycle of deprivation* (London, 1974)

K. Joseph, 'Address' in *Report of the First National Conference of the Association of Directors of Social Services* (1972)

B. Kahan, 'Preventive work by Children's Departments, Part II' *Social Work*, 18 (1961)

—— 'Prevention and rehabilitation', *Approved Schools Gazette*, 55 (1961)

—— 'The child care service', in P. Townsend (ed.), *The Fifth Social Service: A critical analysis of the Seebohm proposals* (London, 1970)

S. Kay, 'The future of family casework in the non-statutory social services', *Social Work*, 23 (1966)

S. Kay, A. Davies and S. Ambrose, 'From psychiatric social work to family casework', *Social Work*, 24 (1967)

M. Keenleyside, 'Developments in casework', *Social Work*, 15 (1958)

J. Kendall and M. Knapp, *The Voluntary Sector in the UK* (Manchester, 1996)

B. Knight, *Voluntary Action* (London, 1993)

R. Kramer, *Voluntary Agencies in the Welfare State* (London, 1981)

—— 'Voluntary organizations, contracting and the welfare state', in J. Batsleer, C. Cornforth and R. Paton (eds), *Issues in Voluntary and Non-Profit Management* (Milton Keynes, 1992)

M. Ladd Taylor, '"Fixing mothers": Child welfare and compulsory sterilisation in the American Midwest, 1925–1945', in J. Lawrence and P. Starkey (eds), *Child Welfare and Social Action* (Liverpool, forthcoming)

R. D. Laing, *The Politics of Experience* (Harmondsworth, 1967)

C. Landry, D. Morley, R. Southwood and P. Wright, 'An analysis of radical failure', in J. Batsleer, C. Cornforth and R. Paton (eds), *Issues in Voluntary and Non-Profit Management* (Milton Keynes, 1992)

M. Lassell, *Wellington Road* (London, 1962)

B. Law and D. Downes, *Disability and Coinless Repayment Meters* (Leicester, 1991)

B. Law, J. Sealy and C. Elliott, *There's No Money In My Meter* (Leicester, 1990)

B. Law, J. Sealy, C. Elliott and P. Cornhill, *Contains No Cash: The experiences and opinions of 50 users of gas key meters* (Leicester, 1990)

M. Lee, *Pacifism On The Doorstep* (London, 1944)

P. Leonard, 'The place of scientific method in social work education', in E. Young-husband (ed.), *Education for Social Work* (London, 1968)

—— 'Explanation and education in social work', *British Journal of Social Work*, 5 (1975)

H. Lewis, *Deprived Children: The Mersham experiment, a social and clinical study* (Oxford, 1954)

J. Lewis, 'Developing a mixed economy of care: Emerging issues for voluntary organisations', *Journal of Social Policy*, 22 (1993)

—— *The Voluntary Sector, the State and Social Work in Britain* (Aldershot, 1995)

—— 'Management consultants and voluntary organisations: The cases of Relate, National Marriage Guidance, the Family Planning Association and the Family Service Units', *Non-Profit Studies*, 1 (1996)

J. Lewis, D. Clark and D. Morgan, *Whom God Hath Joined Together: The work of marriage guidance* (London, 1992)

J. Lewis and J. Welshman, 'The issue of never-married motherhood in Britain, 1920–1970', *Social History of Medicine*, 10 (1997)

E. J. Lidbetter, *Heredity and the Social Problem Group* (London, 1933)

Liverpool Council for Social Service, *Problem Families: The report of a conference convened by the Liverpool Council of Social Service* (Liverpool, 1946)

—— *The Outlook for Voluntary Social Service on Merseyside* (Liverpool, 1950)

K. Lloyd, 'The Family Centre of Hackney, I', *The British Journal of Social Work*, 1 (1971)

London County Council Health Committee, *Problem Families: Employment of social workers* (London, 1959)

R. Lowe, *The Welfare State in Britain since 1945* (London, 1993)

M.L.D., 'From dependence to independence: A case study', *Case Conference*, 4 (1958)

D. R. MacCalman, 'The changing nature of family casework problems', *Social Work*, 10 (1953)

C. McCreadie, *Home School Liaison: Report of an experimental project in community work* (London, 1985)

V. McDonagh, V. Myers, F. Walker and W. Hallas, 'Towards the eradication of the problem family: A symposium', *Journal of the Royal Sanitary Institute*, 73 (1955)

N. McGaughan (ed.), *Groupwork Learning and Practice* (London, 1978)

O. McGregor, *Divorce in England: A centenary study* (London, 1957)

E. McKie, *Venture in Faith: The story of the establishment of the Liverpool Family Service Unit and the development of work with problem families* (Liverpool, 1963)

J. Macnicol, 'The effect of the evacuation of schoolchildren on official attitudes to state intervention', in H. L. Smith (ed.), *War and Social Change: British society in the Second World War* (Manchester, 1986)

—— 'In pursuit of the underclass', *Journal of Social Policy*, 16 (1987)

A. Maluccio and D. Marlow, 'The case for the contract', *Social Work (USA)* 19 (1974)

K. Mann, *The Making of an English 'Underclass': The social divisions of welfare and labour* (Milton Keynes, 1992)

H. Marsh, 'The agency: Its history and its clients', in J. Miller and T. Cook (eds), *Direct Work with Families* (London, 1981)

S. Martel (ed.), *Direct Work with Children* (London, 1981)

—— *Supervision and Team Support* (London, 1981)

A. Martin, 'Child neglect: A problem of social administration', *Public Administration*, 21 (1944)

G. Martin, *Social Policy in the Welfare State* (New Jersey, 1990)

M. May, 'A tradition of partnership', in R. Whelan (ed.), *Involuntary Action: How voluntary is the voluntary sector?* (London, 1999)

J. Mayer and N. Timms, *The Client Speaks: Working class impressions of casework* (London, 1970)

J. B. Mays, *Penelope Hall's Social Services of England and Wales*, 10th edition (London, 1983)

J. Maxwell, 'Children and state intervention: Developing a coherent historical perspective', in A. M. Rafferty, J. Robinson and R. Elkan (eds), *Nursing History and the Politics of Welfare* (London, 1997)

P. Mazumdar, *Eugenics, Human Genetics and Human Failings: The Eugenics Society, its sources and its critics in Britain* (London, 1992)

H. Mellor, *The Role of the Voluntary Sector in Social Welfare* (London, 1985)

S. Mencher, 'Factors affecting the relationship of the voluntary and statutory child-care services in England', *Social Service Review*, 32 (1958)

N. Middleton, *When the Family Failed* (London, 1970)

S. Middleton, K. Ashworth and R. Walker, *Family Fortunes: Pressures on parents and children in the 1990s* (London, 1994)

J. Miller and T. Cook (eds), *Direct Work with Families* (London, 1981)

S. Miller, 'Social science and social pathology', *Social Work*, 16 (1959)

F. Mitchell, 'Towards a more unified service', *Social Work*, 18 (1961)

—— 'Clients' expectations of a family casework agency', *Social Work*, 20 (1963)

J. Mitchell, *Psychoanalysis and Feminism* (London, 1974)

R. Mitchison, *British Population Change Since 1860* (London, 1977)

A. Montagu, *Man's Most Dangerous Myth: The Fallacy of Race* (New York, 1974)

M. Morris, *Voluntary Work in the Welfare State* (London, 1969)

A. Mullender, 'Drawing up a more democratic contract', *Social Work Today*, 11 (1979)

R. Mullin, *Present Alms: On the corruption of philanthropy* (Birmingham, 1980)

G. Murphy, *Voluntary Social Work: Some questions, some comments* (Leicester, 1972)

C. Murray (ed.), *The Emerging British Underclass* (London, 1990)

—— *Underclass: The crisis deepens* (London, 1994)

G. Murray, *Voluntary Organisations and Social Welfare: An administrative impression* (Edinburgh, 1969)

National Council for Voluntary Organisations, *Meeting the Challenge of Change: Voluntary action into the 21st century* (London, 1996)

New Society, 'Helping out the family', *New Society*, 43 (March, 1978)

S. Nicholls and B. Law, *The BIG Report: Setting up and running a claimants' self help group* (London, 1989)

Notes, *The Eugenics Review*, 45 (1956)

M. O'Farrell, review in *Social Work* 10 (1953) of C. P. Blacker (ed.), *Problem Families: Five enquiries* (London, 1952)

F. O'Malloy, 'Leicester FSU "drop-in centre" for parents with young children', *Social Work Service*, 29 (1982)

T. O'Neill, *A Place Called Hope: Caring for children in distress* (Oxford, 1981)

J. Packman, *The Child's Generation* (Oxford, 1981)

M. Paneth, *Branch Street: A sociological study* (London, 1947)

R. Parker, *Away from Home: A history of child care* (Ilford, 1990)

N. Parton, *Governing the Family: Child care, child protection and the state* (Basingstoke, 1991)

R. Paton and C. Cornforth, 'What's different about managing in voluntary and non-profit organizations?', in J. Batsleer, C. Cornforth and R. Paton (eds), *Issues in Voluntary and Non-Profit Management* (Milton Keynes, 1992)

M. Payne, 'Relationships between theory and practice in social work: Educational implications', *Issues in Social Work Education*, 10 (1990)

A. Penn, 'The Management of Voluntary Organisations in the Post-War Period' (unpublished DPhil thesis, University of Sussex, 1992)

H. Perlman, 'The lecture as a method in teaching casework', in E. Younghusband (ed.), *Education for Social Work* (London, 1968)

P. Phillimore, *Families Speaking: A study of fifty-one families' views of social work* (London, 1981)

A. F. Philp, *Family Failure: A study of 129 families with multiple problems* (London, 1963)

A. F. Philp and N. Timms, *The Problem of 'the Problem Family': A critical review of the literature concerning the problem family and its treatment* (London, 1957)

A. Pincus and A. Minahan, *Social Work Practice: Model and method* (Illinois, 1973)

R. Pinker, 'The threat to professional standards in social work education: A response to some recent proposals', *Issues in Social Work Education*, 4 (1984)

D. Plowman, 'What are the outcomes of casework?', *Social Work*, 26 (1969)

A. Pope, 'Investigation into the problem of the tired mother', *Social Welfare*, 7 (1949)

R. Popplestone, 'Staff assessment in Family Service Units', *Social Work Today*, 6 (1975)

—— 'Moving the balance from administration to practice', *Social Work Today*, 8 (1977)

M. Power, 'Mental illness and the law', *Social Work*, 14 (1957)

—— 'Varieties of casework', *Social Work*, 19 (1962)

M. Preston-Shoot, 'Reports on a questionnaire survey of evaluation practice and needs in Family Service Units', *FSU Quarterly*, 36 (1985)

—— 'An evaluation of policy of family involvement in one Family Service Unit from families' perspectives', *FSU Quarterly*, 36 (1985)

A. Price, 'School for mothers', *Child Care: Quarterly Review of the National Council of Associated Children's Homes*, 28 (1954)

F. Prochaska, *Royal Bounty: The making of a welfare monarchy* (London, 1995)

—— 'Swimming into the mouth of Leviathan: The King's Fund and the voluntary tradition', in R. Whelan (ed.), *Involuntary Action: How voluntary is the voluntary sector?* (London, 1999)

A. Querido, 'The problem family in the Netherlands', *Medical Officer*, 75 (1946)

G. Rankin, 'Family casework in a local authority', *Social Work*, 16 (1959)

—— 'Professional social work and the campaign against poverty', *Social Work Today*, 1 (1971)

—— 'Personal view: Supervision and assessment, science – art-therapy – mumbo-jumbo', *Social Work Today*, 5 (1974)

—— 'Personal view', *Social Work Today*, 6 (1975)

T. Ratcliffe and E. Jones, 'Intensive casework in a community setting', *Case Conference*, 2 (1956)

E. Rathbone, *The Disinherited Family: A plea for the endowment of the family* (Bristol, 1986),

D. Reay, M. Lowe and C. Bowker, *Before It's Too Late: An account of the Pakeman School Unit* (London, 1984)

W. Reid, *Task-Centered Casework* (New York, 1972)

D. Reith, 'I wonder if you can help me?', *Social Work Today*, 6 (1975)

—— 'Family in turmoil: A case of self-determination', *Social Work Today*, 8 (1977)

B. Reynolds, *Learning and Teaching in the Practice of Social Work* (New York, 1942)

D. Riley, *War in the Nursery: Theories of the child and mother* (London, 1983)

A. Robinson, B. Nesbitt and C. Perry, 'The Local Authority Social Services Bill: Comments from three social workers', *Social Work*, 22 (1970)

B. Rodgers, 'The administration of the social services and the family caseworker', *Social Work*, 17 (1960)

B. Rodgers and J. Dixon, *Portrait of Social Work: A study of social services in a northern town* (Oxford, 1960)

B. Rodgers and J. Stevenson, *A New Portrait of Social Work: A study of the social services in a northern town from Younghusband to Seebohm* (London, 1973)

F. Rodger and M. Lawson (eds), *Dear Heart: Letters to and from two conscientious objectors* (Sheffield, 1997)

C. Rojek, 'The subject in social work', *British Journal of Social Work*, 16 (1986)

C. Rojek and S. Collins, 'Contract or con trick?', *The British Journal of Social Work*, 17 (1987)

—— 'Contract or con trick revisited: A reply to Corden and Preston-Shoot', *British Journal of Social Work*, 18 (1988)

## 264    Bibliography

C. Rolph, 'Derelict families', *New Statesman and Nation* (May, 1950)

W. Roper, *When the Family Fails* (London, 1947)

J. Rose, *For the Sake of the Children: Inside Dr Barnardo's: 120 years of caring for children* (London, 1987)

N. Rose, *Governing the Soul: The shaping of the private self* (London, 1989)

R. Roseman and J. Cooke, 'Social groupwork with children in a family casework agency', *Social Work*, 21 (1964)

J. S. Rowntree, *Poverty and Progress: A second social survey of York* (London, 1941)

M. Ruddock, *The Bridge Project, Thamesmead FSU: An interim report* (Thamesmead, 1985)

K. Russell, S. Benson, C. Farrell and H. Glennerster, *Changing Course* (London, 1981)

M. Rustin, 'Social work and the family', in N. Parry, M. Rustin and C. Satyamurti (eds), *Social Work, Welfare and the State* (London, 1979)

E. Sainsbury, *Field Work in Social Administration Courses: A guide to the use of field work placements in the teaching of social administration in basic social studies courses* (London, 1966)

—— *Social Work with Families: Perceptions of social casework among clients of a Family Service Unit* (London, 1975)

—— 'A national survey of FSU families', *FSU Quarterly*, 8 (1975)

—— *The Personal Social Services* (London, 1977)

—— 'Diversity in social work practice: An overview of the problem', *Issues in Social Work Education*, 5 (1985)

S. W. Savage, 'Intelligence and infant mortality in problem families', *British Medical Journal*, 2 (1946)

—— 'Rehabilitation of problem families', *The Medical Officer*, 75 (1946)

—— 'Rehabilitation of problem families', *Journal of the Royal Sanitary Institute*, 66 (1946)

H. and E. Schaffer, 'Child care and the family', *Occasional Papers in Social Administration*, 25 (1968)

B. Schlesinger, B. Ayres and F. Trakousky, *The Multi-Problem Family: A review and annotated bibliography* (Toronto, 1963)

J. A. Scott, *Appendix on Problem Families in London* (London, 1956)

—— 'Problem families in London', *The Medical Officer*, 100 (1958)

G. R. Searle, *Eugenics and Politics in Britain, 1900–1914* (Leyden, 1976)

—— 'Eugenics and politics in Britain in the 1930s', *Annals of Science*, 36 (1979)

A. Sedley, *The Challenge of Anti-Racism: Lessons from a voluntary organisation* (London, 1989)

P. Seed, *The Expansion of Social Work in Britain* (London, 1973)

L. Selby, 'The fieldwork supervisor as educator', in E. Younghusband (ed.), *Education for Social Work* (London, 1964)

—— 'Typologies for caseworkers: Some considerations', in E. Younghusband (ed.), *New Developments in Casework* (London, 1966)

J. Seth-Smith, 'The new look in family casework', *Social Work*, 15 (1958)

B. Sheldon, *The Use of Contract in Social Work* (Birmingham, 1980)

M. Sheridan, 'The intelligence of 100 neglectful mothers', *British Medical Journal*, 1 (1956)

—— 'Neglectful mothers', *Lancet*, 2 (1959)

C. Sherrington, 'The NSPCC in Transition 1884–1983: A study of organisational survival' (unpublished PhD thesis, University of London, 1984)

M. Sherwood, *Pastor Daniels Ekarte and the African Churches Mission* (London, 1994)

T. S. Simey, *Principles of Social Administration* (Oxford, 1937)

—— *Our War-Time Guests* (London, 1940)

A. Sinfield, 'Which way for social work?', in P. Townsend (ed.), *The Fifth Social Service: A critical analysis of the Seebohm proposals* (London, 1970)

J. N. Sissons, 'Planning Air Raid Precautions in the City of Liverpool, 1935–1940: A study of politics and administration' (unpublished MPhil thesis, University of Liverpool, 1985)

C. Smart, 'Disruptive bodies and unruly sex: The regulation of reproduction and sexuality in the nineteenth century', in C. Smart (ed.), *Regulating Womanhood: Historical essays on marriage, motherhood and sexuality* (London, 1992)

C. Smith and A. Freedman, *Voluntary Associations: Perspectives on the literature* (Harvard, 1973)

D. M. Smith (ed.), *Families and Groups: A unit at work* (London, 1974)

G. Smith, 'Control in a voluntary organisation', *Social Work*, 27 (1970)

G. Smith and J. Corden, 'The introduction of contracts in a Family Service Unit', *British Journal of Social Work*, 11 (1981)

J. Smith, *Growing Together: Innovatory work with a whole family* (London, 1985)

Society of Housing Managers, 'Unsatisfactory tenants and applicants', *Quarterly Bulletin*, 17 (January, 1955)

—— *Solving Family Problems: A statement of theory and practice* (Leicester, 1981)

M. L. Somers, 'The small group in learning and teaching', in E. Younghusband (ed.), *Education for Social Work* (London, 1964)

Southampton Discussion Group, 'The neglectful mother', *Social Work*, 12 (1955)

J. Spence, *One Thousand Families in Newcastle upon Tyne: An approach to the study of health and illness in children* (Oxford, 1954)

M. Spring-Rice, *Working-Class Wives: Their health and conditions* (London, 1939)

S. Stainforth, 'Some aspects of casework in Westminster since the war', *Social Work*, 2 (1942)

C. O. Stallybrass, 'Problem families', *The Medical Officer*, 75 (1946)

—— 'Problem families', *Social Work*, 4 (1947)

A. Stanton, *Invitation to Self-Management* (Ruislip, 1989)

P. Starkey, *'I Will Not Fight': Conscientious objectors and pacifists in the North West during the Second World War* (Liverpool, 1992)

—— 'The Medical Officer of Health, the social worker and the problem family: Family Service Units, 1943–1968', *Social History of Medicine*, 11 (1998)

—— 'The feckless mother: Women, poverty and social workers in 1940s Britain', *Women's History Review*, 9 (2000)

T. Stephens, *Problem Families: An experiment in social rehabilitation* (London, 1945)

O. Stevenson and P. Parsloe, *Social Service Teams: The practitioner's view* (HMSO, 1978)

J. Stroud, *The Shorn Lamb* (London, 1960)

E. Studt, 'Worker–client authority relationships in social work', in E. Young-husband (ed.), *New Developments in Casework* (London, 1966)

M. Taylor, 'Voluntary action and the state', in D. Gladstone (ed.), *British Social Welfare: Past, present and future* (London, 1995)

N. R. Tillett, 'The derelict family', *New Statesman and Nation* (April 1945)

N. Timms, 'Casework with difficult cases', *Social Work*, 11 (1954)

—— *Social Casework: Principles and practice* (London, 1964)

—— *Casework in the Child Care Service* (London, 1962)

—— 'Problem families in England', *The Times* (September 4 1980)

—— 'Value talk in social work: Present character and future improvement', *Issues in Social Work Education*, 6 (1986)

R. M. Titmuss, *Commitment to Welfare* (London, 1968)

—— 'The social environment and eugenics', *Eugenics Review*, 36 (1944–45)

—— *Problems of Social Policy* (London, 1950)

—— *Essays on the Welfare State* (London, 1963)

—— *The Gift Relationship: From human blood to social policy* (London, 1970)

C. C. Tomlinson, *Families in Trouble: An enquiry into families in trouble in Luton* (Luton, 1946)

W. L. Tonge and D. S. James, *Families Without Hope: A controlled study of 33 families in Ashford* (Ashford, 1975)

C. Towle, 'A social work approach to course in growth and behaviour', in E. Younghusband (ed.), *Education for Social Work* (London, 1964)

P. Townsend, 'The objectives of the new social service', in P. Townsend (ed.), *The Fifth Social Service: A critical analysis of the Seebohm proposals* (London, 1970)

A. F. Tredgold, *Mental Deficiency* (London, 1908)

M. Valk, 'Imaginative literature and social work education: An extended comment on Barker', *Issues in Social Work Education*, 3 (1983)

D. Vincent, *Poor Citizens: The state and the poor in twentieth-century Britain* (London, 1991)

F. E. Waldron, 'A choice of goals in casework treatment: A case study', *British Journal of Psychiatric Social Work*, 6 (1961)

A .Walker, 'Blaming the victims', in C. Murray (ed.), *The Emerging British Underclass* (London, 1990)

C. Walker and M. Church, 'Poverty by administration: A review of supplementary benefits, nutrition and scale rates', *Journal of Home Nutrition*, 32 (1978)

R. Walpole, 'The future policy of voluntary casework agencies', *Social Work*, 7 (1950)

J. Warham and S. McKay, 'Working with the problem family', *Social Work*, 16 (1959)

L. Waterhouse, 'The relationship between theory and practice in social work training', *Issues in Social Work Education*, 7 (1987)

W. Webster, *Imagining Home: Gender, 'race' and national identity, 1945–64* (London, 1998)

P. Wedge and H. Prosser, *Born to Fail* (London, 1973)

J. Weeks, *Sex, Politics and Society: The regulation of sexuality since 1800* (London, 1981)

J. Welshman, 'In search of the "problem family": Public health and social work in England and Wales 1940–70', *Social History of Medicine*, 9 (1996)

—— 'Evacuation and social policy during the Second World War: Myth and reality', *Twentieth-Century British History*, 9 (1998)

—— 'The social history of social work: The issue of the "problem family", 1940–1970', *British Journal of Social Work*, 29 (1999)

—— 'Evacuation, hygiene and social policy: The "Our Towns" report of 1943', *The Historical Journal*, 42 (1999)

M. Whale, 'Problem families: The case for social casework', *Social Work*, 11 (1954)

R. Whelan, *The Corrosion of Charity* (London, 1996)

—— 'How voluntary is the voluntary sector?', in R. Whelan (ed.), *Involuntary Action: How voluntary is the voluntary sector?* (London, 1999)

N. Whiteside, 'Creating the welfare state in Britain, 1945–60', *Journal of Social Policy*, 25 (1996)

R. Whitworth, *Merseyside at war: A day-by-day diary of the 1940–1941 bombing* (Liverpool, 1988)

R. Wilkes, *Social Work with Undervalued Groups* (London, 1981)

H. Williams, 'Problems of family casework in a statutory setting', *Social Work*, 24 (1967)

H. C. M. Williams, 'Problem families in Southampton', *Eugenics Review*, 47 (1956)

P. Willmott, *A Singular Woman: The Life of Geraldine Aves 1898–1986* (London, 1992)

F. M. G. Willson, *Administrators in Action: British case studies* (London, 1961)

A. T. M. Wilson, 'The development of a scientific basis in family casework', *Social Work*, 4 (1947)

D. Wilson, 'Organizational structure in the voluntary sector: A theoretical overview', in J. Batsleer, C. Cornforth and R. Paton (eds), *Issues in Voluntary and Non-Profit Management* (Milton Keynes, 1992)

H. Wilson, 'Juvenile delinquency in problem families in Cardiff', *British Journal of Delinquency*, 9 (1958)

R. Wilson, 'Social work in a changing world', *Social Work*, 7 (1950)

R. C. Wofinden, *Problem Families in Bristol*, Eugenics Society occasional paper (London, 1950)

—— 'Problem families', *Public Health*, 57 (1944)

—— 'Problem families', *Eugenics Review*, 38 (1946–47)

—— 'Homeless children: A survey of children in the scattered homes, Rotherham', *The Medical Officer*, 77 (1947)

—— 'Unsatisfactory families', *The Medical Officer*, 94 (1955)

J. Wolfenden, *The Future of Voluntary Organizations: Report of the Wolfenden Committee* (London, 1978)

Women's Group on Public Welfare, *Our Towns, A Close Up: A study made during 1939–1942 with certain recommendations by the Hygiene Committee of the Women's Group on Public Welfare* (Oxford, 1943)

—— *The Neglected Child and His Family: A study made in 1946–47 of the problem of the child neglected in his own home, together with certain recommendations by a subcommittee of the Women's Group on Public Welfare* (Oxford, 1948)

K. M. Wood and L. L. Geismar, *Families at Risk: Treating the multi-problem family* (New York, 1989)

B. Wootton, *Social Science and Social Pathology* (London, 1959)

C. H. Wright, 'Problem families', *The Medical Officer*, 94 (1955)

S. Wyatt, 'Poverty and the wage stop', *Case Conference*, 11 (1965)

## 268    Bibliography

M. Wynn, *Family Policy* (London, 1970)

E. Younghusband, *Report on the Employment and Training of Social Workers* (Edinburgh, 1947)

—— *Social Work in Britain: A supplementary report on the employment and training of social workers* (Edinburgh, 1951)

—— 'Trends in social work education', *Social Work*, 13 (1956)

—— 'Social work education in the world today', *Social Work*, 13 (1956)

—— 'Student learning in a family casework agency', *Social Work*, 13 (1956)

—— 'Social work in public and voluntary agencies', *Social Work*, 17 (1960)

—— *Basic Training for Casework: Its place in the curriculum* (London, 1962)

—— 'The teacher in education for social work' in E. Younghusband (ed.), *Education for Social Work* (London, 1964)

—— *Social Work and Social Change* (London, 1964)

—— *New Developments in Casework* (London, 1966)

—— *Social Work and Social Values* (London, 1967)

—— 'The future of social work', *Social Work Today*, 4 (1973)

—— *Social Work in Britain: 1950–75*, 2 vols (London, 1978)

# Index